FANTASTIC SPIRITUALITIES

FANTASTIC
SPIRITUALITIES

*Monsters, Heroes and the
Contemporary Religious Imagination*

J'ANNINE JOBLING

t &t clark

Published by T&T Clark International
A Continuum Imprint
The Tower Building, 11 York Road, London SE1 7NX
80 Maiden Lane, Suite 704, New York, NY 10038

www.continuumbooks.com

British Library Cataloguing-in-Publication Data
A catalogue record for this book is available from the British Library

Typeset by Pindar NZ, Auckland, New Zealand
Printed and bound in Great Britain by the MPG Books Group

ISBN 13:   978-0-567-03046-7 (Hardback)
           978-0-567-03047-4 (Paperback)

CONTENTS

Acknowledgements

vii

CHAPTER 1

Introduction. Fantasy and Spirituality

I

CHAPTER 2

Transforming Selves. Harry Potter: *'A highly unusual boy'*

22

CHAPTER 3

Transforming Selves. Earthsea: *'The Eaten One'*

45

CHAPTER 4

Metaphysics and Transcendence. His Dark
Materials: *'The Republic of Heaven'*

63

CHAPTER 5

Metaphysics and Transcendence. Earthsea: *'Only in silence the word'*

84

CHAPTER 6

Transforming Worlds. Buffy the Vampire Slayer: *'Bite me'*

103

CHAPTER 7

Transforming Worlds. Harry Potter*: 'Toujours Pur'*

128

CHAPTER 8

The Good and the Monstrous. His Dark
Materials*: '. . . and ye shall be as gods'*

147

CHAPTER 9

The Good and the Monstrous. Buffy the Vampire
Slayer*: 'From beneath you, it devours'*

168

CHAPTER 10

Conclusion. Shadows of the Divine

189

Bibliography

203

Index

213

ACKNOWLEDGEMENTS

I WOULD LIKE TO thank all my friends and colleagues who have supported me in the production of this book: you are too numerous to name! In particular, I am grateful to my managers, Dr Terry Phillips and Professor Kenneth Newport for their constant encouragement. I must also make mention of Revd Dr Sharon Jones, in conversation with whom this whole project arose. Ursula Leahy, as ever, gets an honourable mention for cat-sitting services while I undertook research trips. My thanks to my editor, Thomas Kraft, for continuing support. As this project drew to completion, I am also indebted to Lucy Kay and Colin Brown for proofing, conversations, and simply being there.

INTRODUCTION
FANTASY AND SPIRITUALITY

Is the fantastic primarily a literature of fragmentation, a subversive literature that reveals our desires in a fun-house mirror, opening an abyss of meaning, questioning the limits of self and society? Or is the fantastic primarily a literature of belatedness, unmoored from reality, innocent, the repository of exploded supernatural beliefs, expressing a yearning for a lost wholeness, promising transcendence?
The answer is yes.[1]

THE RELATIONSHIP BETWEEN THE fantastic and spirituality has long been acknowledged. Ursula K. Le Guin considers fantasy to be the natural and appropriate language for the 'recounting of the spiritual journey and the struggle of good and evil in the soul.'[2] This should not be surprising. As mode, fantasy is radically open to the imagination of new potentialities, whether feared, desired, or subversive.[3] Fantasy frequently deploys mythic patterns and archetypes, thus resonating with culturally deep-rooted questions, impulses and anxieties. Folklore and fairy tale, Romantic literature, and mythologies from around the world all leave their traces in fantasy texts. What is more, with postmodern enthusiasm for bricolage, Loki can rub shoulders quite happily with Spider Woman.

---

1   David Sandner, *Fantastic Literature: A Critical Reader* (London: Praeger, 2004), 1.
2   Ursula K. Le Guin, *The Language of the Night: Essays on Fantasy and Science Fiction*, edited and with introductions by Susan Wood, 2nd edn (London: The Women's Press, 1989), 64.
3   For fantasy as subversive, see in particular Rosemary Jackson, *Fantasy: Literature of Subversion* (London: Routledge, 1981).

The basic premise of this book is that religious sensibility in the Western world is in a process of transformation, but that we see here change, not decline. Paul Heelas, for example, argues that we see a turn to spiritualities organized around diverse conceptions of the 'authentic' life, rather than religions traditions centred around God. Against this back-cloth, I read fantastic forms in popular culture as prime examples of how contemporary spiritual emphases are implicitly (and sometimes explicitly) explored and expressed. Steve Bruce, following Weber, has it that Western consciousness is becoming religiously 'unmusical' as religion fragments into the individualistic and piecemeal: 'it means nothing to us.'[4] To the contrary, I would argue that spiritual themes continue to have enormous resonance, even if not played out in the mass social arena, and this is one of the drivers for the popularity of the fantastic.

The converse of this hypothesis is that the production and consump-tion of the fantastic in popular culture can offer an illuminating window on to spiritual trends and conditions. What modes of being and what values are applauded, admired, embraced, deplored? Or exert an uncanny fascination? What fictions seem to tap deeply into the contemporary cultural consciousness? I would contend that attentiveness to spiritual themes in cultural icons could offer the student of theology and religions insight into the framing of the moral and religious imagination in the late twentieth and twenty-first centuries; this can prompt traditional religions to reflect on whether their own narratives are culturally framed in a way resonating with the 'signs of the times'. I hope to provide some examples of how spiritual themes might be explored within fantasy texts, asking how selected examples navigate philosophically waters of truth, morality, authority, selfhood and the divine. It is argued that we see potent models of the authentic journey of the self emerge, which are evocative of traditional religious frameworks. However, the dislocation from religious communities and religious ends could arguably make the comparison with liberalized and individualistic spiritual forms more telling, and one might expect congruence with the psychoanalytical models typical of New Age metaphysics. This is without foreclosing on the possibility of other modes of spiritualities emerging in the textual conversations.

Thus, what I aim to do in this book is explore and theoretically analyse spiritual and theological themes in J. K. Rowling's *Harry Potter* series, Philip Pullman's *His Dark Materials*, Joss Whedon's television spin-off

4   Steve Bruce, *Religion in the Modern World: from Cathedrals to Cults* (Oxford: Oxford University Press, 1996), 234.

Buffy the Vampire Slayer and Ursula K. Le Guin's *Earthsea* cycle. I have chosen those particular case studies first because of their influence in the contemporary field. All are products of the late twentieth and early twenty-first century (although the first book in Le Guin's series actually goes back to 1968). All could also reasonably be termed cross-over fiction – by which I mean, they are read by both adults and young adults. The television series *Buffy the Vampire Slayer* is the creation of Joss Whedon and a spin-off from the film of the same name, enjoying a seven-season run from March 1997 to May 2003 and a cult following. Buffy is the Chosen One. As the opening credits tell us: 'Into each generation a slayer is born. One girl in all the world, a chosen one. One born with the strength and skill to fight the vampires.' Buffy lives in Sunnydale, California, which just happens to be the Hellmouth. The librarian of her High School is her Watcher – despatched by the Watchers' Council in London to manage her life as a Slayer and induct her into her duties and responsibilities. She and her friends – who come to be known as the 'Scooby Gang' must battle various vampires, demons and other examples of the 'Big Bad' in their quest to protect the human world from evil incursions. Although she is called a Vampire Slayer, in fact her remit is rather more broadly ranging across the realms of the demonic.

J. K. Rowling's *Harry Potter* series has enjoyed phenomenal success and has also provoked a quite startling backlash from right-wing Christian groups, accusing her of encouraging occult activity. This is particularly ironic because, of all the authors under discussion here, Joanne Rowling is publicly open about the fact that she is a churchgoer. Harry is an orphan, brought up by unpleasant and abusive relatives, who at age 11 suddenly finds himself transported into the magical world of wizardry and away from the so-called Muggle world, the realm of the non-magical. He attends the school Hogwarts in the company of his best friends Ron and Hermione. Gradually Harry's mysterious destiny is revealed: as a baby he defeated the evil Lord Voldemort and is the only known survivor of a killing curse; upon Voldemort's return from apparent death, he continues to survive repeated encounters with the Dark Lord, which coincide nicely with the cycle of each school year. Ultimately, it is prophesied that Harry must either kill the Dark Lord, or himself be killed. That is his destiny and his burden.

The *Earthsea* cycle is penned by one of the most acclaimed science fiction and fantasy writers of the late twentieth century and beyond – Ursula K. Le Guin. Earthsea is a fully realized alternative universe, with a detailed geography and cosmology of its own. In it, we have a poor rustic boy, Duny, who likewise discovers he is a wizard and ends up at a school for wizardry – Roke. There he is known as Sparrowhawk, although throughout the book I will refer to him by his final and truest name, Ged. Ged, through his own fault, unleashes a dreadful evil, a shadow, upon the world; he must go through various vicissitudes to stem the threat. Thereafter, he engages in various other quests. The second book of the series features the priestess Tenar as a protagonist. One of the interesting points about the *Earthsea* cycle is that it was originally a trilogy written between 1968 and 1972. In 1990, Le Guin returned to Earthsea. This was directly as a result of a feminist consciousness – again, of which more later. In *Tehanu*, and the 2001 volume *The Other Wind*, there is stinging critique of traditional gender roles and the emphasis moves away from Ged and on to female Tenar, and the girl child Therru.

The material is then explored thematically, under four headings: 'Transforming Selves'; 'Metaphysics and Transcendence'; 'Transforming Worlds'; and the 'Good and the Monstrous'. I consider two of my case studies under the rubric of each theme. Why those themes? 'Transforming Selves' offers a heroic analogue to the spiritual journey, each of which entails a quest, self-growth, personal transformation and re-integration (whether with self, society, or God). This section is deliberately planned as a 'gendered pair', in which the hero quest of Harry Potter is set alongside the hero quest of Le Guin's Tenar. This is because of the substantial body of feminist literature on the androcentric nature of the traditional hero quest.

'Metaphysics and Transcendence' allows an exploration of the imaginary cosmologies and ontologies in *Earthsea* and in the multiverse of Philip Pullman. In both cases the social, ethical and political implications of these metaphysical frameworks are also considered. The section 'Transforming Worlds' looks at socio-political issues – social stratification in the case of *Harry Potter* and flows of power and structures of authority in *Buffy*. This is because the model of spirituality adopted here does not confine itself only to personal transformation, although that is certainly part of it. Spiritualities have both socio-political contexts, and socio-political implications. Finally, I consider the nature of the good and the monstrous in relation to *His Dark Materials* and *Buffy*. This section focuses on what is held to be good – that is of cultural value and virtue – and what monstrous. The latter signifies what is repressed, outcast or considered the shadow-side of humanity. The monstrous does not necessarily reside externally to humanity: it can, in fact, be humanity's own face that is monstrous. The closing section, 'Shadows of the Divine', reflects on the spiritual motifs, themes and frameworks emerging. It considers the extent to which these fantastic worldviews (not framed in religious terms) can be seen as humanistic spiritualities, and to what extent they can be seen to be marked by a sense of the transcendent. These themes are related to features posited of contemporary conditions of 'postmodern' spirituality.

By way of background, I now go on to talk briefly about two of the contexts for this study: first, the mode or genre of fantasy; second, the secularization debate. Manlove defines fantasy as 'fiction, evoking wonder, and containing a substantial and irreducible element of supernatural worlds, beings or objects with which the mortal characters in the story or the readers become on at least partly familiar terms.'[5] However, Laetz and Johnston rightly note that wonder is dependent upon the reader as much as the text, and that some styles within the genre – such as dark fantasy, with graphic depictions of violence and sexuality – are probably not intended to be wondrous in that way. Nevertheless, the expectations of fantasy fiction are that it departs from consensus reality and opens on to worlds of supra-mundane possibility, typically but not always featuring elements of magic or the supernatural, and often located in secondary or alternate worlds.

That fantasy is not simply mimetic has led, indeed, to a tendency to dismiss fantasy as being 'unrealistic', trivial or merely escapist. Thus, the fantastic has often been neglected as subject for critical study, or marginalized as literature. That much fantasy literature has traditionally been for children has exacerbated this trend. And yet, there is, of course, a necessary connection between fantasy and reality. Fantasy negotiates a boundary between the actual and the incredible, the real and the illusory. Fantasy, in fact, is inevitably a commentary on or counterpart to reality. As intimated, fantasy is related to myth, legend, folk tales, religion and the occult – all of which can be seen as expressions of deep human drives. This book seeks to consider certain examples of young adult fantasy texts in relation to spiritual themes, motifs and frameworks.

The fantastic, and fantasy as a literary genre, both defy simplistic definition and resist easy evaluation. We need, in fact, to separate out these two terms to begin to shed any clarity on the matter. Each has its own ideological history, and has been used in various (and sometimes contradictory) ways. Manlove identifies 'elusiveness' as integral to the nature of fantasy.[6] The 'fantastic' is used for a range of non-realistic effects

5   Colin N. Manlove, *Modern Fantasy: Five Studies* (Cambridge: Cambridge University Press, 1978), 12. See also Brian Laetz and Joshua J. Johnston, 'What is Fantasy?', *Philosophy and Literature* 32, no. 1 (2008): 161–72.
6   Colin N. Manlove, 'The Elusiveness of Fantasy', in O. H. Saciuk (ed.), *The Shape of the Fantastic: Selected Essays from the Seventh International Conference on the Fantastic in the Arts* (Westport, CT: Greenwood Press, 1990), 53–65.

in texts from across the genres, including magic realism, surrealism and fabulation, as well as providing the adjectival form for 'fantasy' as a genre. Tzvetan Todorov uses the term in a much more restrictive way, to denote a hesitation or uncertainty when confronted by an inexplicable event:

> In a world which is indeed our world, the one we know . . . there occurs an event which cannot be explained by the laws of this same familiar world. The person who experiences the event must opt for one of two possible solutions: either he is the victim of an illusion of the senses, of a product of the imagination – and the laws of the world then remain what they are; or else the event has indeed taken place, it is an integral part of reality – but then this reality is controlled by laws unknown to us.[7]

The fantastic occupies the duration of the hesitation, between 'the uncanny', where the event is assimilated into real-world laws and discourses, and 'the marvellous', where the situation is resolved with a supernatural explanation. In practice, the narrowness of this definition means it is not widely applicable.

If one considers fantasy as a genre, its roots go back far. While it is generally considered to have become established as genre only in modern times, its antecedents run deep and are plentiful; Clute has named this rich stock of myths, fairy tales, legends, ballads, romances and the like 'taproot texts'. The term fits well, and has taken hold in critical literature. Notwithstanding its ancient roots, fantasy is widely considered to have begun the transformation into its modern manifestation in the Romantic period. This coincided, indeed, with the dawn of modernity itself; the Romantic period is, of course, generally understood to have blossomed in reaction against the rationalism of the Enlightenment. The emphasis on creativity, imagination and the sublime led to a fascination with fairy tales, folk legends, mediaeval romances and the like. This was not without contestation, however, and by the late Victorian period, the realist novel was firmly in the ascendant as literary form. As Attebery notes, initially realism, psychological suspense and science fiction came from the crucible of nineteenth-century romance literature in America.[8] Fantasy was largely redirected into children's literature, or periodicals.

---

7 Tzvetan Todorov, *The Fantastic: A Structural Approach to a Literary Genre* (Ithaca, NY: Cornell University Press, 1975), 25.
8 See John Clute and John Grant (eds), *The Encyclopedia of Fantasy* (New York, NY: St Martin's Griffin, 1999), 921-22; Brian Attebery, *The Fantasy Tradition in American Literature: From Irving to Le Guin.* (Bloomington, IN: Indiana University Press, 1980).

Fantasy has been associated with a number of undesirable features. It is presumed to be childish, and the implication is intended to be derogatory. It is assumed to represent the 'non-rational' because of its association with 'supernatural or impossible worlds, beings or objects'.[9] It has been deemed escapist (therefore trivial), irrelevant (because not 'realist') and formulaic. Yet there has been an undeniable explosion of interest in the genre at the popular level since Tolkien blazed the trail. Book outlets in the high street, airport lounges and train stations will all typically have a healthy portion of their available space for stock reserved for 'Fantasy and Science Fiction'. This popular thirst for fantasy literature and its sibling SF contrasts markedly with its position in the literary academy; while there has been a flow of serious studies of fantasy since the Second World War, it has until recently been marginal to the discipline. Olsen, writing in 1990, refers to fantasy as 'the country very few critics – especially American ones – visited until about ten years ago'.[10] The critic Rottensteiner, reviewing Le Guin's *Language of the Night*, commented:

> Polemically it could be said that the psychological basis of modern fantasy lies not in its power of individuation but, on the contrary, in its appeals to common symbols . . . i.e., its appeal to the mass mind.[11]

The rise of cultural studies assayed a profound challenge to traditional notions of the canon and to literary criticism in the mould of Bloom or Leavis.[12] Cultural studies provided a fertile ground for the development of explicitly ideological critical approaches (such as feminism and Marxism), and for interdisciplinary study incorporating insights from sociology, anthropology, philosophy, psychoanalysis and so on. It also pulled the rug from under the distinction between the elite and the popular. This invites us to raise questions about the cultural location of fantasy texts: why is fantasy so popular? What cultural trends and currents does it tap into – or promote, illuminate or subvert? Once examined in this light, the charges of escapism and irrelevance on the part of some critics seem distinctly short-sighted. If it is escapism, what are the readers and viewers

9   Manlove, *Modern Fantasy*, iv.
10 Lance Olsen, 'The Country Nobody Visits: Varieties of Fantasy in Strand's Poetry', in O. H. Saciuk (ed.), *The Shape of the Fantastic: Selected Essays from the Seventh International Conference on the Fantastic in the Arts* (Westport, CT, Greenwood Press, 1990), 3–8.
11 Franz Rottensteiner, 'Review: Le Guin's Fantasy', *Science Fiction Studies* 8, no. 1 (1981): 87–90 (88).
12 Ibid.

of fantasy seeking to escape from, and to? One hypothesis is that fantasies offer a sense of meaning, purpose and value which accords with spiritual concerns, anxieties and desires.

Spirituality is a very 'baggy' term and notoriously difficult to define, as it comprehends so many variant interpretations. I do not propose to survey here all the possible permutations of what could be included or excluded under its rubric. Rather, I shall 'set out my stall' in terms of the particular interpretation I am taking in dialogue with selected commentators. For Carrette and King, spirituality in advanced capitalist and consumerist societies has become the 'brand-label' for the search for meaning, values, transcendence, hope and connectedess.[13] Genealogically, drawing upon Walter Principe's analysis, they identify four main phases of the term's history and pre-history. The first is early biblical times, in which life in the 'spirit' (*pneuma* in Greek) represented life according to the Spirit of God, in contradistinction from life according to the 'flesh' (*sarx* in Greek). Such a distinction is moral, not ontological, and refers to modes of existence. The second use, by contrast, draws the distinction between spirit and matter according to a philosophical dualism. The Gnostic movements of early Christian Hellenistic times are famed representatives of this kind of thinking. A third usage, found in the mediaeval period, categorized persons and properties as either spiritual or temporal according to whether or not they fell under ecclesiastical jurisdiction or ownership. The fourth is the emergence of the modern use of the term, with the appearance of the word *spiritualité* in French. Spirituality then became associated with the interior life and subjective religious experience.[14] The development of psychology in the late nineteenth century further interiorized spirituality and located it within the individual self.[15] This constituted the first privatization of religion, and funded the development of individualized, consumeristic spiritualities. Carrette and King argue that, from the 1980s, spirituality underwent a second privatization – this time, however, in economic terms, as a servant to business success and corporate goals:

> In this climate, 'spirituality' becomes one of a number of ways of shaping individual sensibilities in terms of a new regime of power, this time dominated by the demands of corporate enterprise and the need for a flexible and compliant workforce. . . . With the emergence of capitalist spirituality the

13 Jeremy R. Carrette and Richard King, *Selling Spirituality: The Silent Takeover of Religion* (London: Taylor & Francis, 2005), 32.
14 Ibid., 34–37.
15 Ibid., 44.

freedom of the individual to express their inner nature through 'spirituality' becomes subordinated to the demands of corporate business culture and the needs of a flexible and competitive economy.[16]

Carrette and King do not suppose that this form of spirituality exhausts either possibilities or actualities, but are highlighting a concern that spiritualities which are not only individualist but capitalist are inimical to valuable aspects of our religious and cultural heritage, such as social justice, community concern, and an ethic of compassion and selfless love.[17] They are therefore advocating models of spirituality which are attentive to such matters and to the politics of knowledge. Embedded in this perspective is an understanding of spirituality as shifting, with no 'authentic' or timeless core definition; rather, spiritualities are constituted within specific contexts and transmute according to changing societal power relations. They invoke Foucault at this point to highlight how the construction of meaning is enmeshed in the history of power.[18] For Foucault, discourses – sets of signifying practices – produce and regulate knowledge and norms. Discourse is constituted in the relations between language, social institutions, power and subjectivity. Spirituality, then, can be understood as operating within discursive domains, and fundamentally related to politics.[19]

Schneiders takes a different approach in delineating the contours of spirituality. She suggests that at its most basic, spirituality is an anthropological characteristic: 'the capacity of persons to transcend themselves through knowledge and love'. This involves reaching out to others and becoming more than a self-enclosed and material monad.[20] However, she also notes that a greater degree of developed and conscious relationality to 'self, others, world, and the Transcendent' would normally be implied.[21] This more self-aware spirituality would nevertheless be profoundly diverse – inflected by location in relation to religious traditions and sub-traditions, historico-cultural contexts, roots in particular discourses such as feminism, mysticism, biblical Christianity or postcolonialism and the unique perspective of a particular individual. Schneiders cites the definition of Peter Van Ness, who looks at spiritualities outside of religious traditions:

16   Ibid., 45.
17   Ibid., 171.
18   Ibid., 172.
19   As Carrette and King (ibid.) point out, if spirituality is defined in apolitical terms, it is in effect supporting the status quo: itself a political posture.
20   Sandra Marie Schneiders, 'Religion vs. Spirituality: A Contemporary Conundrum', *Spiritus: A Journal of Christian Spirituality* 3, no. 2 (2003): 163–85 (165).
21   Ibid.

'the quest for attaining an optimal relationship between what one truly is and everything that is.'[22] She then offers her own particularization of this: 'the experience of conscious involvement in the project of life-integration through self-transcendence toward the ultimate value one perceives.'[23] For Schneiders, this self-integration involves: personal lived reality; conscious involvement ('an ongoing conscious approach to life as a consciously pursued and ongoing enterprise'); the holistic life-integration of body and spirit, emotions and thought, the active and passive and the social and individual; and finally it is consistent self-transcendence towards ultimate value. Such ultimate value might be conceived as, for example, God, social justice, life itself, or personal and social well-being.[24]

For purposes of this study, I adopt a modified version of Schneiders' definition, expanded by insights drawn from Carrette and King. The modification lies in a caveat: individual spiritualities may be neither coherent nor consistent, but nonetheless share in the other features of life experience identified above by Schneiders. Spiritualities are dynamic, and may therefore change; people may also combine beliefs from different sources and experiences, which, examined rigorously, do not cohere into an integrated system. Also, spiritualities perceived as incoherent need not be identified with the 'bricolage' model of personal spiritual amalgams outside of established traditions. For example, it is precisely on grounds of epistemological incoherence, as well as ethical concerns, that Christianity is rejected by post-Christians such as Daphne Hampson.[25] Individual adherents to specific traditions may also incorporate syncretistic and hybridized elements into their spiritual landscapes. Furthermore, spiritualities may not be wholly conscious in the psyche, but still a real, potent and shaping force in individual lives and experiences. Indeed, it is often the beliefs and orientations held below the level of conscious articulation which are most persistent and influential, precisely because they are unexamined.

Building on the definitions sketched in above, I propose to work with the following parameters for understanding spiritualities:

1 Spiritualities are the actualization of the capacity for self-transcendence through, for example, knowledge and love.

22 Peter Van Ness, 'Introduction: Spirituality and the Secular Question', in Peter Van Ness (ed.), *Spirituality and the Secular Quest*, vol. 22 of *World Spirituality: An Encyclopedic History of the Religious Quest* (New York, NY: Crossroad, 1996); cited in Schneiders, 'Religion vs. Spirituality', 165.
23 Schneiders, 'Religion vs. Spirituality', 165.
24 Ibid., 166.
25 Daphne Hampson, *After Christianity* (London: SCM Press, 1996).

2   Such self-transcendence operates within and towards the horizon of an explicitly or implicitly perceived 'ultimate value'. This ultimate value may not be reducible to one concept ('God', 'justice', 'love', 'self-actualization', etc.), but comprise an intimately interrelated nexus of values which are mutually constitutive.

3   Spirituality may be expressed within or outside organized religious traditions.

4   Even when explicitly and consciously understood as integrative and coherent systems, spiritualities may nevertheless feature elements that are tensive or sometimes contradictory, in common with other complex patterns of thought and practice.

5   Spiritual belief-matrices, like other sets of beliefs, may be formative at subconscious as well as conscious levels.

6   Spiritualities are discourses – sets of signifying practices, in Foucauldian terms – and both produce and are regulated by knowledge and norms in the social field.

7   Spiritualities may be collective or individual, but are not wholly privatized or internalized because they are sited within a discursive field.

Included above is a statement that spiritualities may be expressed both within traditional religion forms and outside of them. It is also understood that specific religious traditions may want to frame spiritualities more distinctively: for example, Christian traditions will probably generate Christomorphic spiritualities. It is also worth pausing at this point to explicate the relationship envisaged between religion and spirituality. A common but not wholly uncontroversial distinction is to identify 'spirituality' with the personal and experiential, and 'religion' with the institutional, ritualistic and dogmatic. This kind of differentiation leads to the increasingly common self-definition as spiritual, but not religious, by those who do not affiliate to a formal religious tradition but consider spiritual matters to be of importance in their lives. However, as spirituality is often understood as a phenomenon *within* religious traditions as well as outside of them, and the concept of religion is not reducible to adherence to a particular set of major institutionalized traditions, the distinctions become much more difficult to uphold. Historically the concept of spirituality arose as an expression of religion; presently, religion is just as likely to be conceived as an expression of spirituality. This reflects the turn to the subject characteristic of modern and postmodern times. Like spirituality, religion is also notoriously difficult to define. Clifford Geertz defined it as a cultural system of meanings embedded in symbols, with pervasive and persistent influence on mood, disposition and understanding of reality;[26] on this kind of understanding, non-traditional spiritualities which have attained to cultural power might equally be deemed religious. In the context of this kind of reading, the sub-title of this book deliberately uses the term 'religious imagination': since I am examining spiritual ideas manifest or discernible in public and popular cultural artefacts, I wanted to locate spirituality not only in the personal and internalized but also the public sphere of shared culture.

There has been a great upsurge of interest in the loose bundle of beliefs and practices typically labelled as 'alternative spirituality'. This includes those often identified as 'New Age' (defined by Paul Heelas as 'Self-Spirituality'),[27] Neopaganism, and alternative spiritualities focused on well-being and social concerns (designated as 'spiritualities of life' by Heelas and Woodhead).[28] The interest is manifest in an outpouring of literature in the 'mind, body, spirit' section of the publishing industry, a thriving market for spiritual retreats and courses, and the move into everyday discourse of concepts and practices such as feng shui, holistic medicine, meditation, manifestation, reiki, angel cards, crystal healing and positive thinking.

In his research into spirituality in America, Wade Clark Roof argues that it is personal meaning rather than social belonging which is currently most religiously potent. A quest culture has developed, where what is sought is 'authentic inner life and personhood.'[29] In the context of a 'crisis of modernity', individuals are spiritual seekers, actively scripting and creating their own religious narratives from available resources.[30] Roof argues that 'the discourse on spiritual "journeys" and "growth" is now a province not just of theologians and journalists, but of ordinary people in cafes, coffee bars and bookstores across the country.'[31] The emphasis, found Roof, was on personal power, transformation and life-direction.[32] Such self-reflexive spiritual seekers voyaged across traditions, time and space.[33]

This apparent spiritual vitality sits in uneasy relation to the idea that

26 Clifford Geertz, *Interpretation of Cultures* (New York, NY: Basic Books, 1977).
27 Paul Heelas, *The New Age Movement* (Oxford: Wiley-Blackwell, 1996).
28 Paul Heelas and Linda Woodhead, *The Spiritual Revolution: Why Religion is Giving Way to Spirituality* (Oxford: Wiley-Blackwell, 2005).
29 Wade Clark Roof, *Spiritual Marketplace: Baby Boomers and the Remaking of American Religion* (Princeton, NJ: Princeton University Press, 2001), 7.
30 Ibid., 12–45.
31 Ibid., 7.
32 Ibid., 82.
33 Ibid.

Western culture is in a process of inevitable religious decline. This is the so-called secularization thesis, and to give further insight into the current religious context, I will now survey some aspects of this and the counter-claim that in fact what we are seeing is sacralization. This is not a sociological study, and it is not my aim here to offer a comprehensive over-view of the complex and long-standing secularization debate. However, I pick out below a limited number of voices in this debate to demonstrate the contested nature of the thesis, and that the term 'sacralization' may be deemed an equally appropriate commentary on certain recent religious dynamics. In fact, of course, the tendencies can operate in tandem, with different varieties of religious forms in varying locations following distinct trajectories. I hope the below also, therefore, underlines the dangers of inattention to geographical and cultural diversity in promulgating univer-salizing theories; this book proceeds from the heritage of liberal, humanist and predominantly Christian thought-streams in the so-called West, which have intertwined more recently with postmodern, postcolonial and feminist currents. It does not pretend to speak from or to a 'neutral' or 'universal' location.

The underlying premise of most secularization theses seems to be that humanity will 'progress' beyond the need for the consolations of religion and be able to adopt a sensibly non-superstitious, thoroughly rationalistic perspective on the world. Certainly this was the kind of outlook espoused by progressive thinkers of the nineteenth and early twentieth centuries, such as Auguste Comte, Max Weber and Karl Marx. Ludwig Feuerbach and Sigmund Freud added into the equation a psychologized account of religious dependency, whereby humanity projected its own needs and desires onto deity. As Müller put this back in 1878:

> Every day, every week, every month, every quarter, the most widely read journals seem just now to vie with each other in telling us that the time for religion is past, that faith is a hallucination or an infantile disease, that the gods have at last been found out and exploded.[34]

The so-called 'secularization thesis' held dominant sway until the 1990s. The detail of extrapolated patterns differed: would religion become completely extinct or restricted to specific enclaves? Was religion on a cataclysmic crash course to obliteration, or was secularization a long, slow affair? However, there was widespread agreement on certain fundamental

---

34 Friedrich Müller, *Lectures on the Origin and Growth of Religion* (London: Longmans, Green, 1878), 218.

issues. Stark points out that proponents of secularization, building on the mood of the 1960s, tended to agree on five key points.[35]

First, the advent of modernity was identified as 'the causal engine dragging the gods into retirement.'[36] The inexorable juggernaut of industrialization, economic development, education, rationalization and urbanization would inevitably lead to religious decline in a predictable and relatively steady negative correlation. The more modernized society became, the less religious it would be. Second, secularization would occur at the level of individual belief and practice, and not only institutional status and authority. Third, scientific advancements are perceived to be pivotal in the development of a secularized worldview. Fourth, it is understood as irreversible if modern cultural conditions prevail.[37] Fifth, it is assumed to be a global phenomenon, although the majority of discussions concentrate upon Western Christianity. 'No one', Stark comments with some acid, 'has bothered to explain this to Muslims': nor, indeed, to other religious communities.[38]

Bruce is one of the most well-known contemporary advocates of the secularization thesis – although in more recent work he prefers to call it a 'paradigm', recognizing the diversity of approaches which can fall under this broad umbrella. He is also careful to delimit his arguments to the 'West'. Nor does he make the assumption that secularization is temporally uniform, inevitable, and culminates in atheism. At the core of Bruce's secularization paradigm are 'individualism, diversity and egalitarianism in the context of liberal democracy [which] undermine the authority of religious beliefs'; thus, 'religion diminishes in social significance, becomes increasingly privatized, and loses personal salience except where it finds work to do other than relating individuals to the supernatural.'[39] It is not only that religion then loses public and social significance; this then has a knock-on effect on the number of people interested in religion within their own lifeworlds. He locates the key historical shift in the Reformation, when both individualism and rationality were in the ascendant; this is important because 'individualism threatened

---

35 Rodney Stark, 'Secularization, R.I.P.', *Sociology of Religion* 60, no. 3 (1999): 249–73.

36 Ibid., 251.

37 Stark notes here that events in Eastern Europe and the former Soviet Union do not bear this supposition out. He cites Andrew M. Greeley, 'St. Vladimir has routed Karl Marx', in Andrew M. Greeley, *Religious Change in America* (Cambridge, MA: Harvard University Press, 1989), 272.

38 Stark, 'Secularization, R.I.P.', 253.

39 Steve Bruce, *God is Dead: Secularization in the West* (Oxford: Oxford University Press): 30.

the communal basis of religious belief and behaviour, while rationality removed many of the purposes of religion and rendered many of its beliefs implausible.'[40] The concept of God becomes, increasingly, a matter for individual negotiation and preference; religion becomes a lifestyle choice. The pattern of religious organization diversifies and fragments into a panoply of alternatives. For Bruce, the 'sacred canopy' – that universal and overarching religious frame – has not merely become rather frayed at the edges: it has disintegrated. The resulting trajectory is towards a profound religious indifference. Nevertheless, religion may still continue to play a functional role, in what Bruce deems to be counter-tendencies to secularization (cultural defence), and as a socializing agent during societal transition.[41]

David Martin was an early pioneer in the problematization of the secularization thesis. Inconvenient data includes: the increase in church membership rates in the United States from the nineteenth century to the twenty-first; failure to demonstrate that Church participation in Europe was actually at a 'high point' from which to decline at the onset of the modern period; and the continuing self-identification of a majority of people as theists in both continents. Counter-critics assert, of course, that while there may well have been no 'Golden Age' of faith and church attendance, it is still historically credible to suggest that a religious cosmology was more widespread and pervasive in pre-modern times than currently.

Davie urges sensitivity to differentiation in social, cultural and religious profile even among those nations customarily grouped together as 'the modern West'. She points out that the Protestant cultures of Northern Europe, with their 'tolerant and well-funded state churches' (such as in Sweden), contrast markedly with the United States, where Protestantism likewise dominates, but in ways both more vibrant and more varied. In between in terms of level of religious commitment are the Catholic states of Southern Europe, and Canada, Australia and New Zealand are each different yet again (according to Davie, displaying a 'half-way position between Europe and the New World'). Is it possible, she asks, that one theoretical approach could accommodate such variation?[42] Davie considers

---

40 Steve Bruce, *Religion in the Modern World: From Cathedrals to Cults* (Oxford: Oxford University Press, 1996), 230.

41 This is partly how Bruce accounts for the 'exceptionalism' of America – high immigration in conjunction with a federal and diffuse structure; homogeneous and closed local sub-cultures may thus be constructed as 'refuges' for conservatives to continue to exert hegemony.

42 Grace Davie, 'Prospects for Religion in the Modern World', *The Ecumenical Review* 52, no. 4 (2000): 455–64 (456).

that the secularization thesis does have valid applicability to certain stages of European development as religion became increasingly privatized. This led, however, to a fallacious conclusion:

> Europe's religious life was considered a prototype of global religiosity; what Europe did today everyone else would do tomorrow. That is, secularization was a necessary part of modernization, and as the world modernized it would automatically secularize.[43]

The obvious differences with the American context in terms of religious enthusiasm and public significance generated opposite explanations. On the one hand, America was seen to be 'exceptional', and a deviation from the norm in respect to the relationship between developed modernity and secularization; on the other hand, commentators such as Berger and Martin argue that it is Europe that defies expectation. This is to leave aside, furthermore, that the non-Western world is as 'furiously religious' as ever,[44] and the complexities introduced by global social movements such as transnational Catholicism, Pentecostalism and 'fundamentalism'.[45]

Presently, the impact of globalization upon religious vitality is receiving considerable attention. Prominent globalization theorist Roland Robertson dismisses the secularization thesis as a 'modern Western myth', and argues that current globalization processes run strongly counter to it.[46] This is flagged to draw attention to the broader context of religious trends and tendencies at this juncture in the twenty-first century. The impact of Western-style globalization in other areas of the world may include modernizing tendencies simultaneously with a desire to rediscover traditional religion. Norris and Inglehart relate this to existential security in their recent revivification of the secularization thesis.[47] For them, it does not operate on a cognitivist model (*à la* Weber), in which the rise of scientific worldviews are the most telling factor; nor a functionalist one (*à la* Durkheim), in which human needs are now met by education and social services rather than through religion. No: for Norris and Inglehart,

---

43   Ibid., 457.
44   Peter Berger, *A Far Glory: The Quest for Faith in an Age of Credulity* (New York, NY: Free Press, 1992), 32.
45   Davie, 'Prospects for Religion in the Modern World', 458–60.
46   Roland Robertson, 'Global Millennialism: A Postmortem on Secularization', in Peter Beyer and Lori G. Beaman (eds), *Religion, Globalization and Culture* (Leiden: Brill, 2007), 9.
47   Pippa Norris and Ronald Inglehart, *Sacred and Secular: Religion and Politics Worldwide* (Cambridge: Cambridge University Press, 2004).

it is levels of risk and vulnerability that mediate a tendency to secularity or religiosity. According to them, this even accounts for the 'exceptional' case of the United States – for, when contrasted with Europe, a major social difference is the quality and extent of welfare support. This does not make secularization mechanistic or inevitable, but it does make it likely and predictable. Allowing for individual variation, it also works as a general principle on the personal as well as social levels:

> [P]eople who experience ego-tropic risks during their formative years (posing direct threats to themselves and their families) or socio-tropic risks (threatening their community) tend to be far more religious than those who grow up under safer, comfortable, and more predictable conditions. In relatively secure societies, the remnants of religion have not died away . . . But in these societies the importance and vitality of religion, its ever-present influence on how people live their daily lives, has gradually eroded.[48]

Yet a further perspective stems from rational choice theory, which remains a major theoretical alternative and proceeds on the dynamics of the marketplace. It is associated especially with the work of Rodney Stark, Roger Finke and Walter Bainbridge. Rational choice theory postulates that being 'religious' is an aspect of human being. Therefore, the 'demand' for religion does not decline with societal change: people still desire 'compensators', i.e. substitutes for the rewards of religion (such as certainty, security, fellowship, comfort, hope for the future and so on). People also recognize that there is a corresponding range of costs (for example conformity, time commitment, money, participation). In societies where change in religious culture has led to the availability of choice, individuals effectively perform a 'cost-benefit analysis' and select their religious affiliation accordingly. Through this theoretical lens, Europe is the exception because it still carries its historical legacy of relatively low levels of religious diversity and monopoly of state religions. Critics, however, contend that such a perspective fails to take account of the relatively high levels of religious pluralism in Great Britain and the Netherlands, coupled with comparatively low participation rates[49] – and the relatively high participation rates

---

48 Ibid., 5.
49 Gill and Lundsgaarde argue that the low participation rates in Great Britain and the Netherlands can be explained by the 'substitution' effects of established welfare state systems. This counterbalances the effects of religious pluralism, which might otherwise be expected to stimulate increased religious 'consumption'. See Eric Gill and Anthony Lundsgaarde, 'State Welfare Spending and Religiosity: a Cross-National Analysis', *Rationality and Society* 16, no. 4 (2004): 399–436.

in 'monopolistic' Catholic countries such as Italy, Ireland and Poland.

Some proponents of secularization have shifted the ground: whereas historically it was understood to comprehend the religious orientation of individuals, later definitions have restricted the term to institutional decline in influence and social power, and a diminishment in the extent to which public space is permeated by religious figurations. Indeed, this conception of secularization is even referred to as 'de-institutionalization'.[50] This does, of course, beg the question regarding the link between the personal and the institutional, both causally and as a factor in the nature of religiosity. Stark is indignant about manoeuvres to exclude individual consciousness from conceptions of secularization, claiming this constitutes a 'breathtaking evasion' of the relevance of 'personal piety';[51] for him, the decline in political power of religious leaders in the West is worthy of scholarly note and study, but does not reach to the heart of what is connoted by 'secularization'.

A broader understanding of what actually comprises secularization allows for arguments against it that point to factors such as the previously noted upsurge in New Age spiritualities in the West as a positive indicator for religious vitality. Critics such as Bruce, however, dismiss the argument that the popularity of 'New Age' spiritualities fatally undermines any theory suggesting religiosity is in long-term decline. He concludes:

> The New Age is eclectic to an unprecedented degree and it is so dominated by the principle that the sovereign consumer will decide what to believe that, even if it were the case that we have some innate propensity to spirituality, we will not get from where we are now to any sort of religious revival. . . . Furthermore, I suspect that the New Age, weak as it has always been, will weaken further as the children of the New Age prove indifferent to the spiritual questing of their parents.[52]

This aligns with Bruce's view that strong community organization is necessary to maintain distinct belief systems and ward off the tides of secularization.

Thus, the debate around secularization and the future of religion in the West is complex and variegated. The Kendal Project, undertaken by Paul

---

50 K. Dobbelaere, 'Some Trends in European Sociology of Religion', *Sociological Analysis* 48 (1987): 107–37; David Martin, *A General Theory of Secularization* (New York, NY: Harper & Row, 1978).
51 Stark, 'Secularization, R.I.P.', 252. Stark is referring specifically here to the commentary of Karel Dobbelaere.
52 Bruce, *God is Dead: Secularization in the West*, 105.

Heelas and Linda Woodhead, was an empirical study focusing in-depth
on the locality of Kendal (Cumbria, UK), in pursuit of evidence about
contemporary religious and spiritual life, and whether a 'spiritual revolution' might be said to be underway.[53] The argument was underpinned by
the premise that modern culture has taken a 'massive subjective turn' away
from life according to external rules, duties, expectations and obligations,
to life according to subjective experiences, capabilities, needs and desires.[54]
It is worth noting that 'subjective experience' should not be identified
solely with the individualistic; it comprehends the relational as well. This
'subjective turn' is visible across a whole set of life-domains – such as, for
example, the development of child-centred education, patient-centred
healthcare, and certain varieties of human resource management. It is
bound up with pluralization, democratization and autonomization,[55]
which underline the specificity of truth, equality of voice and self-
determination, respectively. Furthermore – building on the predictions of
John Maynard Keynes – it is related to the development of affluence in
increased proportions of Western populations, freeing up resources and
time to pursue the 'art of life'.[56] The conclusion of the project was that
'tectonic shifts' are underway in the landscape of the sacred; although
the so-called 'holistic' milieu 'currently caters for a relative small market
niche',[57] there is potential for its expansion to an equivalent size as the
'congregational milieu' within 40 or so years.[58] This indicates at least the
potential for a spiritual revolution in Britain in the future. While a study
such as this has inevitable limitations in scope, it adds to the evidence base
that the Western spiritual milieu is transforming, not withering.[59]

Christopher Partridge supports the notion that the contemporary
religio-cultural milieu is best understood in terms of *both* secularization
and sacralization. Furthermore – in a claim highly relevant to the context
of this book – he argues that the milieu of alternative spiritual awakening
'both resources and is resourced by popular culture'; specifically, an 'occult
milieu', which he describes as 'occulture'.[60] By 'occult', Partridge intends
to comprehend a broad and flexible range of beliefs and practices which

53 See http://www.lancs.ac.uk/fss/projects/ieppp/kendal/index.htm; Heelas and
    Woodhead, *The Spiritual Revolution: Why Religion is Giving Way to Spirituality*.
54 Ibid., 2.
55 Ibid., 130.
56 Ibid., 131.
57 Ibid., 138.
58 Ibid., 149.
59 Ibid., 150.
60 Christopher Hugh Partridge, *The Re-Enchantment of the West: Alternative Spiritualities,
    Sacralization, Popular Culture and Occulture*, vol. 1 (London: Continuum, 2005), 4.

are 'sourced by Eastern spirituality, Paganism, Spiritualism, Theosophy, alternative science and medicine, popular psychology, and a range of beliefs emanating out of a general interest in the paranormal.'[61] This spiritual milieu is diverse, contradictory, dynamic and generally disrespectful of borders. The forms of spirituality embraced are frequently hybridized, forming bricolages of beliefs and practices. This may include heavily re-interpreted assimilations of older ideas about the occult, and of traditional religions. Partridge argues that 'idealized, neo-Romantic, detraditional-ized concepts of spiritual powers and entities are being constructed.'[62]

This shifting and complex set of divergent spiritualities is infrastruc-turally supported by practitioner networks. This includes the fair and festival circuit, workshops, retreats, courses and local community groups (such as healing circles, meditation groups, or psychic circles). In certain spheres there are professional associations, especially in therapeutically oriented practices. It also includes the networks and associations found in cyberspace – listservs, blogs, forums, social networking site groups and the like. Ideas and information are also exchanged through the media, popular cultural forms such as art, music and literature, and through the publishing industry. Major bookstores normally have burgeoning sections on 'mind, body and spirit', covering topics ranging across angelology, faery, demonology, numerology, crystal healing, reiki, tarot cards, psychic devel-opment, psycho-spiritual literature, mediumship, aura reading, Atlantis, alien abduction, apocalyptic prophecies, the nature of soul connections, manifestation and so on. Such networks facilitate the development and persistence of shared discourses.

It is these shared discourses that constitute Partridge's occulture. With reference specifically to the relationship between popular culture and occulture, he argues:

> (1) that occultural worldviews have been an important source of inspiration for popular culture, (2) that popular culture has in turn been an important source of inspiration for the formation of occultural worldviews, and con-sequently (3) that popular culture is beginning to have a shaping effect on Western plausibility structures.[63]

This posited relationship between spiritual cultures and popular cultures forms the backcloth for this study. It is not a direct exploration of influence

61 Ibid.
62 Ibid., 1:129.
63 Ibid., 1:126.

and impact – either of socio-cultural contexts upon the texts, or vice versa. It is rather a consideration of selected dimensions of spirituality as defined above within selected texts drawn from the fantasy literature field. If such texts can be considered part of the resource-base from which contemporary spiritualities may be drawn, this brings to critical attention spiritual themes and philosophies which may be perceived within them. Conversely, if such texts can be considered in some respects as mirrors of the religio-cultural milieu, then particular respects in which this might be so are brought to the surface.

Let us turn now to the texts.

TRANSFORMING SELVES
HARRY POTTER: 'A HIGHLY UNUSUAL BOY'

HARRY POTTER IS NO ordinary boy. Yet it could be said that the navigation between the ordinary and the extraordinary is just what makes the
series so widely appealing. Scholarly analysis locates the books in relation
to a range of genres and literary forms, including fantasy, the boarding school novel, the fairy tale and the mythic. It can also be deemed
a contemporary example of the *Bildungsroman* tradition, charting the
development of its protagonist from youth to maturity. The formal
structure of the series clearly lends itself to such a categorization, with
each of the seven texts structured in relation to the approach of a new
school year. The reader follows Potter from the advent of his eleventh
birthday – in the British educational system, the typical moment of
transition from 'junior' to 'senior' school – through to what would have
been his final year at Hogwarts, which commences with Harry turning 17
and thereby 'coming of age' as a wizard. Thus, the span of the books not
only chronicles Harry's induction into and development within the realm
of the extraordinary (as the 'Boy Who Lived' in the wizarding world),
but also the ordinary challenges and triumphs of adolescence: developing
sexuality, relations with peers, examinations, sporting endeavours and so
on. In this respect, the temporal and individual development characteristic
of the novel of formation intertwines with the quest narrative typical of
heroic fantasy. This is commonly found in the young adult fantasy genre,
and is found in association with the sub-category of 'magician's apprentice'
literature: a tag which could also legitimately be applied to the *Harry
Potter* books.

Coming-of-age literature of this kind, then, commonly engages themes consonant with the 'hero's journey'. This is taken as the primary framework for this chapter in order to explore themes relating to the development and transformation of selfhood within the *Harry Potter* cycle. Such self-transformations may be understood as expressions of spirituality on the definition outlined in Chapter One, involving purposeful striving, self-integration and self-transcendence. The specific model of the 'hero's journey' used for this analysis is drawn from Joseph Campbell's classic pattern as set down in his 1949 work *The Hero with a Thousand Faces*. Campbell's schema is not the only such, of course. Edward Tylor (1871) and Johann Georg von Hahn (1876) were early contributors to the study of common patterns in hero myth and folklore, with Otto Rank's *The Myth of the Birth of the Hero* (1909), Vladimir Propp's *Morphology of the Folk Tale* (1928) and Lord Raglan's *The Hero* (1936) also attempting to chart common elements and structures in mythic corpora. Jann Lacoss tabulates Propp's model as applied to *Philosopher's Stone* and *Goblet of Fire*; M. Katherine Grimes considers Potter's life in relation to Otto Rank's categories of hero birth and development.[1]

Where psychoanalytic theory is explicitly applied to analysis of the 'hero's journey', the development of the individual is placed firmly in the centre of the viewing pane, making such models particularly useful to an analysis focused on portrayal of personal growth and transformation. Rank, for example, used Freudian Oedipal motifs (and to a lesser extent his own emergent emphasis on the pre-Oedipal birth experience) to explicate the life cycle of the hero. Campbell, by contrast, also drew heavily on the thought of Carl Jung, and Jung's predecessor Adolph Bastian.[2]

In selecting Campbell's account as the main structuring principle for the following analysis, limitations of his work as a mythographer must be duly acknowledged. Dundes argues that the narratives Campbell analyses are properly folk tales and legends rather than myths; he considers the 1968 volume *Creative Mythology* to be one 'of essentially wide-ranging literary criticism.'[3] Campbell believed that the essentials of his hero pattern

---

1   Jann Lacoss, 'Of Magicals and Muggles: Reversals and Revulsions at Hogwarts', in Lana A. Whited (ed.), *The Ivory Tower and Harry Potter: Perspectives on a Literary Phenomenon* (Columbia and London: University of Missouri Press, 2004), 67–88 (86). M. Katherine Grimes, 'Harry Potter: Fairy Tale Prince, Real Boy and Archetypal Hero', in Lana A. Whited (ed.), *The Ivory Tower and Harry Potter: Perspectives on a Literary Phenomenon* (Columbia and London: University of Missouri Press, 2004), 106–20.

2   Bastian's account of common elements in myth prefigured Jung's development of archetypal theory.

3   Alan Dundes, 'Folkloristics in the Twenty-First Century (AFS Invited Presidential

were universally discernible across all cultures, leading him to identify it as the 'monomyth', a term he gleaned from James Joyce's *Finnegan's Wake*. This is dismissed by Dundes as both a 'vacuous portmanteau neologism' and a wholly unsustainable concept.[4]

I make no claim for the universal validity of Campbell's thesis in either anthropological or literary terms, but rather adopt it as a tool to map key stages in the narrative arc of the *Harry Potter* series as it relates to the character maturation of the protagonist. Campbell's model of the hero's journey lends itself to such an analysis because it is overtly concerned with the applicability of the model to personal life-journeys:

> The passage of the mythological hero may be over-ground, incidentally; fundamentally it is inward – into depths where obscure resistances are overcome, and long lost, forgotten powers are revivified, to be made available for the transfiguration of the world.[5]

Furthermore, Campbell constantly relates his hero's outward macro-quest and inward micro-quest to spirituality. Upon accomplishment of the quest:

> [L]ife no longer suffers hopelessly under the terrible mutilations of ubiquitous disaster, battered by time . . . Something of the light that blazes invisible within the abysses of its normally opaque materiality breaks forth, with an increasing uproar. The dreadful mutilations are then seen as shadows, only, of an immanent, imperishable eternity . . .[6]

The hero is seen to have an inherent link to spiritual concerns. For writers such as Campbell, the divine within as well as outside of our selves is disclosed in the heroic journey, and we are invited to share it. The hero reflects the face of the divine to the world, and is reborn as the 'eternal man'; in listening to the hero's story, we encounter the Imperishable within ourselves.[7] The hero may be a model for emulation, or a symbol for contemplation; in either case, the hero is a doorway to the divine. It is not only what the hero might inspire in terms of action, if following in

---

Plenary Address, 2004)', *Journal of American Folklore* 118, no. 470 (2005): 385–408 (395).

4 Ibid.

5 Joseph Campbell, *The Hero with a Thousand Faces* (Novato, CA: New World Library, 2008), 22.

6 Ibid.

7 Ibid., 243.

their steps is possible, but what the hero represents. For Thomas Carlyle, the hero is 'a natural luminary shining by the gift of Heaven; a flowing light-fountain'.[8] Heroes inspire a sense of human potentiality. Campbell comments that 'by a like miracle, so will each whose work is the difficult, dangerous task of self-discovery and self-development be portered across the ocean of life.'[9]

Northrop Frye distinguishes between three types of hero. The first is superior in kind, and is therefore to be considered a divine being: in that sense, Frye deems such a hero to fall into the realm of myth ('in the common sense of a story about a god') and to fall outside of ordinary literary categories. The second type of hero is superior in degree but not kind, and is therefore a human being, but one endowed with extraordinary powers. This is the hero of romance, where the ordinary laws of nature do not wholly apply: 'enchanted weapons, talking animals, terrifying ogres and witches, and talismans of miraculous power violate no probability once the postulates of romance have been established.' The third type of hero is also superior in degree, but operates in an environment ordered by recognizable laws of nature and society. This, he suggests, is the hero of the high mimetic mode, and can be considered a leader-figure.[10] If Frye's categories are applied to Harry Potter, we have a conflation of the second and third categories of hero, as Harry moves between the Muggle world and the 'wainscot' world of magic, inhabiting its interstices.

A hero may be such in a range of realms – as warrior, artist, scientist, world-redeemer, lover, saint, ruler and so on. It is not the realm of activity but the quality of orientation towards life. Nor must a hero be of immortal stature. This nature of the hero is a contextual matter, and may vary in different epochs. Segal posits that:

> Far from divine, the contemporary hero is hopelessly human – mortal, powerless, amoral . . . Persistence replaces success, survival replaces achievement. Old-fashioned heroic virtues like courage and duty give way to new ones like irony and detachment.[11]

This is in contradistinction to the romantic and bourgeois hero-types of the nineteenth century; Segal gives the examples of Byron's Childe Harold

---

8   Thomas Carlyle, *Sartor Resartus (1831). Lectures on Heroes (1840)* (London: Chapman and Hall, 1858), 185.
9   Campbell, *The Hero with a Thousand Faces*, 17.
10   Northrop Frye, *Anatomy of Criticism: Four Essays* (Princeton, NJ: University of Princeton Press, 1957), 33.
11   Robert Alan Segal, *Hero Myths* (Oxford: Wiley-Blackwell, 2000), 8–9.

and Flaubert's Emma Bovary respectively. He also points to the emergence of new forms of hero – the comic, the absurd, the outcast and the simply ordinary.[12] Human vulnerability is important in the hero, and arguably it is the hero with flaws and contradictions who offers most scope for personal identification and the possibility of emulating the quest for self-mastery. Nevertheless, as Segal also points out, societies continue to transform humans into virtual gods by conferral of divine attributes – citing celebrity culture in Hollywood and sport as examples.[13]

So the hero, as hero, is both a model of and inspiration for personal transformation, which in Campbell's account has overt linkages to spirituality. This is partly because the hero figure participates in the hero archetype. Archetypes are primal images or symbols; for Carl Jung, these archetypes are universal, primordial and emerge from a collective unconscious. In Campbell, the archetypes – while universal – can also be interpreted as social and/or psychoanalytic in origin. In literary analysis, archetypes can be understood as culturally common symbols and thought-structures which evoke deep-rooted resonances of meaning. For an image or figure to tap into archetypal structures itself adds a richness and complexity of texture that lends itself to spiritual interpretations (as speaking to and from deep-rooted structures in self and society).

It can also be noted that Campbell's hero journey is particularly apt for a study of late twentieth- and twenty-first-century fantasy because it has been utilized in a number of influential outputs of the genre, notably including *Star Wars*. Christopher Vogler's popular guide *The Writer's Journey: Mythic Structure for Writers* was also based on Campbell's work, and the broad outline of his hero's journey has been discerned in a whole range of works from the *Matrix* trilogy to *The Lion King*. Without making strong assertions regarding its general applicability, it can certainly be proposed more cautiously that it accords with a pattern of the hero quest very familiar in modern Western popular film and literature. It should also be noted that Campbell's work has been criticized for both ethnocentricity and gender bias. That, of course, does not preclude it from consonance with popular literary and filmic forms! Issues of this nature are recognized here, but taken up more fully in the chapter examining the world of Harry Potter from a socio-political vantage point.

Aside from a narratological similarity at the structural level between Campbell's hero journey and fictional quest narratives, it is possible in fact to go further and assert that, with respect to speculative fiction in

12   Ibid., 8.
13   Ibid., 7.

particular, there is quite commonly a mythic dimension. The category 'myth' is, of course, itself deeply fractured. It is variously understood as a foundational story, a falsehood, a moral charter, a psychological projection, a functionalist vehicle of socially explanatory power, an attempt to understand and account for human existence, as religious genre, as legitimation of social institutions, as a codification of the symbols structuring a cultural world, or as sacred story. Myths at the social level are typically culturally resonant, of archetypal or over-arching significance and may form part of a cosmic drama. It can be argued therefore, that even where the sacred or divine is not specifically featured, myths evoke a transcendent dimension.

Thus, in evoking the fantastic, writers may call upon the mythic symbolic field to instil a sense of monumental time[14] – that is to say, the sense of an epic, cosmic drama whose import transcends a transient moment of linear history. This relates also to the very common apocalyptic trope in speculative fiction, where the fate of the world or even the universe hangs in the balance. Myth, like fantasy, also deals with the supranatural or the supra-human. Expanding the envelope of the mythic category from its anthropological roots, Ursula K. Le Guin also puts forward the category of 'submyth' to incorporate images and motifs which are collective, alive and powerful but not part of the 'great living mythologies of religion and power'; this enables her to locate Superman, for example, within the mythic sphere.[15] In Chapter Ten, the notion of mythopoesis will be explored – that is to say, the deliberate elaboration and reworking of mythological themes to create new myth-type forms.

To turn, then, to Campbell's account of the 'hero's journey'. At its most basic this model is patterned on a 'separation-initiation-return' schema. This has the following sub-categories:[16]

---

14 I use 'monumental time' here in a sense more closely allied to Julia Kristeva's definition than Paul Ricoeur's. For Ricoeur, monumental time is the secretion of monumental history and relates to contexts of power and authority (see Paul Ricoeur, *Time and Narrative*, trans. Kathleen Blarney and David Pellauer, 3 vols [Chicago: University of Chicago Press, 1985]). By contrast, Kristeva relates monumental time more to life-cycles and repetition in the context of eternity, and makes specific reference to myths of resurrection. For more on this, see Chapter Three.

15 Ursula K. Le Guin, *Language of the Night: Essays on Fantasy and Science Fiction*, edited and with introductions by Susan Wood, 2nd edn (London: The Women's Press, 1989), 64. Le Guin is speaking with specific reference to science fiction, but the comment holds for fantasy also. However, I disagree that such sub-myths 'have no religious resonance and no intellectual or aesthetic value' (ibid.).

16 These categories are based on the subdividing of the journey found in Campbell, *The Hero with a Thousand Faces*, 41–209.

Departure
- The Call to Adventure
- Refusal of the Call
- Supernatural Aid
- The Crossing of the First Threshold
- The Belly of the Whale

Initiation
- The Meeting with the Goddess
- Woman as the Temptress
- Atonement with the Father
- Apotheosis
- The Ultimate Boon

Return
- Refusal of the Return
- The Magic Flight
- Rescue from Without
- The Crossing of the Return Threshold
- Master of the Two Worlds
- Freedom to Live

It is easy to see how some of the primary features of classic hero journeys are replicated both within the individual books and in the story arc of the *Harry Potter* series as a whole. Campbell's hero journey begins with the call to adventure, assuming a chronologically older starting point than Rank, whose account of the hero journey begins at birth. Nevertheless, Campbell does comment on the childhood of the human hero: 'the tendency has always been to endow the hero with extraordinary powers from the moment of birth, or even the moment of conception.'[17] However, it is a time spent in exile or lowliness of estate: 'the child of destiny has to face a long period of obscurity. This is a time of extreme danger, impediment, or disgrace.'[18] This maps well, of course, onto the childhood of Harry Potter, in exile from the world of magic of which he is a part, abused by his adoptive family, and with origins already shrouded in the legends of the 'Boy Who Lived', of which he is ignorant. The trademark lightning scar marks him out, a process further reinforced when knowledge of the prophecy made before his birth becomes available. The scar operates in the

17 Ibid., 274.
18 Ibid., 280.

manner of the *pharmakon*, both remedy and poison: it is simultaneously primal wound and primal signifier of his 'chosen' status.

Campbell described the call to adventure in the following terms:

> This first stage of the mythological journey – which we have designated the 'call to adventure' – signifies that destiny has summoned the hero and transferred his spiritual center of gravity from within the pale of his society to a zone unknown.[19]

This is frequently followed by a refusal of the call: 'Walled in boredom, hard work, or "culture," the subject loses the power of significant affirmative action and becomes a victim to be saved.'[20] In the case of Harry Potter, this call/refusal dyad is represented by the increasingly insistent messages from Hogwarts, and his uncle's increasingly frantic attempts to ward them off. Mr Dursley thus acts as the hostile guardian of the boundary which the hero must negotiate to proceed on the journey. When letters finally begin to stream 'like bullets'[21] down the kitchen chimney, an infuriated Mr Dursley whisks the whole family away, ultimately to a shack on a rock out at sea. Harry is literally 'walled in' by his relatives and his age-related dependence upon them. This emphasizes the limitations upon Harry's agency at the outset of his journey.

The shack on the rock at sea evokes a number of mythic carceral 'towers' – typically, however, it is a daughter or stepdaughter who is imprisoned.[22] This aligns Harry with a lack of autonomy and victim status associated with the traditionally feminine. Issues around gender portrayals, both feminine and masculine, are explored in more detail in Chapter Seven. Certainly, at this point, Harry's deliverance is entirely externally provided in the person of Hagrid. Hagrid represents the helpful supernatural aide assisting the hero to navigate the threshold of adventure – arriving on a magic flying motorbike and hexing Dudley Dursley with the tail of a pig. 'If he [Harry] wants to go, a great Muggle like you won't stop him', Hagrid growls at Mr Dursley: but it is Hagrid, not Harry, who effects his departure; Harry does not even voice an active acceptance of the offer made to him, but simply follows Hagrid. Hagrid's words to the Dursleys

---

19 Ibid., 48.
20 Ibid., 49.
21 J. K. Rowling, *Harry Potter and the Philosopher's Stone* (London: Bloomsbury, 1997), 35.
22 Indeed, the recurrent nature of this motif has led to it being classified as 'The Maiden in the Tower (type 310)' in the Aarne-Thompson system of categorizing folklore.

are prophetic in this regard: 'Seven years there [Hogwarts] and he won't know himself.'[23]

Hogwarts itself is certainly reminiscent of Campbell's account of the unknown zone to which the hero is called: a 'fateful region' with both treasure and danger; a place which may be a 'distant land, a forest, a kingdom underground . . . or profound dream state', but always a place marked by the presence of 'strangely fluid and polymorphous beings, unimaginable torments, superhuman deeds, and impossible delight.'[24] Hogwarts occupies the spatial centre of the novels, a place of secrets to which even Dumbledore is not always privy. Its location in Scotland is magically hidden, and 'unplottable'. The very building is polymorphous, with rooms and stairs that change location, and filled with portraits whose subjects can move around, snore, sing, scream and speak to you. For those familiar with the works, Hogwarts as locus for torment, delight and heroic deed needs no exposition: it is integral to the entire sequence.

Given the symbolic centrality of Hogwarts, even though extended narrative sequences do take place elsewhere (particularly in the later books, notably *Deathly Hallows*), it is fitting to consider the school as the primal threshold over which Harry crosses in his entry into the magical world. It is prefaced by annunciation scenes: first by Hagrid himself in disclosing to Harry the initial inklings of his true identity, history and significance; second in the general acclamation of Harry in the Leaky Cauldron pub: 'Harry Potter . . . what an honour', whispers the old barman.[25] Boundary crossings prior to arrival at Hogwarts include entry into Diagon Alley, through the literal construction of a portal in the wall of the pub courtyard: 'The brick he [Hagrid] had touched quivered – it wriggled – in the middle, a small hole appeared.'[26] Harry is also accepted into the economy of the magical world; his key to the family vault in Gringotts bank, handed over by Hagrid, is verified as authentic.[27] Running through the magical barrier at King's Cross Station to arrive at Platform Nine and Three-Quarters represents yet a third significant boundary crossing. However, all of these are staging points in Harry's journey to his true destination, Hogwarts.

As we saw above, Campbell's hero journey sequence includes a point of transition between 'Departure' and 'Initiation' labelled as 'The Belly of the Whale', an image of the 'worldwide womb'.[28] This is representative of

23 Rowling, *Harry Potter and the Philosopher's Stone*, 47.
24 Campbell, *The Hero with a Thousand Faces*, 48.
25 Rowling, *Harry Potter and the Philosopher's Stone*, 54.
26 Ibid., 55–56.
27 Ibid., 57.
28 Campbell, *The Hero with a Thousand Faces*, 78.

a fundamental reconstruction of identity, in which the hero symbolically dies and is reborn. In the *Harry Potter* series it is surely significant that only the new first years are conveyed to the school by means of boats across the lake.[29] The other students are conveyed in carriages. The narrative tells us that, having crossed the lake, the little boats carrying the new initiates pass through a curtain of ivy shrouding a dark tunnel in the cliff face, and carry them 'right underneath the castle' until they emerge at the other side in an underground harbour. Hagrid knocks three times on the huge oak front door: and they are granted admittance.[30]

The Sorting Hat ceremony provides the final stage of entry in the initiatory journey, in which the students are allocated to the four Houses: Gryffindor, Hufflepuff, Ravenclaw and Slytherin. It is even described as 'some sort of test' by Ron in his efforts to explain it to Harry, although it would be more accurate to describe it as 'some sort of evaluation', of which House best suits an individual's aspirations and qualities. Having passed through 'the gates of metamorphosis',[31] the 'road of trials' follows. The hero embarks on the path to transformation, encountering on the journey mentors and arch-enemies, helpers and antagonists. Aid or hindrance may be in forms other than the human, including the animal, supernatural and the talismanic.[32] The path is perilous, and it is long: 'Dragons have now to be slain and surprising barriers passed – again, again, and again.'[33]

A reading of the seven books provides a straightforward account in plot terms of the trials and quests-within-quests which Harry and his companions must undergo, which equate to Campbell's 'road of trials'. Underlying that is a more psychoanalytic framework for considering Harry's personal development. Relationships with father and mother figures are generally considered key in such development – albeit differently theorized in, for example, major thinkers such as Freud, Klein and Lacan. Mills analyses this in Oedipal terms: 'The Oedipal struggle between father and son is also an internal struggle within Harry to bring to consciousness, and thus resolve, shadowy contents of his personal unconsciousness.'[34] Following the later,

---

29 Grimes notes this and relates Harry's journey to Hogwarts to rebirth symbolism. See 'Harry Potter: Fairy Tale Prince, Real Boy and Archetypal Hero', 119.

30 Rowling, *Harry Potter and the Philosopher's Stone*, 84.

31 Campbell, *The Hero with a Thousand Faces*, 87.

32 Examples abound. With respect to the animal world, one can think of Aragog, Buckbeak, Hedwig and Crookshanks; in terms of talismans, the Sorting Hat, the Sword of Gryffindor and the Invisibility Cloak spring to mind. There are many others.

33 Campbell, *The Hero with a Thousand Faces*, 90.

34 Alice Mills, 'Archetypes and the Unconscious in *Harry Potter* and Diana Wynne Jone's *Fire and Hemlock* and *Dogsbody*', in Giselle Liza Anatol (ed.), *Reading Harry Potter* (Columbia and London: University of Missouri Press, 2004), 3–14 (5).

post-Freudian Rank, the story could still be read in terms of child-parent conflict resolution, but with a greater emphasis on the mother-infant dyadic union as the object of desire rather than sexual longing for the same-sex parent. Whatever reading is taken, father and mother relations are crucial to the child's navigation to adulthood. Therefore, it is to this network of father and mother figures that I now turn.

First, there is the complex of structural relations between Harry, his father-figures, and Voldemort. On the one hand, there is James, Harry's biological father. On entering the wizarding world, Harry learns that his father was not a wastrel, as the Dursleys had told him, but apparently a figure to admire and revere. This reinforces what Freud would consider a child's natural propensity to phantasize about being an adopted child whose biological parents are superior to the adoptive ones. As James is dead, Harry is free to constitute him as an ego-ideal and model:[35] a double of Harry himself, in fact, likewise in the mode of ego-ideal. This is textually played out in *Harry Potter and the Prisoner of Azkaban*; under attack by Dementors, Harry sees what he believes to be the Patronus[36] of his dead father. 'For a moment, Harry saw, by its brightness, somebody welcoming it back . . . raising his hand to pat it . . . someone who looked strangely familiar . . . but it couldn't be . . .'[37] Only a short narrative sequence later, returned to the same scene by the Time Turner, revelation arrives: 'And then it hit him – he understood. He hadn't seen his father – he had seen *himself* –'.[38] This recognition of himself in the idealized father figure represents an important moment in Harry's own development, and he finally produces a powerful Patronus of his own – which is, in fact, in the same stag-shape as his father's Animagus form. At this significant moment, when Harry is entering puberty and is beginning to integrate the father-ideal into his own identity, Lisa Damour's comment is amusingly apposite: 'the idea of a milky-white patronus leaping from the end of one's wand is, after all, nothing if not phallic.'[39]

35 Ibid., 4.
36 A 'Patronus' is the conjuration of an animal form. It is a protective surge of positive energy, and takes a shape reflecting the nature of the spellcaster. Its solidity depends on the skill and strength of the witch or wizard. Advanced magic, it is used to deflect Dementors. Patroni can also be used to send messages of unbreakable security against the Dark.
37 J. K. Rowling, *Harry Potter and the Prisoner of Azkaban* (London: Bloomsbury, 1999), 282.
38 Ibid., 300.
39 Lisa Damour, 'Harry Potter and the Acquisition of Knowledge', in Giselle Liza Anatol (ed.), *Reading Harry Potter*. 15–24 (21).

If James is the 'point of origin' in terms of father-figures, there are a number of reflections or doubles of him in Harry's world, beside Harry himself. Dumbledore is the obvious example of the 'good double', but Lupin and Sirius are among others who act towards Harry in that capacity. In terms of the 'bad double', in the Muggle world there is Harry's guardian and uncle Vernon Dursley: blustering, unloving and abusive. Yet Dursley is but a pale shadow of James's 'bad double' in the magical world: Lord Voldemort.

Alice Mills suggests that Voldemort 'functions as a compensatory, monstrous father-figure repeatedly irrupting from the unconscious in terror and malignancy.'[40] This is in keeping with psychoanalytic theories of 'splitting', whereby all goodness is attributed to an idealized object, and all that is painful or experienced as bad to a persecutory one. The identification of Voldemort as 'tied' to Harry and not simply an external, unrelated force is reinforced in the narrative by constant reference to the binary linkages between them. There is Harry's unique position as the 'Boy Who Lived', overthrowing Voldemort while a baby. This dynamic remains, even though it transpires that the causal agency is actually not intrinsic to Harry, but emerges from the protective enchantment cast by his mother's mortal sacrifice. In *Harry Potter and the Philosopher's Stone*, we also find out very early that the 'brother' of Harry's wand belongs to Voldemort.[41] In *Harry Potter and the Chamber of Secrets*, Harry is revealed as a Parselmouth,[42] the only other apart from Voldemort since Slytherin himself. In the same book, the avatar of the young Voldemort, Tom Riddle, himself comments to Harry: 'Because there are strange likenesses between us, Harry Potter. Even you must have noticed. Both half-bloods, orphans, raised by Muggles. . . . We even *look* something alike.'[43]

The connections between Harry and Voldemort/Riddle grow stronger as the series progresses. *Harry Potter and the Goblet of Fire* has the onset of a mental tie between the two, causing Harry's scar to hurt despite physical distance from Voldemort and giving him occasional flashes of knowledge about Voldemort's activities. The culmination of this book sees the bodily reconstitution of Voldemort from the bone of his father, the flesh of his servant, and the blood of his enemy: Harry.

---

40 Mills, 'Archetypes and the Unconscious in *Harry Potter* and Diana Wynne Jone's *Fire and Hemlock* and *Dogsbody*', 4.

41 This is on the basis of the two wands being the only ones in existence to have tail feathers from one particular phoenix as their magical 'core'.

42 A Parselmouth has the ability to talk to snakes.

43 J. K. Rowling, *Harry Potter and the Chamber of Secrets* (London: Bloomsbury, 1998), 233.

In the fifth book, *Harry Potter and the Order of the Phoenix*, Voldemort literally irrupts in Harry, who 'lives' the attack on Arthur Weasley in the consciousness of Voldemort's snake. This instalment also reveals an even deeper layer of connection between Voldemort and Harry, preceding even Harry's birth, through revelation of the prophecy which induced Voldemort to attack Harry as a baby in the first place. The prophecy predicted the birth of a child who would have the power to vanquish the Dark Lord and who would be marked by him as his equal. Furthermore, 'either must die at the hands of the other for neither can live while the other survives.'[44]

In *Harry Potter and the Deathly Hallows*, we have the culminatory revelation in this regard: in the act of attempting to murder baby Harry, Voldemort had dislodged a fragment of his own soul and left it lodged in Harry, who thereby became a Horcrux.[45] Thus Voldemort had some of Harry's blood, and Harry had part of Voldemort's soul. In this way, Dumbledore tells Harry at the end of the series, Voldemort had wrapped their '. . . destinies together more securely than ever two wizards were joined in history.'[46] In Oedipal terms, as Mills comments, the interactions between Harry and Voldemort can be understood as between 'the son, ignorant of the whole truth about his past, and the monstrous father-figure, out to destroy his son before his son kills him.'[47]

At the same time, Voldemort can also be understood as a brother figure. This is especially the case when considering his manifestation as Tom Riddle, the youthful Voldemort, but arguably in general, since even the adult Voldemort is, as Trites notes, 'something of a teenager run amok'.[48] An impression of underlying sibling hostility between Voldemort and Harry is also implied in their contrasting relations with Dumbledore, who stood in a position of authority to both of them at school. To Voldemort's fury, Dumbledore also rejected his application for

44 J. K. Rowling, *Harry Potter and the Order of the Phoenix* (London: Bloomsbury, 2003), 741.
45 In Rowling's fictional universe, a Horcrux is a means of attaining immortality, for it allows a wizard to separate a part of the soul from the physical body and hide it safely elsewhere. The magic requires murder to achieve. Voldemort, in already creating six Horcruxes, had rendered his own soul unstable: thus the involuntary fragmentation of his soul in attacking Harry.
46 J. K. Rowling, *Harry Potter and the Deathly Hallows* (London: Bloomsbury, 2007), 569.
47 Mills, 'Archetypes and the Unconscious in *Harry Potter* and Diana Wynne Jone's *Fire and Hemlock* and *Dogsbody*', 4.
48 Roberta Seelinger Trites, 'The Harry Potter novels as a test case for adolescent literature,' *Style* 35, no. 3 (Fall 2001): 427–85.

the Defence Against the Dark Arts teaching position. Riddle/Voldemort's hostility to Dumbledore is reproduced in their hostility to Dumbledore's protégé, Harry, 'Dumbledore's man through and through.'[49]

Mills puts the case that in assimilating part of Harry's blood, Voldemort has also in fact placed himself in a filial relationship to Harry. However, I suggest that a more potent reading of this takes cannibalism as the hermeneutic lens. Harry is, perplexingly to Voldemort, the most resist-ant 'Other' in opposition to him: as was seen in *Harry Potter and the Philosopher's Stone*, when sharing Quirrell's body he could not even touch Harry without searing pain.[50] Voldemort seeks to absorb the spirit of his enemy in assimilating Harry's blood – his life essence – and thereby ingest his power; in this case, the protective charm inscribed in Harry's blood by the sacrifice of his mother. As Voldemort says when the ritual has returned him to human form: 'I can touch him now.'[51]

Harry undergoes ambivalence in his relations with both James and Dumbledore, which form a significant part of the plot texture in *Order of the Phoenix* in particular. The movement towards reconciliation is gradual, and fully achieved with Dumbledore only at the very conclusion of the books: this is examined in more detail below. Coming to terms with the flaws and weaknesses in both James and Dumbledore is a crucial part of Harry's own maturation process. The most ambivalent of Harry's associations with male authority figures is his relationship with Severus Snape, an ambivalence mirrored in structural terms by Snape's position as double-agent. Snape's love for Harry's mother is what motivates him to join the Order of the Phoenix and to protect Harry, but the loathing between him and Harry is mutual and on Snape's side grounded in deep antipathy towards James. For his part, Harry's attitude towards Snape appears unambivalently hostile – but he was deeply attracted to the Half-Blood Prince, annotator of his helpful Potions book, before he realized the tendency of some of the curses therein inscribed towards darkness, and the identity of the Prince as the youthful Snape. At the end of the book, Harry is able to transcend his loathing of Snape to recognize his bravery and contribution – naming, indeed, one of his sons after him.

So far, selected significant male points of reference in Harry's life have been considered and related to his maturation and individuation in

---

49 J. K. Rowling, *Harry Potter and the Half-Blood Prince* (London: Bloomsbury, 2005), 326.

50 Rowling, *Harry Potter and the Philosopher's Stone*, 213–14.

51 J. K. Rowling, *Harry Potter and the Goblet of Fire* (London: Bloomsbury, 2000), 566.

the course of his 'hero journey'. Turning to their female counterparts, it must first be acknowledged that Campbell's work has been subjected to significant feminist critique. This is on two counts: not only is the model of personal development presented taken from a 'masculine' model, but also within that the role of the 'feminine' is patriarchally presented. The classic account of the hero journey according to Campbell has two primary roles for female characters: the meeting with the goddess, and the woman as temptress.

The meeting with the goddess represents the experience of unconditional love, and can be considered a projection of an idealized infant-mother experience. The goddess-figure is 'the reply to all desire, the bliss-bestowing goal of every hero's earthly and unearthly quest. She is mother, sister, mistress, bride.'[52] Everything that seemed to offer the potential for joy has been in anticipation of the goddess, who incarnates a promise of perfection and an assurance to the soul that the bliss once known would be known again: 'the comforting, the nourishing, the "good" mother – young and beautiful – who was known to us, and even tasted, in the remotest past.'[53] At the same time, recollection of the 'bad' mother – absent, smothering, punishing and/or the object of forbidden desire – also persists. The two modes of the remembered mother are mythologically incorporated into universal cosmic representations of the goddess, as giver and taker of life: 'the womb and the tomb: the sow that eats her farrow.'[54]

For Campbell, the goddess is incarnate in every woman.[55] 'Woman' represents the totality of what can be known: the hero is the knower.[56] The man who can take her as she is 'without undue commotion, but with the kindness and assurance she requires, is potentially the king, the incarnate god, of her created world.'[57] This is evidently constructed from traditional understandings of the preferred male-female relationship, with the female occupying the symbolic polarity of passive/nature and the male that of active/god. The world may be her creation, but it is he who rules it.

In the *Harry Potter* series, Lily is clearly the primary 'good goddess' maternal figure. She is the epitome of perfect mother-love, extending the mother-infant union with Harry beyond the grave; the potent trace of her protective sacrifice is carried in his very blood. Unlike his relationship with

52 Campbell, *The Hero with a Thousand Faces*, 92.
53 Ibid.
54 Ibid., 95.
55 Ibid., 99.
56 Ibid., 97.
57 Ibid.

James, Harry's relationship with Lily never undergoes crisis, but remains as an unconditional constant. Petunia Dursley is equally clearly her sister's 'negative' double, a poor mother-substitute who colludes in the abuse and neglect of Harry in the Muggle environment. Unlike Vernon, however, both Petunia and Dudley do have a moment pointing in a redemptive direction as Harry leaves their house for the last time. Dudley acknowledges that Harry had saved his life; Petunia gives Harry the 'strangest feeling' that she wished to say something to him, but failed to do so.[58]

In the magical world, Mrs Weasley, mother of six sons and one daughter, embodies most fully the 'good' maternal principle. She is an obvious 'earth mother', generous with food and love, and her interactions with Harry develop to include the physical expression of maternal affection that Lily was unable to provide: Harry had 'no memory of ever being hugged like this, as though by a mother.'[59]

Within the magical world, it is Bellatrix LeStrange who mirrors the 'dark mother' to fullest extent. The primary antagonist position to Harry is already taken by Voldemort, but Bellatrix is an able female lieutenant. She is obsessively attached to Voldemort, speaks to him 'as if to a lover'[60] and considers herself his 'most loyal servant'.[61] She helped torture Harry's classmate Neville's parents into insanity, and also tortures Neville and Hermione. Her killing tally includes such significant characters as Sirius Black, Dobby and Nymphadora Tonks. Mills, in a 2004 publication, sees the 'wicked adult female' as missing in Harry's life and that 'there is no way in which Harry confronts this feminine agent of evil.'[62] The first statement clearly cannot be sustained once Bellatrix emerges fully onto the scene in the later books. The second is sustainable in part, in that he cannot summon the necessary ill-will to apply a successful Cruciatus curse upon her, even after she has killed Sirius. On the other hand, she is the first person against whom he is even moved to attempt it. Her relative structural location as the anti-maternal principle is reinforced by the manner of her death at the hands of Mrs Weasley. She has narrowly missed Ginny Weasley with a killing curse:

'NOT MY DAUGHTER, YOU BITCH!'
Mrs Weasley threw off her cloak as she ran, freeing her arms. Bellatrix

58 Rowling, *Harry Potter and the Deathly Hallows*, 41.
59 Rowling, *Harry Potter and the Goblet of Fire*, 620.
60 Rowling, *Harry Potter and the Deathly Hallows*, 580.
61 Rowling, *Harry Potter and the Order of the Phoenix*, 715.
62 Mills, 'Archetypes and the Unconscious in *Harry Potter* and Diana Wynne Jones' *Fire and Hemlock* and *Dogsbody*', 6.

spun on the spot, roaring with laughter at the sight of her new challenger
. . .

'What will happen to your children when I've killed you?' taunted
Bellatrix . . . 'When Mummy's gone the same way as Freddie?'

'You – will – never – touch – our – children – again!' screamed Mrs
Weasley.[63]

Bellatrix has previously vanquished far superior duellists to Mrs Weasley,
but Rowling's narrative once more offers a strong corroboration of
maternal power. Ultimately, of course, Mrs Weasley is to become Harry's
mother-in-law; Ginny is the goddess in her incarnation as desire.

So that is woman as mother-destroyer, the first of Campbell's feminine
archetypes in his account of the stages in the hero's journey. To become
capable of possessing her, and taking the father's place,[64] the hero must
undergo the trials which represent the expansion of his consciousness. In
so doing, he becomes shockingly aware of the 'pushing, self-protective,
malodorous, carnivorous, lecherous fever' which is the true nature of
human existence. Realizing that all is tainted by the flesh, the hero may
well experience a revulsion: 'the acts of life, the organs of life, woman
in particular as the great symbol of life' become intolerable to the 'pure,
pure soul.'[65] If this revulsion is not transcended, the woman, the body and
the world all become symbols of defeat, and an ascetic, world-negating
ethical system ensues. However, not even desert remoteness or monastic
enclosure can defend against the presence of the female; Campbell notes
that all the hermit-resorts of history have been troubled by apparitions
'with loins of irresistible attraction and breasts bursting to be touched.'[66]
These represent the temptations, distractions and confusions which lie
along the path and are summed up by Campbell in his second feminine
archetype: woman as temptress.

This is a symbol, and need not be manifested literally in the shape of
a seductress or indeed a woman of any kind. The patriarchal framing of
such a symbol, and its association of the female with sin, temptation and
fleshy distraction have, of course, received critical attention, but as issues
of gender in relation to the heroic model are considered in some detail in
Chapter Three, I shall not linger on the point here. Accepting this stage
as representing simply 'temptations along the journey', how might it be

63 Rowling, *Harry Potter and the Deathly Hallows*, 589–90.
64 Campbell, *The Hero with a Thousand Faces*, 101.
65 Ibid., 101–2.
66 Ibid., 104.

interpreted in relation to Harry Potter? Ginny, the primary love interest in the story arc, is a goddess figure. She is also 'woman as temptation', since Harry feels unable to pursue a relationship with her while committed to the dark and dangerous path inherited from Dumbledore. He weakens once and kisses her, but I would argue, in fact, that Rowling's portrayal of Harry never shows him faltering in constancy of purpose. However, his purposes are potentially compromised by personal qualities and character-istics, the overcoming of which is part of his 'hero journey'. One primary 'flaw' she bestows upon her hero is a tendency towards risky behaviour without sufficiently analysing consequences, especially when emotionally stirred up; if rushing in where angels fear to tread is the act of a fool, then Harry acts the part of a fool on a number of occasions. A second is an overdeveloped sense of personal responsibility and protectiveness, such that he attempts to thwart the efforts of his friends to assist him if he can. As *Bildungsroman* literature, it is not surprising that Harry is presented as progressively mastering these failings and moving to a position of mature judgement and gracious acceptance of help.

Following these encounters, the hero enters the stage of 'atonement with the Father', which is the centre-point of the journey. The 'Father' represents authority in the aspects of both ogre and god, which are equally projections of the psyche. For Campbell:

> Atonement (at-one-ment) consists in no more than the abandonment of that self-generated double monster – the dragon thought to be God (superego) and the dragon through to be Sin (repressed id). But this requires an abandonment of the attachment to ego itself; and that is what is difficult.[67]

Attaining atonement with the Father enables apotheosis: a pattern of the divine state attainable when the human hero has vanquished the last terrors of ignorance, transcended parochial and falsely oppositional thinking, and focused the mind on the centrality of universal love. In its fullest expression, it is a recognition of the divine in the other, and the other in oneself. Having been sundered from the maternal union, chewed into fragments by the world-annihilating ogre, we are then reborn into a new state of being in which childhood images of parents, 'good', and 'evil' have been surpassed. It is also an acceptance of mortality in the affirmation of life, recognizing the co-incidence of eternity and time, knowledge and love, male and female. Apotheosis enables the completion of the quest,

---

67   Ibid., 109–10.

codified as the granting of the ultimate boon. Campbell notes how frequently this is a misguided desire for personal immortality, when instead illumination could be sought.[68] This 'agony of breaking through personal limitations' is the agony of spiritual growth past restrictive horizons into 'spheres of ever-expanding realization'.[69]

The hero-quest accomplished, there follows the return, which may initially be refused, and may also require a flight if the boon was taken without consent of its guardians or return to the world denied. External assistance may be required at this point. The first 'return' Harry makes is from the realm of the dead. If we look at the structure of the closing chapters of the *Harry Potter* series, this is embedded within a three-fold 'atonement with the Father' sequence. First, Harry goes alone to meet Voldemort, as a willing sacrifice so that the fragment of Voldemort's soul he harbours will be destroyed. The Christological undertones are patent, and were in fact publicly heralded by Rowling before the final book was even published. However, the killing curse does not quite work because Voldemort, in taking Harry's blood into himself in *Goblet of Fire*, kept 'alive' Lily's protective enchantment. Harry, not sure whether he is dead or alive, then encounters Dumbledore in a 'dream sequence' which resolves a number of unanswered questions and represents Harry's final coming to peace with Dumbledore through gaining in understanding and acceptance. Harry has the choice at this point; in Campbell's terms, he could refuse the return. However, he takes the heroic route:

> Leaving this place would not be nearly as hard as walking into the Forest had been, but it was warm and light and peaceful here, and he knew that he was heading back to pain and the fear of more loss.[70]

Harry's third and final 'atonement with the Father' scene is, appropriately, set in the Great Hall of Hogwarts. Believing him dead, Voldemort has his body carried back in triumph to Hogwarts as the final battle commences. Revealing himself to be alive, the last battle of all also appropriately takes place between Harry and Voldemort alone. 'It's just you and me', Harry tells Voldemort. He seeks to offer Voldemort the opportunity to show remorse, which of course he is incapable of doing, and in the end Voldemort is defeated by his own killing curse. Harry does not have to use magic stronger than an 'Expelliarmus' against him, for Harry is the

---

68   Ibid., 162–63.
69   Ibid., 163.
70   Rowling, *Harry Potter and the Deathly Hallows*, 579.

true master of the Elder Wand which Voldemort wields, and it will not function against him.[71]

This concluding sequence represents the culmination of Harry's hero quest. A number of significant motifs can be drawn from this to illustrate the manner in which Harry, truly, has undergone apotheosis in his self-transcendence and attainment of the full maturity of his powers. Rachel Falconer also sees in this Harry's attainment to power in exercising choice over destiny.[72] In particular, one can pick out: Harry's relationship with his father-figures; Harry's attainment to control over his own destiny; and Harry's reconciliation with death.

Just prior to his march to Voldemort to receive death at his hands, Harry has witnessed his murder of Snape to acquire the Elder Wand. Snape gifts Harry with his memories, and entrusts him as steward thereof. In meeting Dumbledore, Harry and he converse as equals; Dumbledore both confesses his own failings, and acknowledges Harry as the 'better man'[73] and the 'worthy possessor of the Hallows.'[74] In the final confrontation with Voldemort, it is Harry who takes charge of the conversation; who calmly states that Riddle has failed to learn from his mistakes; points out his misapprehensions; and finally offers Voldemort the opportunity for remorse. 'You dare –?' he replies. 'Yes, I dare', says Harry, before Voldemort dies by his own rebounded killing curse.

This whole Christomorphic sequence points to the shift in Harry from one who not infrequently wins out through lucky circumstances or accidents, to one who wins through wise choices. It includes a recognition by Harry that the death of his mother to save him was no accident; nor were his choices to fight Voldemort; nor was his choice on this occasion not to defend himself. Harry's readiness to die to save others has extended a mantle of protection over them, as Lily's did for him. Indeed, it is the relationship with death which appears as perhaps the most important theme in Harry's final attainment to 'Master of Two Worlds', and it is with a reflection on this that I will conclude.

First, one may consider the Resurrection Stone; one of the three

---

71 Another of the Deathly Hallows, the Elder Wand will only give its allegiance to one who wins it. Voldemort took it from Snape, not knowing that Snape had never defeated Dumbledore, the previous holder. It was Draco to whom Dumbledore yielded the wand, and Harry had already shown himself victor over Draco. Thus the wand recognized him as its master.

72 Rachel Falconer, *The Crossover Novel: Contemporary Children's Fiction and its Adult Readership* (London: Taylor & Francis, 2008), 70–72.

73 Rowling, *Harry Potter and the Deathly Hallows*, 571.

74 Ibid., 577.

Deathly Hallows, it returns the dead to a quasi-life. As such, it relates to an appropriate relationship with the dead. For the youthful Dumbledore's erstwhile friend Grindelwald, it had represented the potential to raise an army of corpses – the Inferi. For Dumbledore at that time, it offered the prospect of bringing his parents back to liberate himself from the care of his sister. For Voldemort, had he recognized it, it would have held little value. Dumbledore observes to Harry: 'whom would he want to bring back from the dead? He fears the dead. He does not love.'[75] For Harry, the situation was different; it is as he walks to sacrifice himself in order that Voldemort's soul-fragment within him would be destroyed that he calls upon his dead: 'he was about to join them. He was not really fetching them: they were fetching him.'[76] James, Sirius, Lupin and Lily: returned not as ghosts, and not as flesh, but most closely resembling the Riddle who had escaped from the diary in *Chamber of Secrets*: 'and he had been memory made nearly solid.'[77] The memory allusion is apposite; for as Sirius assures Harry, they are part of him, and invisible to anybody else; but 'their presence was his courage, and the reason he was able to keep putting one foot in front of the other.'[78]

The incident also represents a further stage in Harry's coming to terms with death, in relation both to the death of those he loved, and to his own death. This is a key moment in Campbell's hero's journey, and it is replicated in the *Harry Potter* books. As Dumbledore says to Harry:

> You are the true master of death, because the true master does not seek to run away from Death. He accepts that he must die, and understands that there are far, far worse things in the living world than dying.[79]

Zimmerman offers an extended analysis of relationships with both time and death in the *Harry Potter* cycle, utilizing the concept of the 'trace'.[80] She cites Ricoeur's definition of this: 'the trace indicates "here" (in space) and "now" (in the present), the past passage of living beings. It orients the hunt, the quest, the search, the inquiry.'[81] The trace, then, is the seam

---

75 Ibid.
76 Ibid., 560.
77 Ibid.
78 Ibid., 561.
79 Ibid., 577.
80 Virginia Zimmerman, 'Harry Potter and the Gift of Time', *Children's Literature* 37 (2009): 194–215.
81 Ricoeur, *Time and Narrative*, 12. Cited in Zimmerman, 'Harry Potter and the Gift of Time', 194.

of the past within the present. How one positions oneself in respect to the trace offers a telling insight into how one positions oneself in respect to time itself. Harry's relations with his dead and with his past are fundamental to the positive construction of his identity; the same is true of Voldemort, but in negative mode, for his only desire in relation to his personal history is to annihilate it: he creates his first Horcrux through committing patricide, and despises his mother for dying in giving birth to him. Harry hordes the small traces he has of his dead family – the photo album from Lupin, the magic mirror from Sirius, and so on. Voldemort picks out 'special' objects to act as his Horcruxes – such as Rowena Ravenclaw's diadem, Helga Hufflepuff's cup and Marvolo Gaunt's ring – but these have value as bearing the trace of status, and are not personally meaningful in a relational sense.

Voldemort and Harry, as can be seen from Zimmerman's analysis, stand at opposing ends of the spectrum in regard to their view of time, history and death. Voldemort, whose very name means 'flight from death', bends his will to the pursuit of immortality. Harry offers himself as a willing sacrifice in order to strike a blow in the war against Voldemort. Voldemort does not value the artefacts of time in his own family history except as trophies; Harry treasures his. Voldemort, ultimately, seeks the transcendence of time, and thereby of the conditions of phenomenal existence. Harry accepts death for the sake of history – that is to say, in order to preserve and protect the time of others, who would survive him.

Harry does, however, also survive his final and decisive encounter with Voldemort. The Boy Who Lived continues to live, as a man. He returns to scenes of acclamation and awe: again the Christological undertones are present, as hundreds of hands reach for him, determined to touch him, recognizing him as their 'saviour'.[82] The extended showdown with Voldemort was his personal, three-fold apotheosis; this is his public one.

> They wanted him there with them, their leader and symbol, their saviour and their guide, and that he had not slept, that he craved the company of only a few of them, seemed to occur to no one.[83]

Even the portraits of headmasters and headmistresses of Hogwarts applaud him – including that of Dumbledore, who is emanating a 'pride and gratitude' that fills Harry with the 'same balm as phoenix song.'[84] In

---

82 Rowling, *Harry Potter and the Deathly Hallows*, 596.
83 Ibid.
84 Ibid., 599.

a final display of heroic wisdom, Harry refuses to take up the deadly and powerful Elder Wand, but lays it to rest in Dumbledore's tomb.

Harry's story, it has been argued here, maps onto Joseph Campbell's hero quest, and represents a spiritual and personal transformation with distinctly Christological sub-texts in places. Now returned to 'normal' existence, the hero must come to terms with the world of the common day and take up a position as 'Master of Two Worlds'. In Campbell's schema, having undergone the supreme ordeal at the nadir of the mythological round, the reward is gained. This may be represented as sacred marriage (sexual union with the goddess-mother), atonement with the father (recognition by the father-creator), apotheosis (his own divinization), or acquisition of the boon that was sought. Intrinsically, however, it is 'an expansion of consciousness and therewith of being (illumination, transfiguration, freedom).'[85] The hero re-emerges from the kingdom of dread (return, resurrection) and the world is restored by the boon that he brings.[86] In the case of Harry, all of the above apply. He has bestowed the boon of post-Voldemort life upon the world, and can now move forward with his own existence beyond the prophecy. Underlining this, the series ends on a generational note. Ginny, Harry, Hermione and Ron are seeing their children off on the train to Hogwarts. The quest over, Harry's scar has not pained him for 19 years.[87] There are the missing. There are also the living, with the flow of everyday existence continuing on. So, also, do the stories and symbols of heroes.

85 Ibid., 211.
86 Ibid.
87 Ibid., 607.

TRANSFORMING SELVES
EARTHSEA: 'THE EATEN ONE'

IT IS CLAIMED THAT the religious elements in many women's literary works have been overlooked, 'due to their variation from the traditional, male-defined concept of spiritual quest as a journey through trials, which, when overcome, result in a transcendent experience.'[1] The traditional heroic quest patterns have been criticized for over-reliance on models of heroism which assume a masculine protagonist in terms of psychoanalytic development and symbolism of life-challenges. It can also be argued that patriarchal values continue to dominate texts even where female characters have a lead role. Qualities commonly identified as 'patriarchal' include physical stature, rational detachment, action, and the capacity to engage as a warrior. Connections drawn between feminist spirituality and fantastic fiction 'recast heroic femininity as a spiritual exercise.'[2] This chapter takes the young adult female hero journey as the focus of consideration, looking at the portrayal of Arha/Tenar in Ursula K. Le Guin's *The Tombs of Atuan*.

This is especially interesting because of Le Guin's own, purposeful revisiting of her original *Earthsea* trilogy specifically in light of a raised feminist consciousness during the intervening years. In the three books produced between 1968–72, the second, *The Tombs of Atuan*, featured a central female character, Arha, who became Tenar. Le Guin returned to Earthsea 18 years later, and over a course of years produced another three volumes. The first of these, *Tehanu*, was flagged (it turned out erroneously)

1   Janice C. Crosby, *Cauldron of Changes: Feminist Spirituality in Fantastic Fiction* (Jefferson, NC: McFarland, 2000), 1.
2   Ibid., 2.

as the 'last book of Earthsea' (1990). It was followed by *The Other Wind* and a collection of short stories, *Tales from Earthsea* (both published in 2001). In a 1992 lecture, *Earthsea Revisioned*,[3] Le Guin articulated the philosophy and rationale underpinning her return to Earthsea. The focus of her talk was gender politics, which she identified as a major driver in her desire to create another *Earthsea* novel – one foregrounding female protagonists. In the opening to her lecture, she drew attention to the gendered nature of hero-tales; 'with rare exceptions . . . women are not heroes. They are sidekicks. Never the Lone Ranger, always Tonto.'[4] Furthermore, she considers that the 'maleness' of the hero-tale has profoundly influenced its structural dynamics. It is about the establishment and validation of manhood; it is about a quest, a conquest, a test, involving conflict and sacrifice. The typical archetypes of mythology as identified by Jung – such as the devouring mother, the wounded king, the wicked witch – are 'immensely useful', but nevertheless 'mindforms of the Western European psyche as perceived by a man.'[5]

There has, therefore, been a call for female heroes who do not simply occupy the traditional heroic mould (doing their own 'hunting, fighting and monster-slaying') while sporting perky breasts and lustrous hair. Such a move expands the envelope of female representation, but does not fundamentally challenge extant models of positive cultural value. Le Guin herself has stated, with reference to science fiction, that the field has shifted from tales of heroes and killers to commentary on human culture; her novels, she says, have 'people', not just 'heroes'.[6]

Therefore, the tale of Arha/Tenar offers an interesting window on to a discussion of heroic self-transformation attentive to gendered dynamics. It is the story, written by a woman, of a young woman on a 'coming-of-age' journey which the author herself subsequently determined was not an adequate account of female development. Le Guin herself readily admits to patriarchal structures embedded in the initial trilogy, although does point out that she attempted to be subversive in her portrayal of ethnicity. 'Only the villains were white. . . . I meant this as a strike against racial bigotry.'[7] Arha/Tenar of the second novel, is the exception: she is Kargish,

---

3   Ursula K. Le Guin, *Earthsea Revisioned* (Cambridge, MA: Children's Literature New England, 1993).

4   Ibid., 5.

5   Le Guin, *Earthsea Revisioned*, 6.

6   See Ursula K. Le Guin, 'The Carrier-Bag Theory of Fiction', in Denise Du Point (ed.), *Women of Vision* (New York, NY: St Martins Press, 1988), 1–9.

7   Le Guin, *Earthsea Revisioned*, 8.

and it was already established that Kargs were white.[8] It seems that Tenar, however, cannot attain the dignity of being named as hero; she is, says Le Guin, a heroine; she is not a free agent; she is complementary to the hero, Ged. Le Guin makes this argument despite critical commentary suggesting that Tenar and Ged are actually interdependent. It is part of the wider structure of her world at the time:

> Communities of men in Earthsea are defined as powerful, active and autono-mous; the community of women in Atuan is described as obedient to distant male rulers, a static, closed society. No change can come, nothing can be done, until a man arrives. Hero and heroine depend on each other in getting free of this terrible place, but the man originates the action of the book.[9]

And, of course, in all three books the power of magic is found only in men who have no sexual contact with women. This aspect will be explored in more detail in Chapter Five. Taking all of this into consideration leads Le Guin to this damning conclusion: 'The establishment of manhood in heroic terms involves the absolute devaluation of women. The woman's touch, in any sense, threatens that heroic masculinity.'[10]

My aim here is to revisit the story of Tenar and to consider it as a 'female' hero journey, taking note of its co-optation into patriarchal symbolisms and structures, but then moving on from that to attempt to suggest ways in which it can be read 'against the grain'. Le Guin felt morally and politically impelled to return to Earthsea and 'revision' it; for what had been innocence, after the feminist revolution, became irrespon-sibility.[11] I should like to intimate other possible avenues for revisioning, which depend on re-reading rather than re-writing.

In the preceding chapter, the primary analytic frame deployed was the hero quest as outlined by Joseph Campbell. It is worth pausing briefly here to relate the concerns of this chapter to Campbell's model, as to do so underlines clearly what the problematic is with traditional accounts of the hero quest from a feminist perspective. Feminist interventions will then be indicated. According to Campbell:

> The male usually has the more conspicuous role, just because of the condi-tions of life. He is out there in the world, and the woman is in the home.

---

8   Ibid.
9   Ibid., 9.
10   Ibid., 11.
11   Ibid., 12.

... Giving birth is definitely a heroic deed, in that it is the giving over of oneself to the life of another.[12]

Campbell, then, is anxious to reclaim a space for female heroism, and emphasizes the heroic value of motherhood – often overlooked because of its lack of novelty. He incorporates in this not only the birth process, but the continuing commitment entailed in mothering. This is, of course, important. However, in so doing he simultaneously restricts the potential heroic role of the female to the 'traditional' feminine realms of birth and domesticity. Heroic discourse is dominated by the transition from boy to man. The woman transforms from maiden to mother ('a big change, involving many dangers'[13]), but for Campbell this is in a sense simply an automatic transition.

> It's harder for the boy than for the girl, because life overtakes the girl. She becomes a woman whether she intends it or not, but the little boy has to intend to be a man. At the first menstruation, the girl is a woman. The next thing she knows, she's pregnant, she's a mother. The boy first has to disengage himself from his mother, get his energy into himself, and then start forth.[14]

Such an analysis diminishes any possibility of a heroic dimension to female development, because it is removed from conscious action and becomes a function of bodiliness.[15] This is, of course, a wholly typical gesture within patriarchal constructs of the female and female value. Unsurprisingly, feminist critics have challenged such accounts of female heroism. One significant contribution in this area is a study of the female hero in American and British literature by Carol Pearson and Katherine Pope, who seek to offer a female-oriented account of the hero's journey, arguing that understanding of 'the basic spiritual and psychological archetype of human life' has been limited, not only by gender, but also in terms of ethnicity and social status.[16] Their study both equalizes the playing field, in asserting that the journey of self-discovery is the same at archetypal

---

12 Joseph Campbell and Bill Moyers, *The Power of Myth*, ed. Betty Sue Flowers (New York: Doubleday, 1988), 153.
13 Ibid.
14 Ibid., 168.
15 In this respect, Campbell appears to be echoing views aired some four decades previously: 'The woman is life, the hero its knower and master' (Joseph Campbell, *The Hero with a Thousand Faces* [Novato, CA: New World Library, 2008], 120).
16 Carol Pearson and Katherine Pope, *The Female Hero in American and British Literature* (New York, NY: R.R. Bowker, 1981), 4.

level for both male and female, and attempts to identify ways in which situational differentiation may require differentiation in heroic models.

There is a distinction here between the female hero and the heroine, who typically exists as a supporting character or within an immanent, pre-defined subjectivity conforming to stereotypical and archetypal expectations of the feminine. The female hero, like her male counterpart, embarks on a voyage of discovery, including discovery of the self. A hero is the artist of her own life. Her situation is emblematic for other women. Her actions have effect. She exceeds the stereotypical as cultural role-model. In short, she has entered a mode of transcendent rather than immanent existence, using de Beauvoir's distinction between 'transcendence' as self-overcoming and 'immanence' as stagnation or subsistence.[1]

For Pearson and Pope, one 'job' of the female hero is to depart from the role prescribed for her, slaying external dragons of patriarchal society, and socially induced internal dragons which inhibit her self-fulfilment. The treasure acquired is her own true self: vital and powerful. Pearson and Pope are also careful to note that men who occupy relatively powerless locations because of class or race may similarly be excluded by a 'macho' account of the hero's journey; in exploring the heroic journeys of such categories of people, an archetypal hero emerges who 'masters the world by understanding it, not by dominating, controlling, or owning the world or other people.'[2]

There is a path here that requires careful navigation. On the one hand, it is an important and affirmative deed to recognize and validate the kinds of activities which do not fall within traditional models of the heroic. This would include revisiting the kinds of qualities which constitute a hero. It might also incorporate acts that are repetitive and everyday, but nonetheless personally demanding and socially significant; caregiver roles and much work-related activity could potentially be described in this way. On the other hand, by legitimating more 'mundane' tasks, one would not wish to occlude the possibility of heroic journeys in a broader range of realms (whether undertaken by women or men). If one role of fiction is to imagine a transformational space, the irruption of the extraordinary or the non-quotidian is one manner in which expansion of consciousness can occur. It is precisely this which, as was indicated in Chapter One, grants fantasy its spiritual power.

In what follows I shall assess *The Tombs of Atuan* as deserving of Le Guin's critique, but also point out ways in which her original story-cycle

---

1   Simone de Beauvoir, *The Second Sex* (New York, NY: Knopf, 1971).
2   Pearson and Pope, *The Female Hero in American and British Literature*, 5.

subverted patriarchal structures even while reflecting and upholding them. This is both an exercise in its own right and a prequel to Chapter Five, which considers Le Guin's feminist refashioning and development of the metaphysical basis of *Earthsea*.

The Tombs of Atuan is set in the Kargad Lands, already established in *A Wizard of Earthsea* as 'Other' to the Archipelago centred around Havnor. A small girl, Tenar, is taken from her family in accordance with custom and ritual; she was born on the night the One Priestess of the Tombs of Atuan died, and is therefore deemed to be her reincarnation. She is destined to become Arha, the Eaten One, whose life and service are dedicated to the Nameless Ones. The Place of the Tombs is a complex of temples set in the desert; it is ruled by the three priestesses who serve the Nameless Ones, the Godking and the Twin Gods respectively. Only women, eunuchs and sacrificial prisoners are allowed within its sacred precincts. As Arha matures, she begins to master her realm – the deep labyrinthine structures lying beneath the Place of the Tombs. She also begins to realize her own lack of power; the centre of theological and political gravity lies not with the Nameless Ones, whose worship is increasingly nominal, but with the Godking who ruled in Awabath.[3]

At this point, there is an unexpected intrusion into the apparently timeless and unchanging rhythms of the Place: Arha finds a man wandering in the labyrinth. He is Ged, hero of *A Wizard of Earthsea*,[4] and now Archmage; he seeks the broken half of the Ring of Erreth-Akbe in order to restore the lost Rune of Peace to the Hardic Kingdom. Arha knows she should have him killed, but cannot quite bring herself to do so. Instead, she continues to see him and converse with him, deceiving her fellow priestess Kossil; she becomes, once more, Tenar. Ultimately, both Ged and Tenar escape from the Tombs and Kossil, together with the ring. The wrath of the Nameless Ones precipitates an earthquake, held at bay by Ged while he and Tenar escape, which obliterates the Hall of the Thrones and topples the Tombs themselves. Ged takes Tenar back to Havnor, city of the lost King.

That, then, is an overview of the story arc in which Arha takes on a new identity as Tenar, and in so doing enters into a whole new realm of being. To that extent, it is classic coming-of-age literature. Within this, Le Guin is direct about the thematic focus.

---

3   The High Priestess of the Godkings, Kossil, tells her: 'They are old. Their worship is forgotten, save in this one place. Their power is gone. They are only shadows. They have no power any more' (Ursula K. Le Guin, *The Tombs of Atuan – The Earthsea Quartet* [London: Puffin, 1992], 259.).

4   A summary of *A Wizard of Earthsea* can be found in Chapter One.

The subject of *The Tombs of Atuan* is, if I had to put it in one word, sex. There's a lot of symbolism in the book, most of which I did not, of course, analyze consciously while writing; the symbols can all be read as sexual. More exactly, you could call it a feminine coming of age. Birth, rebirth, destruction, freedom are the themes.[5]

The sexual dynamic is implicit; no sexual activity or declarations take place between Ged and Tenar. However, as Le Guin says, the book is replete with sexual symbolism and can certainly be read as the story of a girl's sexual awakening and precipitation from childhood concerns to a more mature acceptance of choice, responsibility and existential uncertainties. Her meeting with Ged thus represents her growth to maturity, which includes the development of sexual awareness and desire. As Le Guin's comment indicates, the symbolic dimensions of the story are key to its unfolding. In contrast to the typical male hero quest, which involves spatial action, the great majority of *The Tombs of Atuan* is spatially confined. This is itself a telling symbolism of the immanence of the feminine. Given this symbolic significance of the spatial context of the story, I shall first turn my attention to that, and consider the winding space at the heart of the story: the labyrinth.

The labyrinth has a long-standing spiritual history. 'Walking the labyrinth' is a contemporary spiritual practice as a metaphor for life's sacred journey, as a tool for meditation, and for prayer or enlightenment. The labyrinth can be identified with the Jungian anima: 'the entangling and confusing representation of the world of the matriarchal consciousness.'[6] Churches of medieval France and Italy frequently sport labyrinthine patterns in mosaic or as carvings. These may be symbols for the cosmos. Four ancient labyrinths are attested by Pliny in *Natural History* (36:13): Cretan, Egyptian, Lemnian and Italian. Herodotus, Diodorus Siculus and Strabo are also among those of Graeco-Roman times who referred to labyrinths. The labyrinth was associated with ceremonial dancing. It is also a place of death – recognized, for example, in the inscription on a mosaic representation of a labyrinth adorning a family tomb in Hadrumentum: 'He who is confined here loses his life.'[7]

5   Ursula K. Le Guin, *The Language of the Night: Essays on Fantasy and Science Fiction*, edited and with introductions by Susan Wood, 2nd edn (London: The Women's Press, 1989), 44.
6   Joseph Henderson, 'Ancient Myths and Modern Man', in Carl Gustav Jung and Marie-Luise von Franz (eds), *Man and his Symbols* (London: Doubleday, 1964), 104–57 (125).
7   Karl Kerényi, *Dionysos* (Princeton, NJ: Princeton University Press, 1996), 94.

Its most famous mythological appearance is surely in the legendary Cretan labyrinth built by Daedalus for King Minos at Knossos, in order to contain the Minotaur. This half-man, half-bull creature was then killed by Theseus with the assistance of Ariadne, who provided him with a sword and thread. Less well known, however, is that a tablet found in Linear B script at Knossos records that a goddess presided over the labyrinth: 'To the gods honey/To the mistress of the labyrinth honey.' Kerényi hypothesizes that the mistress in question is Persephone, Queen of the Underworld.[8] The 'mistress' is also associated with Ariadne in mythological remnants, which suggests she was a goddess. The Minotaur myth is the one with most resonance with Le Guin's account of the labyrinth in *The Tombs of Atuan*. Like most myths, it has many forms, but a common rendering is that Ariadne helped Theseus because she had fallen in love with him and subsequently ran away with him. In one version Theseus then abandons her on the Isle of Naxos and the god Dionysos rescues her. In another, her assistance to Theseus constitutes a betrayal of Dionysos, and she is killed for this by the goddess Artemis.

Therefore, the labyrinth has deep and rich symbolic value in mythological and spiritual spheres, having associations with the divine, the monstrous, the feminine, death, the underworld, journeying and transformation. The myth of Theseus and Ariadne adds to this further mythic layers: of murderous penetration (Theseus 'conquering' the labyrinth to kill the Minotaur), and of betrayal (the betrayal of her country and/or Dionysos by Ariadne, and of Ariadne by Theseus). The labyrinth in *The Tombs of Atuan* carries with it all of these connotations. Of particular interest for the purposes of this study is the specific location of the labyrinth in Le Guin's text as the sacred heart of a female religious cult. In particular, I would like to explore the problematic inscribed in this, given the extremely negative portrayal of that cult. While on the one hand the 'femaleness' of the cult could be seen as narratologically contingent, I would first like to put the case that the association of the cult with deeply feminine symbolism essentializes religion in the feminine mode as dark, devouring, empty, irrational, meaningless, stagnant and sterile.

This is particularly telling if Atuan is compared to Roke, the island of wizardry and a male citadel. Roke is presented as the guardian of wisdom and truth. It is an island, forested, fecund, where the air is 'bright with enchantments'.[9] It could not form a stronger foil for Atuan

---

8   Ibid., 106.
9   Ursula K. Le Guin, *A Wizard of Earthsea – The Earthsea Quartet* (London: Puffin, 1992), 32.

with its bitter and narrow-minded priestesses, its empty, joyless rituals and its dark underways. Furthermore, Atuan is marginal and withering within the Kargish Empire; Roke is central to the power structures of the Archipelago. From a feminist point of view, the alignment of these contrasting modes of being with a feminine/masculine division is especially unfortunate. *The Tombs of Atuan*, then, could be seen to present the 'subliminal message that women living without men must become twisted and purposeless, while men living without women can be productive and strong.'[10] This side of the argument will now be explored in relation to a number of symbolic and signifying fields.

Language itself is implicated in this gendered symbolic divide. As shall be explored more extensively in Chapter Five, the wizardry of Roke is based on a correspondence between truth of name and truth of thing when utilizing Old Speech rather than the vernacular. This is the basis of magic. It is an efficacious speech-act because of an ontological identity between word and world. In Karg, there is no magic, because the Kargs do not use Old Speech. In *Tombs*, this leads to a fundamental linguistic meaninglessness. The priestesses 'chant tunes made of babble'; speech 'cannot work to change the physical world because the signifiers used by the priestesses are not magically linked to any specific signifieds.'[11]

This vacuity at the centre of the religion is reinforced at every turn. The gods are nameless, and unnumbered. The throne in the Hall is empty. The Tombs are by nature a place of death, sited in the middle of the desert: both features evoke the lifeless, the sterile, the dry and the barren. While the Tombs are held to be full of meaning, 'there was no saying what they meant.'[12] The place is populated by virgins and eunuchs. The rituals are repeated cyclically, with no sense of change or efficacy or even meaning. The ritual consecrating Tenar as Arha, the Remaking of the Priestess, was filled with the chanting of a word that is empty, a word 'so old it had lost its meaning, like a signpost still standing when the road is gone.'[13] Arha's attitude towards the powers she serves and their labyrinth is occasionally marked by fear, or desire for the power her service to them might confer on her, but not devotion.

10 Cordelia Sherman, 'The Princess and the Wizard: The Fantasy Worlds of Ursula K. Le Guin and George MacDonald', *Children's Literature Association Quarterly* 12, no. 1 (1987): 24–28 (26).

11 Laura B. Comoletti and Michael D. C. Drout, 'How They Do Things with Words: Language, Power, Gender, and the Priestly Wizards of Ursula K. Le Guin's Earthsea Books', *Children's Literature* 29 (2001): 113–41 (121).

12 Le Guin, *The Tombs of Atuan*, 187.

13 Ibid., 179.

She, the High Priestess herself, is the emptiest signifier of all. Her very name is taken away from her. She is simply Arha: the Eaten One. This effacement of identity through consumption resonates unpleasantly with constructs both of the devouring maternal and, when taken in conjunction with the womb-like Undertomb, of the 'vagina dentata' – the toothed vagina, classic symbol of male fear of castration during sex, or more broadly of re-assimilation and obliteration of identity through return to the womb. Mithu M. Sanyal offers a cultural history of the vulva which shows it to be a void both semantically and symbolically – a 'gate to Hell', behind which the vagina dentata threatens.[14] In fact, the only men allowed in the Undertomb were eunuchs, and captives who had their tongues cut out. The deliberate obliteration of speech is another kind of identity efface-ment and a return to the pre-linguistic. While the Nameless Ones are not gendered, Nodelman shows that they are suggestively coded as feminine, because 'the dark powers worshipped by women in the tombs of Atuan clearly relate to Jungian archetypes of the feminine – they are irrational, passive, and below consciousness, and their place is dark, labyrinthine, womblike.'[15] As has been noted by a number of feminist critics, Jung's archetypal gender qualities play into the stereotypical; women 'are either exterior containers for male projections or subordinate elements of the male personality.'[16]

These negative accounts code a fear of the feminine and of the maternal that is reminiscent of Kristeva's theory of the abject. Abjection is caused by 'what disturbs identity, system, order. What does not respect borders, positions, rules. The in-between, the ambiguous, the composite.'[17] The primal abjection is of the maternal, which must be rejected and repressed in order to achieve separation from the mother's body; this matricide is a pre-condition of individuation. The maternal body evokes both fascina-tion and fear, particularly of engulfment.

The void in signification is also interesting given the association of the maternal with the pre-linguistic in psychoanalytic accounts of human development, where entry into the symbolic order and realm of language is

14 Mithu M. Sanyal, *Vulva* (Berlin: Wagenbach, 2009), as discussed in Ulrike Baureithel, 'The Origin of the World', *signandsight.com*, 16 June 2009. Online: http://www.signandsight.com/features/1885.html
15 Perry Nodelman, 'Reinventing the Past: Gender in Ursula K. Le Guin's *Tehanu* and the *Earthsea* "Trilogy"', *Children's Literature* 23 (1995): 179–201 (184).
16 Annis Pratt, *Archetypal Patterns in Women's Fiction* (Bloomington, IN: Indiana University Press, 1981), 8.
17 Julia Kristeva, *Powers of Horror*, trans. Leon S. Roudiez (New York, NY: Columbia University Press, 1982), 4.

effected by submission to the Law of the Father. This can also be related to different accounts of temporality. I shall quote here at length from Julia Kristeva on 'Women's Time':

> At the same time female subjectivity would seem to provide a specific measure that essentially retains *repetition* and *eternity* from among the multiple modalities of time known through the history of civilizations. On the one hand, there are cycles, gestation, the eternal recurrence of a biological rhythm . . . whose stereotyping may shock, but whose regularity and unison with what is experienced as extrasubjective time, cosmic time, occasion vertiginous visions and unnameable *jouissance*. On the other hand, and perhaps as a consequence, there is the massive presence of a monumental temporality, without cleavage or escape . . . All-encompassing and infinite like imaginary space . . .[18]

In *Tombs*, time is presented as cyclical, ordered to a ritualistic rhythm. 'Time did not mean very much, here in the desert land, under the unchanging Stones, leading a life that had been led in the same way since the beginning of the world.'[19] Therefore, this cosmic, cyclical, repetitive mode of temporality can be related to Kristeva's 'women's time'; this is significant in part because of its distinction from linear time, the temporality of agency, action and teleology. This reinforces the immanence of Tenar's subject location, enclosed by monumental temporality with no exit route.

Comparing the contextual presentation of Tenar and Ged, the masculine/feminine imagery along traditional dualistic lines is clear:

> Throughout *Tombs*, Le Guin makes traditional connections between femininity and receptivity, silence, darkness, touch, and emotion, on the one hand, and between masculinity and authority, speech, light, sight, and reason, on the other.[20]

Thus, Ged wields his staff and bears light; Tenar is mistress of the dark, uterine Undertomb.

It has been noted already that Le Guin considered her portrayal of

18 Julia Kristeva, 'Women's Time', trans. Alice Jardine and Harry Blake, *Signs* 7, no. 1 (1981): 13–35 (16).
19 Le Guin, *The Tombs of Atuan*, 195.
20 Perry Nodelman, 'Reinventing the Past: Gender in Ursula K. Le Guin's *Tehanu* and the Earthsea "Trilogy"', *Children's Literature* 23 (1995): 179–201 (188).

Ged, Tenar and their world such that, in all feminist conscience, she felt a responsibility to return to Earthsea and revision it. The analysis above demonstrates the extent to which the symbolic field for Tenar's feminine 'quest' could be said to reinforce negative portrayals of a spiritual world coded in the feminine, from which the girl coming of age needs liberation through the agency of a masculine principle, who delivers her into the adult socio-political world of patriarchal relations. However, let us consider some further dimensions to Tenar's story and see if a more fruitful pattern for feminine development can be discerned.

Looked at in another way, the narrative arc of *Tombs* actually represents a rejection of modes of femininity which stifle the formation and development of subjectivity and agency, and endorses a transition to greater freedom, choice and self-determination. In that sense, *Tombs* can be seen as a story of self-actualization and a young woman's development to agency and individuation. At the same time, the midwife of this change is a man, and it could be said that this returns her to a position of dependency – but this time in the 'adult' world of male-female relations rather than the 'childhood' world enclosed by the maternal. It seems that she has accepted Ged's valuation of her situation and herself, and taken her name back from him. Nodelman declares that: 'Vision has triumphed over touch, light over darkness, naming over namelessness – male over female. And in the process, both masculinity and femininity have been defined.'[21]

This is true also of the macro-level. Tenar did not choose the darkness, but she believes it to be the source of her power; her choice is to relinquish that power and emerge from the darkness – but only at the catalyst of the external intrusion of a man. Ged, through his own hubristic actions, chose to invite in the darkness, thus precipitating an active pursuit of it. His pivotal choice is to accept the darkness, the Shadow, and name it with his own name; in this way he attains his own power. 'Her goal is separation', comments Nodelman, 'his, wholeness ... she triumphs by giving up power, he by regaining it.'[22] This has obvious points of contact with a patriarchal model of male and female 'proper' roles and identities. Furthermore, Ged's 'salvation' is fundamentally a solitary act, albeit witnessed by Vetch. Tenar's 'salvation' is dependent upon Ged. Understood this way, Tenar does not even qualify as a 'female hero' on the Pope and Pearson model – she does not 'slay the dragons' of female inferiority in patriarchy or of her inner self-valuation, she does not connect positively

21 Ibid., 190.
22 Ibid., 187.

with female tradition and community, and she does not liberate herself from patriarchally dependent relations.

However, the extent of this dependency is debatable. Nodelman opines that 'Tenar is saved by Ged, whereas Ged saves himself.'[23] If this is so, truly Tenar's rite of passage is from a position of dependent 'girl' in one sphere of existence to dependent 'woman' in another. However, this is not the only possible reading of Tenar's story. It can be argued that Ged's salvation in *Tombs* is as dependent upon Tenar as hers is on him.[24] Without Tenar's protection, Ged would either have died in the labyrinth or met with a summary execution. Without Tenar's guidance, he would not have been able to navigate his way to freedom. Ged pays tribute to Tenar's salvific capacity: 'I was dying of thirst when you gave me water, yet it was not water alone that saved me. It was the strength of the hands that gave it.'[25] It is also true that without Ged, Tenar would probably never have attained either the will or the desire to leave Atuan. What this boils down to on both sides is trust.

The Ring of Erreth-Akbe is likewise a potent symbol of the trusting union between Ged and Tenar. One half resided in the treasure room at Atuan; Ged had already found the other half. Arha removes Ged's from him at an early point in the story; Ged locates the other half when imprisoned. So Ged has Tenar's half of the ring, and she has his. Together, the lost rune of peace can be reconstructed. Ged names trust as the important thing between him and Tenar and in recognition of this, he gives Tenar both his true name and the Ring of Erreth-Akbe.[26] It is in response to these gestures of trust that Tenar decides she will accompany him. The significance of this is fully acknowledged by Ged: '"You have set us both free," he said. "Alone, no one wins freedom."'[27]

It can be said that Ged gives Tenar her name, thus replaying an Adamic exertion of power (Gen 2.20). However, this is not strictly true. It is more accurate to say that Ged discerns her name, an ability he has as an aspect of his magely arts. The name itself is already Tenar's. This is important, because it can be argued that Ged's recognition of Arha as Tenar actually leads to a more ultimate catalyst moment: Tenar's reconnection with her

---

23 Ibid.
24 For other readings in support of this view, see for example Holly Littlefield, 'Unlearning Patriarchy: Ursula Le Guin's Feminist Consciousness in *The Tombs of Atuan* and *Tehanu*', *Extrapolation* 36, no. 3 (Fall 1995): 244–58 and Susan Hopkins, *Girl Heroes: The New Force in Popular Culture* (Sydney: Pluto Press, 2002), 3.
25 Le Guin, *The Tombs of Atuan*, 265.
26 Ibid., 273.
27 Ibid., 274.

own mother. Immediately following the scene where Ged names her, we are told that Tenar dreams of the dead souls on the walls of the Painted Room:

> One of them came up quite close to her. She was afraid at first and tried to draw away, but could not move. This one had the face of a bird, not a human face; but its hair was golden, and it said in a woman's voice, 'Tenar', tenderly, softly, 'Tenar'.
>
> She woke. Her mouth was stopped with clay. She lay in a stone tomb, underground. Her arms and legs were bound with grave clothes and she could not move or speak.[28]

This, then, is the 'good', nurturing maternal reasserting itself over the 'bad', destroying maternal, whose realm is suddenly perceived by Tenar as a living death: a stasis with no breath or life or movement. It is this dream which prompts her announcement: '"I am Tenar," she said, not aloud, and she shook with cold, and terror, and exultation, there under the open, sun-washed sky. "I have my name back. I am Tenar!"'[29] Above, a hawk circles. The hawk is recurrently used as a symbol of Ged, whose use-name is Sparrowhawk: the hawk here is witness, but the reclamation of Tenar's name is her own in matrilineal descent. In this respect, Tenar's self-annunciation can be seen to map onto the model of the female hero journey promulgated by Pearson and Pope, whereby reintegration with or discovery of the maternal world and female traditions is a culminating point. Tenar has found a way to a warmer conception of maternally generated identity.

However, her journey outward is only beginning and is marked both by loss of faith and fear. She suffers a crisis of identity in the confusions precipitated by her conversations with Ged, which is explicitly related to spiritual crisis: 'I am not Tenar. I am not Arha. The gods are dead, the gods are dead'.[30] This association of loss of self-identity and the death of the gods is akin to the dissolution of meaning foreseen by Nietzsche with the death of God. It is pointing to the radical reconstruction of her world, where all the old certainties are falling away. This is a mirror for child development and acceptance of ambiguity, ambivalence and questioning of previously accepted boundaries. This transformation of Arha into Tenar is also explicitly related to the mythic trope of death of the old self

---

28 Ibid., 257.
29 Ibid., 158.
30 Ibid., 264.

and rebirth to the new. 'To be reborn one must die, Tenar,' Ged tells her. And Tenar makes her choice. She will be Tenar. '"I will come with you," she said.'[31]

Their exit from the underground caverns has overtones both of first-time sex and of birth. All the exits are blocked. Ged strikes his staff down 'against the red rock of the shut door', which 'burst asunder.' Earlier, that same doorway had been described in terms evocative of the vaginal entrance – as a 'narrow slit', with the darkness upon entry pressing like 'wet felt'.[32] Now, in leaving, Tenar 'crouched on hands and knees there between the earth and sky', caught between the old world and the new, writhing back 'into the crumbling, lipless mouth of the Tombs.'[33] Enjoined by Ged in the name of the Ring of Erreth-Akbe – a bond of trust, and of peace – she rises, puts her hand in his, and goes with him. Behind them, the Tombstones collapse and are swallowed into the earth.

Tenar feels 'newborn.'[34] Travelling to the coast with Ged, she begins to learn the language of the Archipelago. While on the one hand, this speaks to entry into potentiality, it also speaks to a great vulnerability and lack of both knowledge and experience. She enters her new world with no compass: '"All I know is of no use now', she says, 'and I haven't learned anything else. I will try to learn."'[35]

At this point, it is pertinent to recall the myth of the Minotaur. It was noted at the outset of this chapter that the story of Tenar and Ged has parallels to the story of Ariadne and Theseus, including Tenar's self-perception that she has betrayed her people.[36] Tenar experiences increasing fear of the unknown as they enter further into civilization: 'She knew nothing of forests, or cities, or the hearts of men.'[37] She asks Ged if he will stay with her when they have arrived in the Archipelago; he is obliged to tell her that he cannot. Tenar is increasingly agitated. 'He had made her follow him. He had called her by her name, and she had come crouching to his hand, as the little wild desert rabbit had come to him out of the dark . . . He would not stay with her. He had fooled her, and would leave her desolate.'[38] This is significant because, of course, Ged has no intention of abandoning her in the manner of Ariadne. At the same time he does

31 Ibid., 273.
32 Ibid., 199.
33 Ibid., 280.
34 Ibid., 287.
35 Ibid., 288.
36 Ibid., 298.
37 Ibid., 291.
38 Ibid., 294.

not stay with her. This is one of the key features marking Tenar's story out from the 'immanent' story of a heroine rather than hero. She is left to make her own way and not conjoined to a rescuer figure just as she is on the threshold of independence. Instead, Ged plans to take her to his own old mentor, Ogion, where she can, in silence, find her own way.[39] It is not the ending that one would have expected. It is radically open. There is no intimation of what Tenar's 'own way' might be.

The sea represents an intimation of these new potentialities. Seen for the first time by Tenar, it is 'a kind of joyous shimmering off on the edge of the world.'[40] As Ged and Tenar approach the sea, however, her anxieties increase – she even toys with a dagger while he sleeps, thinking to stab him and redeem herself. The sea is movement and vibrancy, but this is alien to Tenar. 'The desert, the mountains: they stood still. They did not cry out forever in a great, dull voice. The sea spoke forever, but its language was foreign to her. She did not understand.'[41]

Finally at sea, the 'dark hand' of the Nameless Ones looses its hold upon her. She weeps, because she is free. Le Guin inserts a didactic narratorial voice at this point:

> What she had begun to learn was the weight of liberty. Freedom is a heavy load, a great and strange burden for the spirit to undertake. It is not easy. It is not a gift given, but a choice made, and the choice may be a hard one.[42]

This is important. The point is explicit: freedom comes by choice rather than gift. This is emphasizing Tenar's own agency and autonomy, over against Ged's patronage. Tenar's contribution is, in fact, repeatedly endorsed by Ged himself. He tells her how he will speak of her to the princes of Earthsea: 'In the place of darkness I found the light, her spirit. By her an old evil was brought to nothing. By her I was brought out of the grave. By her the broken was made whole . . .'[43]

I would therefore suggest that Tenar is ultimately responsible for her own self-transformation. Ged clearly plays a pivotal role. However, this should not be seen to denigrate Tenar's journey. Ged, in fact, could also be read as Tenar's *animus*, in Jungian terms, in which he represents Tenar's own principle of autonomy, leadership and movement towards sexual

39 Ibid., 299.
40 Ibid., 289.
41 Ibid., 292.
42 Ibid., 295.
43 Ibid., 299.

integration. This would be a reversal of dominant scholarship, which tends to consider Tenar as Ged's *anima*.[44] The two are not mutually exclusive. Indeed, to read Tenar as Ged's *anima* would in itself point towards an enhanced feminist consciousness, in recognizing the incompleteness of Ged's self-actualization at the conclusion of *A Wizard of Earthsea*, where he has yet to form positive relations with a female except for big-brotherly interchange with Vetch's sister.

I would argue, then, that the most appropriate way to read *Tombs* is as moving away from the concept of the solitary, self-sufficient hero towards a partnership model. This is entirely in keeping with trajectories of feminist thought on the female hero, which tend to emphasize the significance of communities and networks in heroic success. Such, indeed, is the model Le Guin moves more explicitly towards when she returns to Earthsea with *Tehanu*. There, however, positive networks among women are explored, as shall be seen in Chapter Five. It is this lack of positive female-female relations which makes *Tombs* so easy to read as a patriarchal myth fostering the notion that women's self-actualization can only come about in dependence upon a man. This is bolstered by the use of feminine symbolism and structures to portray a restrictive, narrow, marginal and destructive Temple community. Again, Le Guin's return to Earthsea generates a whole new paradigm of feminine symbolism, as shall be seen later in the book. Perhaps, then, the second *Earthsea* trilogy is best read not as a repudiation of the worldview inscribed in *Tombs*, but a development of it. Just as Ged's journey at the end of *Wizard* is not complete, nor yet is Tenar's. Neither the heroic nor spiritual journey cease at some pre-marked threshold in a coming-of-age narrative, but spiral forward into different contexts and stages of life.

Sue Vaughn speaks of 'the hero which is not one'.[45] This might be expanded to denote models of personal spiritual becoming which, likewise, 'are not one'. Elizabeth Wulf, building on Vaughn's work, has sought to establish an alternative mode of the heroic which emphasizes situational action (rather than acting according to a pre-given heroic 'blueprint'), and the significance of becoming rather than being to heroic identity. This is to frame spatiality in temporality. Crucially, becoming 'refuses to stop or remain fixed on a particular perspective or stance of viewing.'[46] The

---

44 See, for example, John H. Crow and Richard D. Erlich, 'Shadows in Earthsea: Le Guin's Uses of a Jungian Archetype', in Joseph D. Olander and Martin Harry Greenburg (eds), *Ursula K. Le Guin* (Edinburgh: Paul Harris, 1979), 220–24.

45 Sue F. Vaughn, 'The Female Hero in Science Fiction and Fantasy: "Carrier-Bag" to "No-Road"', *The Journal of the Fantastic in the Arts* 4, no. 4 (1991): 83–96 (86).

46 Elizabeth Wulf, 'Becoming Heroic: Alternative Female Heroes in Suzy McKee

alternative hero is therefore multiple and eludes hierarchical categories. A further dimension to this is the rejection of binary identity, whether cast in terms of mind/body, feminine/masculine or any other dualistic distinction. This is to recognize that each human being is unique, and 'any body can be heroic'.[47] Applying these insights to Le Guin's *Earthsea* cycle, the movement between Tenar in *Tombs* and Tenar in *Tehanu* and *The Other Wind* should not disturb us, but instead be seen as a model of the imperfect becoming hero in circumstances which are imperfect and in states of flux. Tenar is unusual in literature for her doubled iteration as young teenager and as mother, while retaining centrality in her story. Tenar is, indeed, a hero who is not one. Feminists should celebrate this. Understanding her hero journeys within the frame of spiritual becoming also points to dynamic, non-binary, multiple and non-hierarchical contexts. Feminists may wish to celebrate this, too.

Charnas' *The Conqueror's Child'*, *Extrapolation* 46, no. 1 (Spring 2005): 120–32 (121).
47 Ibid., 123.

METAPHYSICS AND TRANSCENDENCE

HIS DARK MATERIALS: 'THE REPUBLIC OF HEAVEN'

PHILIP PULLMAN IS NOTORIOUSLY unsympathetic towards organized religion: 'This is the religion I hate, and I'm happy to be known as its enemy.'[1] However, he also acknowledges the centrality and significance of the religious impulse in human life and experience: 'It is part of being human, and I value it. I'd be a damn fool not to.'[2] While *His Dark Materials* offers a stinging critique of the institutional Church, it is also replete with themes associated with spirituality and the religious – such as the metaphysics of being, sin, evil, love, death, salvation, free will, moral choice and moral responsibility. It offers a non-theistic recapitulation of Milton's *Paradise Lost* and explores fundamental themes of the Christian Fall narrative, including the passage from innocence to experience. It culminates, however, in the rejection of the Kingdom of Heaven in favour of the so-called 'Republic of Heaven'. Although Pullman states that he is telling a story – not writing a philosophy, sermon or treatise[3] – the trilogy is infused with philosophical and religious ideas. There has been

---

1   Philip Pullman, 'The Worlds: Religion', in *Philip Pullman: Other Writing*. Online: http://www.philip-pullman.com/pages/content/index.asp?PageID=110
2   Ibid.
3   Philip Pullman, 'A Dark Agenda?', interview by Susan Roberts, *Surefish: the community website from Christian Aid*, November 2002. Online: http://www.surefish.co.uk/culture/features/pullman_interview.htm

much focus on Pullman as promulgator of anti-religious mythology and atheism;[4] this chapter seeks to show how Pullman's magisterial moral and metaphysical vision is steeped in the spiritual. In so doing, there is a particular exploration of resonances with certain traditions of Eastern origin, in particular Buddhism. It is nevertheless acknowledged that Pullman's metaphysical categories and concepts locate his universe within the Western context of a post-Christian humanism. He himself says:

> I was brought up in the Church of England, and whereas I'm an atheist, I'm certainly a Church of England atheist, and for the matter of that a 1662 Book of Common Prayer atheist. The Church of England is so deeply embedded in my personality and my way of thinking that to remove it would take a surgical operation so radical that I would probably not survive it.[5]

It does not seem problematic, then, to call Pullman 'post-Christian'. More contentious is ascribing to him a 'spiritual' philosophy. He asserts that he never uses the words 'spirit', 'spirituality', or 'spiritual' because he 'can see nothing real that seems to correspond with them.' All the overtones are for him entirely negative, even repulsive: portraits of saints and martyrs as 'grubby old men with rotten teeth', or 'martyrs having their flesh ripped from their bones as they gaze upwards with an expression of fanatical fervour.'[6] Yet, as discussed in Chapter One, spirituality can be seen to exist both inside and outside of the contexts of specific religious traditions; it implies a reference to the frameworks of value, purpose and meaning according to which people orient their lives. Understood in this way, spirituality may or may not entail reference to the divine. Therefore, I will continue to use the language of spirituality for the purposes of analysis, with the understanding that this does not necessarily entail reference to the divine or specific religious traditions.

Pullman's vision is informed by many and various sources. He acknowledges a particular debt to three: William Blake, John Milton and Heinrich von Kleist, but this far from exhausts the materials and mythologies that Pullman has made use of. The eclecticism and enormous scope of influences implicitly and explicitly discernible within *His Dark Materials* are

---

4   For an argument that the trilogy is both deeply theological and more specifically, deeply Christian, see Donna Freitas and Jason King, *Killing the Imposter God* (San Francisco: Jossey Bass, 2007).
5   Philip Pullman, 'The Republic of Heaven', *The Horn Book Magazine*, December 2001. Online: http://www.hbook.com/magazine/articles/2001/nov01_pullman. asp
6   Ibid.

widely recognized. In the acknowledgements to *The Amber Spyglass*, he states himself that he has stolen from every book he has ever read, and that his dæmon would appropriately be either a magpie or jackdaw: 'One of these birds that pick up bright shining things and doesn't distinguish in terms of shininess between the diamond ring and the KitKat wrapper.'[7] Lines from writers such as Samuel Taylor Coleridge, Emily Dickinson, John Keats and Rainer Maria Rilke provide the epigraphs; textual allusions can be found to the Bible, Gnosticism, paganism, Norse mythology, Hermeticism, Kabbalism, alchemy, the story of Odysseus, Doré, Dante and Wagner – among many others! While the religious belief systems introduced to us are narratologically dominated by the Church and Magisterium, there are also references to Shamanism, Zoroastrianism, the tiger gods of the Tartars and the deities of witches. Pullman's intertextuality sits, then, on a deeply eclectic base. In the analysis below I add the less obvious dialogue partner of Buddhism.

Why Buddhism? Pullman makes little reference to this worldview,[8] and it is unlikely it acted as an overt influence. Pullman's Republic of Heaven also differs from traditional forms of Buddhism in significant respects. Furthermore, Hartney argues that Pullman has failed to incorporate Eastern thinking and that this represents a lost opportunity – emanating from a pervasive Western imperialism, nationalism and conservatism in *His Dark Materials*:

> The East remains exotic; rather than a viable alternative consciousness within which problems posed by monoliths such as his Church simply fall away. If Pullman was less Oxonian in his outlook he may have realised that Eastern thinking permits a way to speak of atheism that avoids being trapped in Christian, Western and nationalist discourse.[9]

It is undeniable that the structures of the trilogy are heavily dependent on Western philosophies and specifically Christian concepts – as indicated, notably the Christian Fall narrative and symbology, which are then inverted; it is a 'fortunate fall' towards love and self-knowledge.

---

7   Philip Pullman, 'I am of the Devil's party', interview by Helena de Bertodano, *Telegraph.co.uk*, 29 January 2002. Online: http://www.telegraph.co.uk/culture/donotmigrate/3572490/I-am-of-the-Devils-party.html

8   There is reference in the *The Amber Spyglass* to a Himalayan monastery Cho-Lung-Se, with its healer Pagdzin Tulku.

9   Christopher Hartney, 'Imperial and Epic', in Carole M. Cusack, Christopher Hartney and Frances Di Lauro (eds), *The Buddha of Suburbia* (Sydney: RLA Press, 2005), 258.

Nevertheless, I would argue that in so doing, Pullman narrativizes a philosophy which does have certain resonances with 'Eastern' themes and modes of conceptualization, specifically in respect to aspects of Buddhism. Buddhism is besides an interesting comparator, given that Pullman with his Republic of Heaven wants to establish a non-theistic mode of conceiving meaning, purpose and morality. Buddhism is the world's primary example of a religion (or according to some 'philosophy of life') which typically does not involve belief in 'God'.[10] It is also worthwhile to consider how Buddhism might inform the construction of a non-theistic ethic. As Powers argues, Buddhism brings a valuable voice to this debate, as 'the appeal of Buddhist ethics is existential – virtue is reasserted not as absolute or transcendent truth but as a pragmatic ground from which to regulate human interaction.'[11]

Loy and Goodhew identify an explicit Buddhist allusion in Pullman's account of God as fraud. Balthamos reveals to Lyra and Will the truth about the Authority.[12] He was never, in fact, the creator, but just another angel – the first, certainly, and the most powerful, but also a being condensed out of Dust. He told the others who came after that he was their creator, but this was not true. In the Brahmajala Sutra of the Pali canon, the Buddha tells the following story (itself a parody of certain Hindu myths). Beings reborn in the Abhassara Brahma world dwell there 'mind-made, feeding on delight, self-luminous, moving through the air, glorious.'[13] One being falls from the Abhassara world into an empty Brahma palace, where he is eventually joined by others. This causes the first being to believe that he had created the others through wishing for their existence. Those beings who came after then accepted this version of events. There are, then, some parallels between the two stories in the account of a 'first being' who convinced subsequent ones of their status as a Creator God.

Further to this, it has also been suggested that William Blake's thinking is reminiscent of Eastern philosophies, and it is well established that Pullman's thinking is indebted to Blake. According to Ferrara:

---

10 Jainism also has no concept of a supreme and ontologically distinct God; every soul is potentially divine.

11 Douglas Powers, 'Buddhism and Modernity: An Ancient Tradition Faces the Twenty-First Century', *Religion East and West* 1, no. 1 (2001): 67–76 (73).

12 Philip Pullman, *The Amber Spyglass* (London: Scholastic, 2001), 33.

13 Quoted in David Loy and Linda Goodhew, *The Dharma of Dragons and Dæmons: Buddhist Themes in Modern Fantasy Fiction* (Somerville, MA: Wisdom Publications, 2004), 110.

The similarities between William Blake's philosophical system and that of Buddhism (particularly the Ch'an(a) or Zen School) are no less than astonishing. One is struck by a fundamental similitude underlying the teaching of the Ch'an school and that of Blake's radical epistemology.[14]

This is not a new observation. Northrop Frye notes that Blake's vision of the ultimate identity of all things corresponds with the ultimate identification of nirvana and samsara in Mahayana Buddhism; it is a rejection of the antithesis between being and non-being, between substance and nothingness.[15] Altizer also asserts that 'the true analogue to [Blake's] vision lies in the world of Oriental mysticism', while believing that 'Blake himself could not possibly have had any knowledge of Buddhist philosophy.'[16] It must also be noted that it was only after the middle of the nineteenth century that 'Buddhism' was constructed in Britain; previously, encounters with Buddhism 'remained in British consciousness merely as disparate accounts of the encounter of the West with indistinct aspects of the Orient – but not of the *Buddhist* orient.'[17]

As a prolegomenon to this analysis, such caveats remind us that Western reception and construction of Buddhist ideas may offer us a blurred and homogenized amalgamation of 'Eastern' modes of conceptualization. Nor should we forget that transcultural exchanges through mission activity, for example, also had effects on indigenous Buddhisms. The distinction between 'West' and 'East' is itself a construct which risks reifying differences and obscuring interchanges. Buddhism is far from monolithic, with historical, devotional, philosophical and cultural-geographic differentiations. The broad distinction into Mahayana, Theravada and Vajrayana traditions itself covers healthy growths of sub-varieties. Therefore, it is

---

14 Mark S. Ferrara, 'Ch'an Buddhism and the Prophetic Poems of William Blake', *Journal of Chinese Philosophy* 24, no. 1 (1997): 59–73 (59). Ferrara also argues that Blake was known to be familiar with Eastern philosophies through the first English edition of the Hindu Bhagavad Gita (translated by Charles Wilkins in 1785); that direct influence can be seen in Blake's catalogue entry for a piece named 'The Brahmins – A Drawing' (*A Descriptive Catalogue of Pictures*, 1809); and cites Blake's opinion that 'The philosophy of the east taught the first principles of human perception' (Northrop Frye, *Fearful Symmetry: A Study of William Blake* [Princeton, NJ: Princeton University Press, 1947], 39). However, even if a case can be made for some Vedic familiarity, it does not thereby demonstrate knowledge of Buddhism.

15 Ibid., 431–32.

16 Thomas J. J. Altizer, *The New Apocalypse: The Radical Christian Vision of William Blake* (Aurora, CO: The Davies Group, 2000), 164.

17 Philip C. Almond, *The British Discovery of Buddhism* (Cambridge: Cambridge University Press, 1988), 14. Interest in Buddhism is, however, evident in the writings of German philosophers Leibniz (1646–1716) and Schopenhauer (1788–1860).

important to bear in mind that the subsequent allusions to Buddhist thinking are selective and intended to identify moments of affinity – 'morphic resonance', let us say – or of illuminative divergence, not to offer a comprehensive and systematic account.

In what follows I shall delineate some of the key contours and concepts in Pullman's narrative of the Republic of Heaven, and relate this where appropriate to Buddhist ideas. Before this, however, let us consider what the Republic of Heaven is a reaction *against*: the traditional religion of the Church and the Authority.

Pullman has stated that the *His Dark Materials* chronicle is about 'killing God';[18] this is the horizon and end-time of the trilogy. The denouement of the final novel is the collapse of the Church's Magisterium and the death of the Authority. The defunct and corrupt 'Kingdom of Heaven' is exchanged for the new age of the 'Republic of Heaven'. The battle is rich in traditional apocalyptic tropes: two dualistically opposing forces in a cosmic drama involving God, rebel angels and humans. This battle, indeed, is situated within the threat of an even greater apocalypse: the multiverse itself is at risk, with the mysterious substance Dust leaking away, thereby endangering life, meaning and consciousness in every world. And both of these apocalypses are actually devices of Pullman's to confront a somewhat different kind of apocalypse – in philosophical terms, the death of God.

The death of God has haunted modernity, stalking philosophy ever since the enthronement of the human subject as the centre of the thinking world. The prospect of the loss of the credibility of God has gone hand in hand with anxieties about the disintegration of truth, meaning and purpose. Kierkegaard asked what would life be but despair, if underlying everything was only a 'bottomless, insatiable emptiness', or if all was produced by a 'wild fermenting force' writhing in dark passions:

> If such were the situation, if there were no sacred bond that knit humankind together, if one generation succeeded another like the singing of birds in the forest, . . . how empty and devoid of consolation life would be![19]

It was Nietzsche, of course, who gave the 'death of God' its classical formulation on the lips of his madman in *Thus Spake Zarathustra*:

---

18 As told to Steve Meacham, 'The Shed Where God Died', *The Sydney Morning Herald*, 13 December 2003. Online: http://www.smh.com.au/articles/2003/12/12/1071125644900.html

19 Søren Kierkegaard, *Fear and Trembling*, ed. C. Stephen Evans and Sylvia Walsh, trans. Sylvia Walsh (Cambridge: Cambridge University Press, 2006 [1843]): 12.

'Where has God gone?' he cried. 'I shall tell you. We have killed him – you and I. We are all his murderers. But how have we done this? How were we able to drink up the sea? Who gave us the sponge to wipe away the entire horizon?'[20]

Nietzsche, like Pullman, not only announces but also embraces this death of God. For Pullman, the demise of traditional Christianity presents not a threat but an opportunity. Such a view plays into trends which are suspicious of transcendence. The fear that a worldview incorporating the transcendent is harmful to humanity is based on a number of factors and perspectives. For example, from a feminist point of view, there is concern that it involves or implies a devaluation of the body, immanence and the material world; that, indeed, it is this very materiality and embodiment that are to be transcended. Furthermore, a transcendent/immanent dualism could be seen to underpin a whole series of hierarchical, patriarchal and anti-materialist dualisms: God/world, spirit/matter, male/female, human/nature, and so on.[21] Marxists suggest that fixing the eyes on an otherworldly horizon detracts necessary attention from this one, perpetuating conditions of socio-economic inequality and injustice. Theorists following Feuerbach argue that projecting the highest values such as goodness, wisdom and love onto a transcendent divine alienates humanity from a true understanding of its own potentialities.

Pullman is keen to reject the concept of a transcendent divine in order to rehabilitate the human subject as a free citizen, not a subservient subject of a celestial monarch.[22] He also wants to revalue the physical, sensuous and material world, such that it becomes the focus of a passionate love. His rejection of 'otherworldly' belief-systems leads him to a scathing rebuttal of the viewpoints inscribed in C. S. Lewis's *Chronicles of Narnia*. He highlights in particular Lewis's treatment of the character Susan, who in the final book, *The Last Battle*, is not permitted to enter the stable which is the doorway to salvation. She is no longer a friend of Narnia, it seems, because she is 'interested in nothing nowadays except nylons and lipsticks and invitations', being 'a jolly sight too keen on being

---

20   Friedrich Nietzsche, *Thus Spake Zarathustra*, trans. R. J. Hollingdale (Harmondsworth: Penguin, 1961), 14.
21   It should be noted here that there is a substantial body of literature refuting this view. Specifically in relation to Christianity, it is argued that a proper understanding of the doctrines of creation, incarnation and resurrection in fact renders the material and the immanent profoundly sacred. Christian feminists put forward that it is not the idea of a transcendent God as such that is the problem, but patriarchal configurations of the nature of God, God-world relations, and the status and role of women.
22   Pullman, 'The Republic of Heaven'.

grown-up.'[23] Pullman sees in this an unhealthy antipathy towards normal sexual development and interest. Furthermore, Aslan informs the other children that there really was a train crash and they and their parents are all 'dead': therefore, 'term' is over, and the 'holidays' have begun. Pullman abhors the notion that having Susan's whole family killed in a train crash while she is still a teenager is morally preferable to liking stockings, and sees in this narrative a contempt for life in this world. 'A railway accident', he comments acidly, 'is not an end-of-term treat.'[24]

Nevertheless, Pullman acknowledges that 'not believing in God is not quite like believing in the tooth fairy': there are bigger consequences.[25] He grants that the death of God can fund a sense of meaninglessness and alienation. So, what is needed is a new myth:

> We need a story, a myth that does what the traditional religious stories did: it must *explain*. It must satisfy our hunger for a *why*. Why does the world exist? Why are we here? . . . There's the [why] that asks *What brought us here?* and the other that asks *What are we here for?* One looks back, and the other looks forward, perhaps.[26]

Hence for Pullman, having stripped the world of divine sacrality, it is necessary to re-mythologize: to find new stories, new ways of seeing which endow life with meaning, purpose, value and a sense that things are right and good. To this end, he ambitiously constructs his Republic of Heaven.

Pullman's claims that he is not writing a treatise or philosophy notwithstanding, he is very clear in his own commentaries and interviews about what values and worldviews are comprehended in the Republic of Heaven. Fundamentally, it is oriented towards the here and now, and a belief in the 'preciousness' of the here and now.[27] There is no 'elsewhere'; humanity is a physical constituent of a physical universe. However, this also entails a feeling of believing, being part of a 'real and important story', connected both to our fellow humans (living and dead) and to the universe itself.[28] It stands for a sense that humanity and the universe have

23 C. S. Lewis, *The Last Battle* (London: The Bodley Head, 1967), 127.
24 Pullman, 'The Republic of Heaven'.
25 Ibid.
26 Ibid.
27 Philip Pullman, 'Carnegie Medal Acceptance Speech', in *Philip Pullman: His Dark Materials*. Online: http://www.randomhouse.com/features/pullman/author/carnegie.html
28 Philip Pullman, 'A Dark Agenda?'.

a common meaning, destiny and purpose and are profoundly interconnected. It signifies joy, and a democracy of free and equal citizens which
it is our duty to preserve and promote.[29] This is the ethical imperative of
the Republic of Heaven: to exercise responsibility and use the qualities
we have to make the world a better place[30] – one open-minded, tolerant,
and in which nobody 'has' the truth.[31]

So that is what Pullman is seeking to articulate. I will now expand
on some of the metaphysical and ethical dimensions of the Republic of
Heaven and where pertinent relate it to Buddhist ideas. The first area for
examination is Pullman's concept of Dust, which he uses as a metaphor for
the metaphysics underpinning the Republic of Heaven. This mysterious
elementary particle clusters around humanity, especially on attainment
of puberty and adulthood. This leads the Church to associate Dust with
original sin and the advent of sexuality; thus the concept of 'intercision'
arises as a means of protecting the individual from sin. There is, in fact, an
interesting analogue here in Jainism: in this religion, karma is understood
as a physical substance, very commonly referred to metaphorically as
'dust'; it is accretion of this karmic dust that locks the soul into the cycle
of rebirth; liberation is only achieved through purifying the soul of this
karmic matter.[32] Passions, indeed, foster the adhesion of this karma, by
creating a 'stickiness'. There are, then, some interesting parallels with the
negative view of the accretion of Dust held by the General Oblation Board
in Pullman's narrative.

As the mysteries of Dust are unravelled, these negative valuations
are shown to be shockingly misguided. It is Mary Malone, in our world,
who discovers the connection between Dust (or Shadows), thinking,
and anything associated with human thought or workmanship. Putting
this together with the historical arrival of Shadows some thirty or forty
thousand years previously leads her to the conclusion that Shadows are
actually 'particles of consciousness'.[33]

Dust in Pullman's narrative can be likened to the atomism of Leibniz's

29 Philip Pullman, 'Interview with Philip Pullman', interview by Joan Bakewell, *Belief*
    series, BBC Radio 3, 23 September 2006. A transcript can be found online at http://
    darkadamant.betterversion.org/BBC_Belief_Philip_Pullman.txt
30 Philip Pullman, 'A Dark Agenda?'.
31 Philip Pullman, 'Are You There. God? It's me', *Book*, December 2002. Online:
    http://web.archive.org/web/20050211151440/http://www.bookmagazine.com/
    issue25/inthemargins.shtml
32 It is also, perhaps, worthy of note that the process of inflow of karmic dust is known
    as 'asrav'. This is intriguingly reminiscent of the mulefa word for Dust: 'sraf'.
33 Philip Pullman, *The Subtle Knife* (London: Scholastic, 2007), 88.

monadology,[34] which has in turn been likened to certain Buddhist under-standings in which the constituent basis of the phenomenal world are 'dharmas' (not to be confused with Dharma: the teachings of the Buddha). Sebastian explains this with reference to the Abhidharma system of taxonomy:

> The conception of dharmas . . . discloses itself as a metaphysical theory developed out of one fundamental principle of existence, which is an inter-play of a plurality of subtle, ultimate, not further analyzable elements of matter, mind and forces.[35]

Furthermore, Dust for Pullman is not simply a neutral, physical fact; it is intimately connected with purpose and value. Pullman states that Dust is his metaphor for 'human wisdom, science and art, all the accumulated and transmissible achievements of the human mind.'[36] Angels are condensa-tions of Dust, who interfered in human evolution for revenge against the Authority, inciting matter to desire to know itself. Dust represents also raw potentiality – this is evident in its designation as 'dark materials', which in Milton's *Paradise Lost* (II, 11.915–16) represent the primal mat-ter ordained by the almighty to create more worlds. It is also associated with contemporary physicists' understanding of 'dark matter', a physical constituent of the mass of the universe.

As in Buddhism, the universe of Dust has no external creator. It is self-organizing, immanent, contingent and relational – process rather than substance. It has been argued that doctrines of creation, understood as either a unitary moment or as transcendent imposition of order on chaotic or passive matter, support philosophies which marginalize chance and naturalize identities. To the contrary, theories of material self-ordering open up possibilities for multiplicities attributed to changes in the arrangement of and relations between immanent elements.[37] Thus a

---

34 Leibniz proposed that 'monads' are the simplest units of being and are characterized by perception and appetition. For a commentary and translation of Leibniz's writ-ings on monadology, see Nicholas Rescher, *G. W. Leibniz's Monadology: an Edition for Students* (London: Routledge, 1992).

35 C. D. Sebastian, 'Theory of Psyche in Buddhism: An Appraisal of Buddhist and Scientific Psychology', *OMEGA: Indian Journal of Science and Religion* 6, no. 1: 39–51.

36 Philip Pullman, 'Philip Pullman – the extended e-mail interview', interview by Peter T. Chattaway, *FilmChat*, 28 November 2007. Online: http://filmchatblog.blogspot.com/2007/11/philip-pullman-extended-e-mail.html

37 John Protevi, *Political Physics: Deleuze, Derrida and the Body Politic* (London: Continuum, 2001), 8.

materialist economy can be asserted which disavows transcendent origins and ordering, and in so doing causes us to rethink matter as simply inert, passive or chaotic.

Dust bridges the disjunction between matter and spirit. As the Shadows tell Mary in a conversation about the nature of Shadow particles, spirit and matter are one: in what they are, spirit; in what they do, matter.[38] Dust is matter that has begun to understand itself, and to love itself. It is this tendency towards love and knowledge that leads Dust to cluster in increasing quantities around humans at puberty, as they embark on the journey of loving and knowing themselves as bodies, as matter. Similarly, it is Dust, in the oil of the seedpod, that enables the mulefa to know themselves as such and not simply be grazers.

Pullman's concept of Dust, then, pictorializes a unity between matter and spirit. It has been suggested by Lois Gresh that Pullman's philosophies might most appropriately be described as 'monist idealist', with reality united in a universal, cosmic consciousness. This is in contradistinction to 'monist materialism', which asserts the epiphenomenal dependence of consciousness upon matter. The designation of Pullman as an idealist is problematic since he himself is on record as a committed materialist. However, Pullman's materialism is a form of panpsychism, for it *includes* consciousness, like mass, 'as a normal and universal property of matter . . . so that human beings, dogs, carrots, stones, and atoms are all conscious, though in different degrees.'[39]

This effort to delineate a philosophy which overcomes the matter/spirit dichotomy brings us to a significant point in a comparison and contrast with Buddhism. Gresh also specifically identifies Buddhism, like Pullman's thought, as an example of monist idealism;[40] however, the application of materialist/idealist categories to Buddhism is fraught with difficulties. It has been likened to asking where the horns of a rabbit came from.[41] Nevertheless, it can be argued that Western interest in Buddhism corresponded with the rise of modern science, a split between faith and

---

38 Pullman, *The Subtle Knife*, 249.
39 Pullman, 'Philip Pullman – the extended e-mail interview'.
40 See Lois H. Gresh, *Exploring Philip Pullman's* His Dark Materials: *An Unauthorized Adventure through* The Golden Compass, The Subtle Knife, *and* The Amber Spyglass (London: Macmillan, 2007), 36–37.
41 Cited in James Bissett Pratt, *The Pilgrimage of Buddhism and a Buddhist Pilgrimage* (New Delhi: Asian Educational Services, 1996), 403. It is inherently risky to consider one thought-system in terms developed by another. While there have been numerous attempts to analyse and classify Buddhist thought according to the schools of Western philosophy, it is debatable whether these categories are appropriate.

reason, and was specifically to meet a need for an "'alternative altar," a bridge that could reunite the estranged worlds of matter and spirit.'[42] So, like Pullman's quest for a post-Christian, humanistic, materialist Republic of Heaven, it can be argued that Buddhism's popularity in the West over the last century has been sparked by a perceived crisis in the capacity of traditional Christianity to inhabit adequately modern and postmodern scientific paradigms. This has exacerbated disjunctions between facts and values, spirit and matter, mind and body. As Dewey put it:

> The problem of restoring integration and cooperation between man's beliefs about the world in which he lives and his beliefs about the values and purposes that should direct his conduct is the deepest problem of modern life.[43]

In Buddhism, knowing is not simply a matter of exercising scientific method, but also of morality, self-cultivation and wisdom:

> What all people desire to know is that [i.e. the external world],
> But their means of knowing is this [i.e. oneself];
> How can we know that?
> Only by the perfection of this.[44]

If we can only know 'that' (the world) by knowing 'this' (ourselves), traditional distinctions between matter and consciousness are indeed confounded. This plays into another theme within Pullman's narrative: the interconnected nature of all being, which likewise undercuts distinctions between subject and object, knower and known. This has epistemological implications evident in the way Lyra discerns truth in the alethiometer. There are clear parallels between Lyra's account of how she reads the alethiometer and meditative insight; it is described as a cessation of mental striving after the truth. This centrality of truth – non-deluded and awakened awareness – is itself a point of contact with Buddhist philosophies.

---

42   Martin Verjoeven, 'Buddhism and Science: Probing the Boundaries of Faith and Reason', *Religion East and West* 1, no. 1 (2001): 77–97 (77). Concerns of this kind, in fact, prompted people like Paul Carus to foster Western interaction with Buddhist thinking. Carus garnered support for Buddhist missionaries to go to the United States in the late 1800s and early 1900s as a response to the perceived spiritual crisis.

43   John Dewey, *The Quest for Certainty* (New York, NY: Minton, Balch & Co., 1929), 255.

44   Verjoeven, 'Buddhism and Science: Probing the Boundaries of Faith and Reason', 95.

When Lyra loses her ability to read the alethiometer through simple grace and is told that she can regain the ability through work the importance of awakened awareness is again visible; she is told that this will lead to a deeper and fuller grace, and better reading, because it would come from conscious understanding.[45]

As Colás suggests, 'truth meter' does not really capture the nature of the alethiometer;[46] the divination of the truth through use of this device is more akin to a dialogic and creative process than accession of truth as 'product'. Furthermore, this mode of knowing truth abolishes the division between 'subject' and 'object' inherent in, for example, correspondence theories of truth: the knower is, instead, inseparably part of an immanent and relational process of truth discernment. Therefore, the mode of knowing is more akin to Heidegger's 'poetic reason', or Keats's 'negative capability': which, as Mary Malone quotes, involves 'uncertainties, mysteries, doubts, without any irritable reaching after fact and reason.'[47] Our own enmeshment in reality makes knowledge contingent, open and participatory.

In Buddhism, this fundamental interconnection is primarily expressed in the doctrine of 'dependent origination'. Basically, everything arises in dependence upon conditions; nothing exists in independence; and everything is in a continuous state of flux and dynamic interaction. Everything is impermanent and dynamic, nothing is fixed. This includes the 'self', which is neither unchanging nor eternal. The human person is comprised of five aspects – bodily forms, feelings, perceptions, dispositions and consciousness – all of which are in a state of constant change. This does not negate the 'self' as such, but renders the notion of 'fixed identity' delusional.

The question of human identity moves us on to Pullman's account of the soul. A preoccupation with and fear of death is often held to be rooted in the Western psyche, leading people to cling to concepts of an afterlife and an eternal soul. Pullman's concern to integrate the spiritual and the material can be seen. He rejects accounts of the soul or fundamental self which see it as separable from the human body, as found in dominant forms of Christianity, Cartesian philosophies and Vedic traditions. This is interesting, since a key innovation in *His Dark Materials* is the idea of the

---

45   Pullman, *The Amber Spyglass*, 455.
46   Santiago Colás, 'Telling True Stories, or The Immanent Ethics of Material Spirit (and Spiritual Matter) in Philip Pullman's *His Dark Materials*', *Discourse* 27, no. 1 (2005): 34–66 (41).
47   Pullman, *The Subtle Knife*, 25. See Colás, 'Telling True Stories, or The Immanent Ethics of Material Spirit (and Spiritual Matter) in Philip Pullman's *His Dark Materials*', 42–43.

'dæmon'; this seems to posit a clear dualism at the heart of his presentation of the 'self'. However, as Bird demonstrates to great effect, actually this apparent dualism points at a deeper level to a primary interrelatedness. As Lyra expostulates: 'Your dæmon en't *separate* from you. It's you.'[48] The externalized dæmon, then, models a differentiation which is nevertheless not dualistic; the two cannot be monistically reduced to one, but nor can they be split apart without violent harm, as seen in the procedure of intercision. Furthermore, Will, Mary and Lyra postulate the existence of a 'third' part, which Mary likens to St Paul's tripartite account of the human as spirit, as well as body and soul.[49] Additionally, in Lyra's world, people also have their own 'death', which accompanies them from the moment of birth.[50]

What happens to this dynamic and relational self upon death? Pullman's account of Lyra and Will's visit to the world of the dead is central both to the storyline in *His Dark Materials*, and to his construction of an alternative worldview. Pullman's rendition is clearly indebted to a number of religious mythologies, from Sheol and Hades to the Christian Harrowing of Hell. According to the latter story, Christ descended into hell after his death, broke down the doors and rescued the souls of all those who had died under the conditions of the Fall. The broad shape of the story, therefore, seems clearly to have its roots in a Christian myth. Given Pullman's eclecticism, however, it is hardly surprising that a range of sources can be discerned, nor that the 'rescue' performed by Lyra and Will leads the souls of the dead to an end very different from the traditional Christian understanding of heaven.

Pullman's version of the world of the dead is bleak indeed. Ghosts, child and adult alike, wander listlessly and mournfully through a landscape bleached of all colour. There is no joy, no meaning, just endless apathy. The ghosts are, prison-camp style, guarded by harpies. Lyra and Will effect the escape of the dead through using the subtle knife to cut a window into the 'outside' world; they persuade the harpies to allow the dead to exit by offering them stories as coin for passage.

For the purpose of this analysis, there are two points of particular interest here. The first is the manner through which Lyra and Will carry out this rescue: by telling stories. However, it is highly significant that these are not just any old stories; they are *true* stories. Similarly, upon emerging from the world of the dead, an old woman ghost tells Mary

---

48 Pullman, *The Subtle Knife*, 25.
49 Pullman, *The Amber Spyglass*, 463.
50 Ibid., 275.

Malone: 'Tell them stories. They need the truth. You must tell them true stories, and everything will be well. Just tell them stories.'[51] As is noted earlier in discussing the significance of the alethiometer, truth – awakened awareness – lies at the very heart of Buddhist philosophy. Furthermore, this shows us the personal development of Lyra herself and her own awakening to a deeper understanding. Lyra's actions are rooted in a wholesome intentionality, guided by insight and compassion, and can be compared to Buddhist conceptions of 'skilful' means.[52]

The second significant point relates to the kind of 'redemption' Pullman describes. He is, as has been seen, thoroughly committed to a 'this-worldly' spirituality, and argues that 'we have to find a way of accepting our own mortality and death.'[53] So, released from the prison of the world of the dead, the ghosts are finally free to embrace a true death, becoming part of the earth, the night breeze, the trees, and all living things, as their particles loosen and float apart.[54] This is the 'death of death'[55] through reintegration into the cycle of life of which death is part. As Lyra encourages the ghosts, they will never vanish, but be part of everything alive again. In the words of the woman who died as a religious martyr, they will be 'glittering in the dew under the stars and the moon out there in the physical world, which is our true home and always was.'[56]

A significant resonance with Buddhism is the importance of 'letting go'; that is why enlightenment is sometimes called the 'great death',[57] for it is about the liberation of the ego-self from its fears and attachments, including fear of death and a grasping attachment to this particular life. This demonstrates a graceful acceptance of impermanence, rather than reification of the transient and contingent. Once more, a resonance with William Blake's work can be discerned:

> He who binds to himself a joy
> Does the winged life destroy;

---

51 Ibid., 455.
52 The principle of 'skilful means' is rooted in the Buddha's compassionate aim to assist people to attain enlightenment; it is 'the way in which the goal, the intentions, or the meaning of Buddhism is correlated with the unenlightened condition of human beings' (Martin Pye, *Skilful Means* [London: Routledge, 2008], 1).
53 Pullman, 'The Republic of Heaven'.
54 Pullman, *The Amber Spyglass*, 455–56.
55 There is an allusion here to 1 Cor. 15.26 and Rev. 21.5; typically, Pullman is ironically playing on the Christian idea of the destruction of death, and giving it a vastly different interpretation.
56 Pullman, *The Amber Spyglass*, 356.
57 Loy and Goodhew, *The Dharma of Dragons and Dæmons*, 115.

> But he who kisses the joy as it flies
> Live in eternity's sunrise.[58]

How does Pullman's account of death accord with Buddhist thinking? This is not an easy issue. Precisely what does happen after death is one of those questions the Buddha chose not to answer. It would appear, however, that here a significant divergence between Pullman's philosophy of existence and Buddhist thought might be identified. In Buddhism, rebirth into another existence marked by suffering (dukkha) is traditionally understood to follow death until liberation is achieved through the realization of nirvana – an awakening that involves 'neither annihilation nor some kind of eternal life after death.'[59] This does not appear to accord well with Pullman's recommendations both to immerse oneself affirmatively in the material world, and to accept the dissolution of self at death.

Pullman lays much emphasis on the significance and value of the sensuous, a 'this-worldly' and material affirmation. Even his angels are envious of human capacity to enjoy the material world – for them to have our flesh and our senses, says Will in *The Amber Spyglass*, would be a kind of ecstasy. This would seem to be in sharp contradistinction to Buddhism, which is often understood to teach asceticism, world-renunciation and the desirability of escaping from the cycle of life, death and rebirth. According to Loy and Goodhew, however, there is a genuine ambivalence regarding this in the Buddhist traditions; they ask whether nirvana amounts to the realization of another reality at the expense of our physicality, or whether it is rather the realization of the true reality of this world, including in bodily and sensuous terms.[60] The Buddha's teachings support the 'Middle Way', navigating a path through asceticism on the one hand and self-indulgence on the other; it is also worth noting that while asceticism forms one strand in Buddhist history and practices, other strands such as the tantric traditions celebrate the sensuality of bodily awakening. So-called 'engaged' Buddhism emphasizes the significance of material conditions and the need for active social compassion. Nevertheless, it should not be overlooked that there are traditions of Buddhism which it would be difficult to reconcile with Pullman's embrace of material, phenomenal immanence.

The concept of rebirth in Buddhism is also subject to debate, with

---

58 William Blake, 'Eternity', in *The Complete Poetry and Prose of William Blake*, ed. David V. Erdman (New York, NY: Doubleday, 1982), 470.
59 Loy and Goodhew, *The Dharma of Dragons and Dæmons*, 104.
60 Ibid., 113.

different schools and philosophies expressing varying views. Since Buddhism disavows the idea of an eternal self (atman), it is no simple matter to determine just what is, in fact, reborn.[61] The Pali text *The Questions of King Milinda* has King Milinda questioning a Buddhist monk, Nagasena. When asked whether a person who is reborn is the same as or different from the person who died, the monk responded that he is neither; just as curds, butter and ghee are not the same as the pot of milk from which they originated, nor are they something other than it. Hence, the second thing arises in dependence upon the first; there is continuity and a conditioned relationship between them, but there is not a shared, fixed or stable essence that is passed along. In such understandings of Buddhism, a fundamental essence, consciousness or soul neither outlasts death nor is annihilated at death; once more Buddhism steers a middle way, this time between the poles of idealism and materialism.

Interpreting this, the modern Western Buddhist Nagapriya suggests it is possible to think of rebirth in this manner:

> At death it is possible that we will just flow out into a great karmic ocean, our identity lost forever. . . . After all, this is what happens to our bodies: they are reabsorbed into the elements. Why should our minds carry on in a discrete form?[62]

There are striking similarities here with Pullman's account in *His Dark Materials*. The mode of liberation from the prison camp of an artificial afterlife also bears a resonance: it is an awakening, an enlightenment, through the hearing and telling of truth. For Pullman this is not simply an abstract and conceptual mode of truth-telling, but based in the narrativization of experience. Likewise, knowledge, and experience *as* knowledge, are important to Pullman. His representation of the myth of the Fall recasts it, in Gnostic fashion, as a move from ignorance to knowledge, from immaturity to maturity: from innocence to experience. This inversion of the traditional Christian understanding leads to a positive valuation of the eating of the forbidden fruit. Pullman identifies this as a primary theme of the books, and comments that, traditionally:

---

61 For this reason, there is a technical difference between the concepts of 'rebirth' and 'reincarnation'; the latter belief is rooted in the concept of a particular self which reincarnates.
62 Nagapriya, *Exploring Karma and Rebirth* (Birmingham: Windhorse Publications, 2004), 128.

[The Fall has] been presented as being a very bad thing and Eve was very wicked and we all got covered in sorrow and sin and misery from then on as a result of this ... well, I just reversed that. I thought wasn't it a good thing that Eve did, isn't curiosity a valuable quality? Shouldn't she be praised for risking this? It wasn't, after all, that she was after money or gold or anything, she was after knowledge. What could possibly be wrong with that?[63]

The centralization of truth and awakened awareness do have resonance with Buddhism; Pullman's 'enlightenment' – as modelled by Will and Lyra at the conclusion of the trilogy – is not directly equivalent, but it does represent a transformation of mind and heart, and is accompanied by heightened insight.

Thus far we have seen points of resonance between Pullman's philosophies and aspects of Buddhism in his metaphysics of Dust, his account of the self, his view of 'afterlife', and his centralization of awakened awareness. Another point of contact between Pullman's philosophy and Buddhism could be located in his environmentalism. This is a persistent theme within *His Dark Materials*, reflecting Pullman's own concerns; in his New Year Message of 2006, he asks 'that everybody would just stop destroying the world so that I can stop fretting about it and get on with my proper work.'[64] Humanity's lack of respect for the integrity of the universe is seen to have caused severe disruption in all the worlds portrayed. Asriel's actions epitomize this; his violent unleashing of the energy created by separating Roger and his dæmon in order to create a bridge between worlds causes climactic upheaval in Lyra's world. Thaws, floods, alterations in migratory patterns testify to an overturning of nature, leaving Serafina Pekkala 'heartsick'.[65] The world of the mulefas is held up as an example of ecological balance gone awry; the years of living 'in perpetual joy'[66] with their trees is under serious threat from the leaking of Dust caused by three centuries of cutting windows between worlds. Pullman's emphasis on

---

63 'Faith and Fantasy', on *Encounter* (ABC Radio National, 24 March 2002). Online: http://www.abc.net.au/rn/relig/enc/stories/s510312.htm

64 Philip Pullman, 'New Year Message 2006', January 2006. This was previously available on Philip Pullman's website, www.philip-pullman.com. Pullman's views about environmentalism can also be found at: Philip Pullman, 'Philip Pullman: New Brand of Environmentalism', interview by Andrew Simms, *Telegraph.co.uk*, 19 January 2008. Online: http://www.telegraph.co.uk/earth/3322329/Philip-Pullman-new-brand-of-environmentalism.html

65 Pullman, *The Amber Spyglass*, 39.

66 Ibid., 139.

environmentalism is consistent with his affirmation of this-world: 'where we are is always the most important place.'[67]

Buddhism, in the popular imagination, is also associated with a holistic and environmentally egalitarian worldview. Swearer cautions that the picture is rather more complex than this, and that five (sometimes overlapping) categories can be identified. These range from holding that environmental ethics are a natural extension of Buddhist worldviews, to actual incompatibility between the two.[68] However, the notion that Buddhism promotes a relational, environmentally aware mode of mindful living amounting to a 'cosmic ecology' is also promulgated. This is rooted in the recognition of interdependence and the disavowal of autonomous, stable and separable identities; all are part of a dynamic, changing set of energies with no dualism between 'life' and 'environment'.[69]

The lineage through Blake's influence on Pullman is, again, also worth mentioning. Derek Wall argues that an examination of Green philosophy takes us back, among other influences, to the inspiration of William Blake as poet and holistic philosopher drawing partly from traditions of Western holism and partly from Eastern philosophies: '[t]he influence of William Blake in synthesising and transmitting such ancient knowledge cannot be understated.'[70] Green philosophy's hallmark is a holism that emphasizes the connection between things, with all life interwoven in transformation and interaction. Wall identifies the importance of the dynamic interplay of opposites and of non-reductive modes of perception in Blake's 'The Marriage of Heaven and Hell' as especially inspirational.

The final area I shall touch upon is the nature of ethical action. I suggest here that Buddhist emphasis on action, will and the significance of intentional conduct aligns with Pullman's humanistic views. Pullman has stated that he has an action-based view of identity: 'What we are is not in our control, but what we do is . . . simultaneously, what we do depends on what we are (on what we have to do it with), and what we are can be modified by what we do.'[71] This can once more be related to Buddhism,

67 Ibid., 548.
68 Donald Swearer, 'An Assessment of Buddhist Eco-Philosophy', paper presented at the CSWR-Dongguk Symposium on Buddhism, Center for the Study of World Religions, Harvard Divinity School, 2005. Online: http://www.hds.harvard.edu/cswr/resources/print/dongguk/swearer.pdf
69 See Allan Hunt Badiner, foreword to *Dharma Gaia* (Berkeley, CA: Parallax Press, 1990), xiv–xv.
70 Derek Wall (ed.), *Green History: A Reader in Environmental Literature, Philosophy and Politics* (London: Routledge, 1994), 90.
71 Philip Pullman, 'Identity crisis', *Guardian* (London, England), 19 November 2005.

specifically in the understanding of karma. Nagapriya cites the Buddha, who was reported to have responded to a student:

> Student, beings are owners of their actions [*karmas*], heirs of their actions; they originate from their actions, are bound to their actions, have their actions as their refuge. It is action that distinguishes beings as inferior and superior.[72]

This rooting of karma in action can, then, be compared to Pullman's conceptualization of action-based identity. Sometimes, karma is understood on a deterministic 'reward and retribution' model. There are a number of philosophical problems with this, including encouraging a passive acceptance of pain and suffering for both oneself and others as 'just deserts'; such an understanding could also be seen to run counter to the centrality of compassion as guiding principle for action. The principle of karma might be more fully understood on a model of 'action and consequence', rather than 'reward and retribution'. Even here it is important to note that 'action' also arises in dependence on conditions, and intentionality or volition is central to this.

As in Buddhism, so in Pullman – right intention and right action are crucial to morality. Duty is an important part of Pullman's ethics in *His Dark Materials*, as is explicit in the angel Xaphania's strictures to Will and Lyra and the hard choice ultimately made by them in the trilogy's conclusion. Citizens of the Republic of Heaven are free and equal but have responsibilities – 'to work hard to make this place as good as we possibly can.'[73] Again, we see here analogies with Buddhism, which Powers describes as individualistic, yes, but an individualism of 'responsibility, not desire.'[74] While Buddhism has an emphasis on individual action and karmic liberation, such actions are never divorced from the larger web of existence. To that extent all action is interaction – 'a vast net of inter-reflecting jewels'.[75] In Buddhism, freedom is not expressed in acting on one's desires or in attaining instant gratifications, which are conceptions common in the consumeristic modern society. The Buddha taught that acting on desire is actually a form of bondage – to those very desires, and patterns of habit conditioning desires.

Online: http://docs.newsbank.com/s/InfoWeb/aggdocs/UKNB/10E015E661AF B3F8/10499C0CF00BD483
72 Nagapriya, *Exploring Karma and Rebirth*, 12.
73 Philip Pullman, 'A Dark Agenda?'.
74 Douglas Powers, 'Buddhism and Modernity: An Ancient Tradition Faces the Twenty-First Century', 69.
75 Ibid., 70.

To conclude: the philosophy of *His Dark Materials* can, in a broad understanding of the term, be considered a spirituality. It postulates a universe vibrant with love, spirit, meaning and purpose even at the level of the elementary particle. It is a material spirituality, or a spiritual materialism: the divide between matter and spirit is not merely bridged but collapsed. It promulgates an ethic of care and responsibility, where the communal good is favoured over individual gratification. It can therefore be argued that Pullman's narrative world in *His Dark Materials* is seeped in spirituality. I have in this chapter identified areas where resonances between the spiritual vision of *His Dark Materials* and aspects of Buddhism can be discerned. This is in no way to suggest that Pullman is some sort of 'anonymous Buddhist'; nor is it to deny that similar ideas to those expressed by Pullman can also be found in philosophies of 'Western' provenance (including particular varieties of Christianity). It is, however, to highlight where Pullman's broad structure of an inverted Christian myth is expanded and enriched by alternative ways of thinking about spirit, matter and being. Resonances between Pullman's post-Christian re-mythologization and Buddhist ideas should not perhaps be surprising. Analysis of the spread and reception of Buddhism in contexts such as Britain and America highlights that it is the very differences from Christianity that render Buddhism appealing, including that it is non-theistic, non-dogmatic and emphasizes spiritual autonomy rather than faith in an external saviour figure.[76] It is possible to identify elements of similarity with a non-theistic humanism which is nevertheless spiritually rich. Therefore, it is argued here that *His Dark Materials* has points of resonance not only with Christian traditions, which it overtly rejects, but with Buddhist traditions to which it makes no explicit reference and are typically classed among the 'organized' religions that Pullman purports to despise.

---

76   David N. Kay, *Tibetan and Zen Buddhism in Britain* (London: Routledge, 2004), 5.

METAPHYSICS AND TRANSCENDENCE

EARTHSEA: 'ONLY IN SILENCE THE WORD'

Only in silence the word,
only in dark the light,
only in dying life:
bright the hawk's flight
on the empty sky.

– The Creation of Éa[1]

LE GUIN ENVISAGES her new world order as one rejecting myths of both gender and race, as a precursor to the possibility of imagining freedom. For her, gender is the 'deepest foundation' of oppression. Fantasy does not escape this politicization. It is part of the real world. 'All the moral weight of it is real weight. The politics of Fairyland are ours.'[2]

Le Guin's fiction is notable for its engagement with both metaphysical and socio-political issues, if the two spheres can indeed be so easily distinguished. The *Earthsea* cycle is no exception. As has been explicated at an earlier point,[3] this set of books is unusual because of the temporal spread over which it was produced. There is both continuity and discontinuity

1   This is the epigraph to Le Guin's *A Wizard of Earthsea*, 12.
2   Ursula K. Le Guin, *Earthsea Revisioned* (Cambridge, MA: Children's Literature New England, 1993), 24.
3   See Chapter Three.

in terms of their thematic foci. Le Guin brought to the final three books (*Tehanu*, *Tales of Earthsea* and *The Other Wind*) a greatly heightened feminist awareness. This was not a new outlook for her; however, in past decades, Le Guin had more faith in the possibility of articulating a 'neuter' subject whose humanity transcended gendered considerations.[4] The last book of the first trilogy, *The Farthest Shore*, introduced the topic of death as a major theme. This continued to be a preoccupation, and is explored in detail once more in the final book, *The Other Wind*. Issues pertaining to gender and death are also intricately linked with the metaphysics of language, magic and dragons.

All of this is framed by Le Guin's personal leanings towards Taoism, which underpin much of her philosophies. Indeed, she asserts that it is important to be clear about the significance of Taoism in her work because 'it's a central theme, period.'[5] The flip side of this is her rejection of monotheistic religion. In *The Lathe of Heaven*,[6] there is a character who refers to the 'Judaeo-Christian Rationalist West', and this can act as shorthand for the sort of worldview Le Guin rejects. Erlich identifies the drive to 'separation' as the most explicit aspect of monotheism which Le Guin discards. Separations – of the sacred and profane, light and darkness, this house from that house, human from the 'world' – are understood to reinforce hierarchies. For her the sacred is not that which is set apart, but that which is expressed in connection. She also rejects sacrifice, of self or other, as a noble or virtuous deed. This is evident both in her provocative short story 'The Ones Who Walk Away from Omelas',[7] and in her meta-fantasy *The Beginning Place*,[8] and reflects her interest in Taoism. In an interview, Le Guin said:

> And Lao Tzu says we should be like Nature. We should not be humane either, in the sense that we should not sacrifice ourselves for others. Now that's going to be very hard for Christian readers to accept, because they're taught that self-sacrifice is a good thing. Lao Tzu says it's a lousy thing.

---

4   Ursula K. Le Guin, *Language of the Night: Essays on Fantasy and Science Fiction*, edited and with introductions by Susan Wood, 2nd edn (London: The Women's Press, 1989), 135–47.
5   Cited in Richard D. Erlich, 'Le Guin and God: Quarrelling with the One, Critiquing Pure Reason', *Extrapolation* 47, no. 3 (Winter 2006): 351–80 (351).
6   Ursula K. Le Guin, *The Lathe of Heaven* (New York, NY: Scribner's, 1971).
7   Ursula K. Le Guin, 'The Ones Who Walk Away from Omelas', in Ursula K. Le Guin, *The Wind's Twelve Quarters* (London: Victor Gollancz, 1975), 275–84.
8   Ursula K. Le Guin, *The Beginning Place* (London: Harper & Row, 1980).

This is perhaps the most radical thing he says to a Western ear. Just don't buy into self-sacrifice.[9]

The figure of Lao Tzu (from the seventh century BCE) is a founding influence in Taoism, to whom the important text, the *Tao te Ching*, is commonly attributed. For him, altruism is the other side of egoism, and one should not turn from self for other, or from other for self. However, Le Guin's primary issue with Christianity is its understanding of life after death, particularly as enmeshed in soul/body dualisms and interpretations of the afterlife in terms of the immortality of the ego.

Taoism differs from traditional monotheistic religions in numerous respects. It is an ancient complex of different schools of thought and practice with its roots in China some 2,000 years ago. There is no overarching organizational centre of orthodoxy. Therefore, the brief account I give here must be understood as a great simplification in order to highlight certain key ideas which are discernible in Le Guin's writings. The 'Tao' is typically translated as the 'Way'; it can also be understood as a creative principle of the universe. There is no God in the sense of an ultimate divine figure as typically understood in Judaism, Islam or Christianity. All things depend on and are unified in the Tao. It is a philosophy of complementary forces – light/dark; action/non-action; masculine/feminine and so on. These are not dualistically opposed, but form a unity of dynamically interdependent polarities often summed up as the 'Yin Yang' principle. The practitioner seeks unity and harmony with nature, community and cosmos; self-development; and to lead a virtuous life. Action should not be ego-driven or arise out of an unbalanced striving, but be part of the harmonious flow rather than an imposition upon it. Compassion, moderation and humility are key qualities in this respect.

Taoism permeates Le Guin's work. For example, *A Wizard of Earthsea* is a classic tale of imbalance, in which lack of balance in Ged's personal being and actions has cosmic repercussions. As Wytenbroek puts it:

In a wonderfully Taoistic scene at the end of the novel, Ged and the shadow meet at the very edge of the world, at the center of the balance of power, the place where light and darkness meet. There Ged, recognizing the shadow for who it is, calls it by his own name, merges with it, and thus becomes whole. He is a man who knows and has acknowledged his evil self as part of him,

---

9   Ursula K. Le Guin, 'The Feminine and the Tao: an interview with Ursula K. LeGuin', interview by Brenda Peterson, *Embrace the Moon: School of Tijiquan and Qigong*, 2003. Online: http://www.embracethemoon.com/perspectives/leguin.htm

but he is master of it and can therefore participate wholly in being, as he can never again be seduced or overcome by evil, or the fear of it.[10]

This is also typically read as Jungian, but it need not be seen as an either/or. Le Guin has explored both philosophies, although she had not read Jung when she wrote *A Wizard of Earthsea*.[11] In Jungian terms, this is an integrative moment, conferring psychic wholeness. 'Ged had neither lost nor won, but in naming the shadow of his death with his own name, had made himself whole.'[12] For Jung, recognizing the shadow is essential for any kind of self-knowledge and reconciliation of opposites. To see a shadow is to see a light, and vice versa, which enables the balancing of these opposites and the location of the antithesis position which sits between urges towards fusion and opposition.

It is not surprising if there are elements of correspondence between Taoist concepts and Jungian philosophies, since Jung was familiar with the work of Lao Tzu and made reference to his teachings. Jung related the notion of complementary opposites to his concept of the conscious and unconscious minds by suggesting that if one polarity in a pair of opposites was ignored, it would assert itself in the unconscious mind. Conscious and unconscious minds together, then, form a balance. The relationship with the complementary opposite is compensatory, as too is the relationship between the conscious and the unconscious. A denied polarity takes on further vitality in correspondence with the energy invested in its pair.[13] It is not difficult to see how Ged's encounter with the shadow can be given a Jungian context for interpretation. The more he ran from it, the greater its hold and strength; only in confronting it, accepting it and naming it with his own name did its power diminish: 'Ged reached out his hands, dropping his staff, and took hold of his shadow, of the black self that reached out to him. Light and darkness met, and joined, and were one.'[14] This also symbolizes Ged's acceptance of death, a factor to be of importance in *The Farthest Shore* when the wizard Cob disturbs the balance between death and life.

10 J. R. Wytenbroek, 'Taoism in the Fantasies of Ursula K. Le Guin', in Olena H. Saciuk (ed.), *The Shape of the Fantastic: Selected Essays from the Seventh International Conference on the Fantastic in the Arts* (New York, NY: Greenwood Press, 1990), 173–80 (174).
11 Le Guin, *Language of the Night*, 34.
12 Ursula K. Le Guin, *A Wizard of Earthsea – The Earthsea Quartet* (London: Puffin, 1992), 166.
13 See, for example, Carl Gustav Jung, *Psychology and the East* (Princeton, NJ: Princeton University Press, 1978).
14 Le Guin, *A Wizard of Earthsea*, 164.

Other Taoist principles also suffuse the books. The elegant pattern-
ing embedded in the structure and prose style as well as in the narrative
arc is one such. Harmony, balance, unity and the interplay of opposites
are all part of Le Guin's metaphysical vision. She also incorporates the
Taoist principle of inaction – that is to say, doing only that which is
necessary: 'The first lesson on Roke, and the last, is *Do what is needful*.
And no more.'[15] Her portrayal of love and compassion similarly resonates
with Taoist understandings. Wytenbroek undertakes an analysis of the
relationship between Ged and his royal protégé Arren in *The Farthest
Shore* to demonstrate this, drawing out the close connection between
love and being: 'For a fully realized, whole, and balanced person expresses
him- or herself in some form of love. Thus Ged, as a whole man, loves.
Arren, in learning love, learns wholeness of being.'[16] Arren's feelings for
Ged develop from an initial glamorized 'ardour' to a love with compassion, 'without which love is untempered, and is not whole, and does
not last.'[17]

Taoism, then, provides an underlying understanding of and perspective
on the nature of being within Le Guin's fiction. This framework is shared
across the fantasy world and the 'real' world. Within her magical realm,
a distinctive feature of Le Guin's creation is the ontology of language.
As well as the vernacular, there is the language of dragons, known as the
Old Speech, which is also the language spoken by Segoy, who made the
islands. This language is a language of true naming and it is the basis of
magic. It is a language to which there is no end.[18]

This connection between language and being forms a major plank
in the metaphysical basis of the crisis presented in *The Farthest Shore*.
Wizardry is going awry. '"I am afraid," said the Patterner to Ged. "There
is fear. There is fear at the roots."'[19] Ged can sense 'a break, a wound'.[20]
The woman who has lost her powers, Akaren, tells Ged and Arren:

> I lost all the things I knew, all the words and names. . . . There is a hole in
> the world, and the light is running out of it. And the words go with the
> light. Did you know that?[21]

15   Ursula K. Le Guin, *The Farthest Shore – The Earthsea Quartet* (London: Puffin,
     1992), 420.
16   J. R. Wytenbroek, 'Taoism in the Fantasies of Ursula K. Le Guin', 179.
17   Le Guin, *The Farthest Shore*, 379.
18   Le Guin, *A Wizard of Earthsea*, 51.
19   Le Guin, *The Farthest Shore*, 312.
20   Ibid., 325.
21   Ibid., 377.

The magic is draining away from the world. People are going mad. There is sickness. People are forgetting words, songs, arts and crafts. The reason is the sorcerer Cob's attempts to gain immortality, in pursuit of which he has opened a door between death and life. Language and creativity and true names are being sucked away. Ged explains to Arren the importance of death, which bestows the gift of selfhood: 'There is no safety. There is no end. The word must be heard in silence. There must be darkness to see the stars. The dance is always danced above the hollow place, above the terrible abyss.'[22] Death is required for life, for without death, there can be no rebirth. The balance is misunderstood as stillness, or as stasis: it is an eternal becoming.[23] Ged attempts to explain to Cob, the sorcerer, why his arts will not work on him after Ged has pursued him into death:

> My name is no use to you. You have no power over me. I am a living man; my body lies on the beach of Selidor . . . And when that body dies, I will be here: but only in name, in name alone, in shadow. Do you not understand?[24]

When dead, the name has no power because no true referent. This is the catastrophe that Cob has brought upon Earthsea; he has sundered its ontological foundations by creating the 'hole in the world', disrupting the linguistic bonds that, in Earthsea, connect signifier with signified. With death infecting life, or life pouring away into death, 'being' is losing its name, its vitality and its creative force.

Hence, I disagree with Philippopoulos-Mihalopoulous, who asserts that 'Ged utters the name of things and slowly inscribes his way towards his personal ideal of society.'[25] This is for two reasons. The first is that this would run counter to Roke's philosophy of balance and needful action. The second is that he bases this analysis on a Whorfian linguistic paradigm, whereby 'nature' is dissected 'along lines laid down by our native languages.'[26] This, says Philippopoulos-Mihalopoulous, is what happens in *Earthsea* – 'faithful to Whorf's idea of language as the tool for nature carving.'[27] However, this seems to be an inversion of the implications of

---

22 Ibid., 410.
23 Ibid., 423.
24 Ibid., 180.
25 Andreas Philippopoulos-Mihalopoulos, 'Between Light and Darkness: Earthsea and the Name of Utopia', *Contemporary Justice Review* 8, no. 1 (2005): 45–57 (50).
26 Benjamin Lee Whorf, *Language, Thought and Reality: Selected Writings*, ed. J. B. Carroll (Cambridge, Mass: MIT Press, 1956), 212.
27 Andreas Philippopoulos-Mihalopoulos, 'Between Light and Darkness: Earthsea and the Name of Utopia', 50.

Le Guin's model of Old Speech in *Earthsea*. Reality is radically given: a named and existent truth which exceeds human perception and naming. This makes reality remarkably resistant to human construction, for it has its own independent truth and identity. Knowing the truth of a thing, in the shape of its name, a mage may alter it. However, this is tampering with the ontological foundations of the universe, which is precisely why it is considered such a weighty and risky act to alter the nature of so much as a pebble.

This is radically disjunctive from, for example, Derrida's concept of signification. In *Of Grammatology*, Derrida argues that signification always refers to other signs, which do not have inherent meaning in and of themselves: there is no self-referential sign. Meaning is both differed – it means in relation to other things which are absent, in a never-ending chain – and deferred; temporally speaking, it never comes to closure or cessation. His notion of 'arche-writing' rests on an understanding of this 'originary' deferral of meaning which means that it can never be fully and definitively present. Thus, there is no ontological relationship between signifier and signified. Language is arbitrary, and signs signify only in relation to other signs. In Old Speech, meaning is neither of these things. *Tolk* is *tolk*, because it is *tolk*, and not in relation to the name for anything else. There is an identity between name and essence which gives Old Speech language a transcendent dimension. It is not a human construction; it is embedded in the nature of being itself.

Children go by baby-names or 'use-names' until the granting of the 'true name' at adolescence. According to Robinson, the 'everyday' use-name by which a child is known prior to the bestowal of the 'true name' is selected for its appropriateness to the characteristics of the individual, and is 'an artistic, emotional and intellectual response to the arbitrariness of the sign and the division of the subject.'[28] It offers the (false) ideal of integrated characters, and leads Robinson to hypothesize that it amounts to a 'representation of the imago from Jacques Lacan's mirror stage.'[29] That is to say, it represents the projection of a unified ego-ideal. This can be compared to Lacan's mirror stage, whereby the child sees its reflection as possessing a coherence and unity.

This ideal image does not of course correspond to the real subject, and is impossible to realize. The child observes its own reflection as both other and same; also, while the imago may possess a coherence and unity, the

---

28 Christopher L. Robinson, 'The Violence of the Name: Patronymy in Earthsea', *Extrapolation* 49, no. 3 (Winter 2008): 385–409 (386).
29 Ibid.

subject does not. The child therefore has an ambivalent relation to its own ideal as constituted by the imago, which is only resolved through entry into the symbolic order. The symbolic order is the regulatory system by which a culture operates, ordered by linguistic and social rules and conventions, and within which subjectivity is articulated. The symbolic order is an all-encompassing network within which subjectivity is constructed; it operates under the Name of the Father to which the developing subject must submit. The passage into the symbolic order is achieved through navigation of the Oedipus complex. As a result of its subjection to the Name of the Father, the subject becomes divorced from the pre-linguistic realm of the real, and is constituted as a linguistic being with no unmediated access to its environment. However, a durable identity is achieved which is stabilized by the proper name, itself regulated by the Name of the Father. Robinson sums this up:

> So, where the imaginary order [at the mirror stage] fosters an illusion of wholeness, but induces a state of ambivalence that inhibits a sense of true and lasting identity, the symbolic order confers a stable identity by virtue of the Name of the Father, but demands in turn a double sacrifice, one that both divides the subject from itself and separates it from others.[30]

Thus, Robinson draws parallels between the states of subjectivity in the imaginary and symbolic orders, and Le Guin's naming system in *Earthsea*. He is postulating that the protagonist's use-name (e.g. Sparrowhawk) is a representation of the imago in an onomastic reconstruction of the imaginary order; the true name, by contrast (e.g. Ged), is a patronym that functions within the symbolic order. As noted, in *Earthsea* the true name is given at adolescence. Robinson observes a gender dynamic in the naming ceremony, whereby an anonymous woman on one bank of a river takes away the boy's juvenile name, while the mage Ogion on the other bank bestows on him his true name, Ged. This leads Robinson to the conclusion: 'Seen in this light, the fiction of a magical language of names becomes a barely distinguished analogy for masculine authority, power and privilege.'[31] This gendered dynamic enables Robinson to add a Kristevan layer to his analysis.

Kristeva highlights how the condition of entry into the symbolic order is matricide – in order to achieve individuation, separation from the maternal must be achieved. Yet the maternal is repressed and abjected

30 Ibid., 388.
31 Ibid., 394.

rather than wholly ejected, such that the act of nomination (a linguistic and individuating process) is 'a more or less victorious confrontation' with the mother, but one that is 'never finished with her.'[32] The act of nomination with Ged is repeated twice more: once when Ogion calls him back from his falcon shape, and once when Ged himself names the shadow creature with his own name. For Robinson, the necessity to repeat the act of naming 'underscores the discontinuous nature of the subject.'[33] What this means in *Earthsea* is that the naming ceremony actually represents sacrificial violence, re-enacting separation from the maternal body and initiating rupture in the subject's own being.

> Henceforth, its drives, desires, and identity will be subordinated to a symbolic order founded upon patronymy, which is represented by or abbreviated in the given true name, *Ged*. In this way, a gender divide comes to be inscribed in the onomastic, as well as the symbolic and physical space of the ceremony . . . Consequently, the violence at work in the naming ceremony turns out to demystify the magical or utopian construction of a mirror-like reflection between name and character.[34]

Here seems a timely moment to interject with three stories running counter to Robinson's analysis. Not incidentally, they are stories about women. First, we can be reminded of Tenar, whose naming was discussed in Chapter Three. Ged, giving Tenar her name, actually simply doubled the originary naming of her mother. The name of the mother therefore preceded the name of the father and was not effaced. Second, we can introduce Irian. Irian is the hero of a short story, 'Dragonfly'.[35] There is much more that could be said about Irian's story, but here I will restrict myself to the bare points. Irian is dismayed to receive the name of her abusive father's domains as her true name. She enters Roke school of wizardry under the guise of a boy (although the Doorkeeper recognizes her), defeats a corrupted revenant mage and transforms into a dragon. This is not shape-shifting into an alien form but an assumption of a true identity. She then flies to 'beyond the west' to receive her name: 'In fire,

---

32 Julia Kristeva, 'Place Names', in Leon S. Roudiez (ed.) and Thomas Gore, Leon Roudiez and Alice Jardine (trans.), *Desire in Language* (New York, NY: Columbia University Press, 1980), 291, cited in Robinson, 'The Violence of the Name: Patronymy in Earthsea', 402.

33 Robinson, 'The Violence of the Name: Patronymy in Earthsea', 402.

34 Ibid., 403.

35 Ursula K. Le Guin, 'Dragonfly', in *Tales from Earthsea* (London: Orion, 2001), 197–265.

not water.'[36] Third, Tehanu, who is Therru, the burned child, receives her name directly from the Maker of All, Kalessin, who is Segoy, and not gendered (although initially referred to as 'he'). These three namings point to a circumvention of patronymy and are further signs of the changing times after the events of *The Farthest Shore*. As Ogion whispers to Tenar on his deathbed, 'All changed!'[37]

These 'interruptions' to the patronymic system are, then, part of a development of a new metaphysic and a new cosmology. Comoletti and Drout argue that: 'In *Tehanu*, Le Guin extends the underlying idea of a creation language in such a way as to work women and their powers and speech into the cosmological and metaphysical workings of Earthsea'[38] – itself a move from the *how* of performative speech to the *who*. In one sense this could be seen to stray from the metaphysical as such to the socio-political. However, the point is that in Le Guin's *Earthsea* they are intimately intertwined. Wizard education and practice, and thus anything more than bastardized knowledge of the Old Speech, is confined to men. This projects a social and political gendered inequity into the metaphysical sphere: or vice versa, it takes as an ontological truth that women have a different metaphysical location from men and uses this to legitimate socio-political inequity.

Magic in Le Guin's universe is deeply gendered. Even Ged is convinced of the incompatibility between womanhood and art magic: 'No woman can be Archmage. She'd unmake what she became in becoming it. The Mages of Roke are men – their power is the power of men.'[39] And yet, the Patterner on Roke prophesied, in response to the question, 'Who shall be the next Archmage?' – 'A woman on Gont.'[40]

The story of the refashioning of *Earthsea* is told through the story of Tenar, so I shall now turn to her. The sustained focus of the following analysis will be the book *Tehanu*, although I will conclude by looking briefly at *The Other Wind* to allow certain threads of thought to be concluded. *Tehanu* offers a remodelling of the hero; in this respect the analysis is a companion to that undertaken in Chapter Three. However, here Le Guin's revisited hero is tied in with a remodelling of the metaphysics and

---

36   Ibid., 264.
37   Ursula K. Le Guin, *Tehanu – The Earthsea Quartet* (London: Puffin, 1992), 23.
38   Laura B. Comoletti and Michael D. C. Drout, 'How They Do Things with Words: Language, Power, Gender, and the Priestly Wizards of Ursula K. Le Guin's Earthsea Books', *Children's Literature* 29 (2001): 113–41 (124).
39   Le Guin, *Tehanu*, 219.
40   Le Guin, 'Dragonfly', 245.

cosmology of *Earthsea*, which is achieved through the life-narrative of Tenar's adopted child, Therru.

The Tombs of Atuan closed with Tenar's advent in Havnor, and her expressed desire not to stay in the 'great cities among foreign men.'[41] In *Tehanu*, written 17 years later, Tenar has abandoned studies with the mage Ogion, and chosen to be a farmer's wife. Why? Le Guin acknowledges the danger that her feminist 'revisioning' could instead be seen as showing female submission to societal expectations and dislike of powerful, independent women. However, Le Guin argues that Tenar has not abdicated power; she is simply exercising it in a different way: 'Her acts and choice do not involve ascendance, domination, power over others, and seem not to involve great consequences.'[42] There is a classic double-bind at work here, for it is precisely those who uphold the traditional division between 'public' and 'private' who might see Tenar's choice as foolish, and her story as 'sadly unheroic'[43] – while Le Guin argues that it is precisely in this rejection of the public role of hero on the masculine model that Tenar's heroism is subversive. However, Tenar's family life as wife to Flint and then subsequently his widow seems to epitomize patriarchal familial relations; certainly, if the son Spark is anything to go by, the concept of a woman deserving respect from men is foreign.

Ged, likewise, has become (in heroic terms) an ordinary man; he has lost his power of magery; he has abdicated his public office as Archmage, and lives in domestic daily life with Tenar – 'weak, ill, depressed.'[44] 'History is no longer about great men.'[45] No longer a wizard, Ged is no longer under a spell of chastity imposing independence from women beyond the dance of formal chivalry: sex comes to *Earthsea* in the shape of a quiet romance between two middle-aged lovers. As Mills puts it: '*Tehanu* thus subverts the classical model of the hero's return, bearing witness instead to the extreme cost in a patriarchal world of honoring embodying the feminine.'[46]

Witches remain mysterious; invisible in the patriarchal system valorizing only the magic of men. There is a saying, oft-repeated in the *Earthsea* cycle – 'Weak as woman's magic, wicked as woman's magic.' The old village witch Moss confides to Tenar:

---

41 Le Guin, *The Tombs of Atuan*, 298.
42 Le Guin, *Earthsea Revisioned*, 13.
43 Ibid.
44 Ibid., 17.
45 Ibid., 13.
46 Alice Mills, 'Burning Women in Ursula K. Le Guin's *Tehanu: The Last Book of Earthsea*', *New York Review of Science Fiction* 7, no. 1 (1995): 3–7 (3).

Oh, well, dearie, a woman's a different thing entirely. Who knows where a woman begins and ends? Listen, mistress, I have roots, I have roots deeper than this island. Deeper than the sea, older than the raising of the lands. I go back into the dark. . . . No one knows, no one knows, no one can say what I am, what a woman is, a woman of power, a woman's power . . . Who'll ask the dark its name?[47]

And Tenar's response is telling. 'I will,' she asserts, 'I lived long enough in the dark.'[48] Also telling is Moss's declaration that the power of women is deeper than the roots of trees, deeper than the roots of islands; what else is called to mind here but the magic embodied in the Immanent Grove on Roke Island, and Roke itself? Mills suggests that we should see in the names of Moss and Ivy (*Tehanu*'s other witch) a paradigm of nature against culture, but one in which the power of nature is pervasive, subtle, 'moistly earthy'.[49]

Crucially for the reframing of the nature of the hero, Tenar does not agree with sacrifice. This, as we saw earlier, is also a Taoist theme. Tenar's soul cannot live in that 'narrow place'; there is a freedom beyond 'payment, retribution, redemption'. She does not die to be reborn, instead she is 'rebearing . . . actively, in the maternal mode.'[50] Yet, having abandoned powers in the 'heroic' mode of the old tradition, both Ged and Tenar find themselves helpless before their enemies at the end of the book. 'Their strength and salvation must come from outside the institutions and traditions. It must be a new thing.'[51]

The child Therru is the key to the 'new thing'. She is on the one hand thoroughly dehumanized by her treatment in society – burned, disfigured, raped, beaten, with one eye blinded and one hand maimed, Therru represents the disempowered and disinherited. In a sense, she is 'everywoman' under patriarchy: 'the child's maiming in the fire represents the general maiming of women in Earthsea, the suppression of sexuality by wizards, and assault upon the anima by most men.'[52] Therru's very name means burning. 'She has nothing left of the girl men want girls to be. It's all been burned away.'[53] The link with sexuality is heightened, Mills reminds us, if one bears in mind the biblical command to pluck out the

47   Le Guin, *Tehanu*, 53.
48   Ibid.
49   Mills, 'Burning Women in Ursula K. Le Guin's *Tehanu*', 4.
50   Le Guin, *Earthsea Revisioned*, 18.
51   Ibid., 19.
52   Mills, 'Burning Women in Ursula K. Le Guin's *Tehanu*', 4.
53   Le Guin, *Earthsea Revisioned*, 24.

right eye and cut off the right hand of women who (sexually) offend. As Mills also percipiently notes, given the symbolic weight thus given to fire, it is interesting that Tenar's dead husband and son are named, respectively, Flint and Spark.[54]

On the other hand, there is a strangeness about her that carries with it the threat or the promise of an overturning. They will fear her, Ogion had told Tenar. What does Therru see? Tenar asks herself; we find out that Therru sees with the eye of spirit as well as flesh. She becomes the guide to the 'new world', a future of wildness and possibility. Tenar herself understands that 'a wrong that cannot be repaired must be transcended';[55] it must be made anew, like the world.

The dragons symbolize wildness; they also represent revolution and change:

> The dragon is the stranger, the other, the not-human: a wild spirit, danger-
> ous, winged, which escapes and destroys an artificial order of oppression.
> The dragon is the familiar also, our own imagining, a speaking spirit, wise,
> winged, which imagines a new order of freedom.[56]

Le Guin insists that if they are archetypes, it is of a 'new world'.[57] Archetypes, furthermore, should be conceived as full of vibrant potentialities, not as fixed forms. Dragons cannot be owned. The rule is that a man should not look into a dragon's eye: but Tenar does: '[S]he knows the rule, but then, she's not a man is she? . . . She and the dragon look at each other . . . They recognize each other.'[58] It is reminiscent of the story told early in the book: the legend of the Woman of Kemay, about a time when dragons and humans were one people, and had then become separated, but might once more become one.[59] Tenar can do this because she chose

---

54 Mills, 'Burning Women in Ursula K. Le Guin's *Tehanu*', 4. It is also interesting that her daughter is named Apple. Mills, however, sees this as more representative of both Therru's and Arha/Tenar's sufferings ('incest, being eaten, dying'); she invokes the traditional imagery of the apple as 'forbidden fruit'.

55 Le Guin, *Tehanu*, 580.

56 Le Guin, *Earthsea Revisioned*, 25–26.

57 Specifically, the dragons are of a 'new world, America, and the visionary forms of an old woman's mind' (ibid., 22).

58 Ibid.

59 This is the vision expressed by Fan's fan: on one side are painted women and men of the royal court, on the other dragons; held to the light, seeing the one image superimposed on the other, 'the men and women were winged, and the dragons looked with human eyes.'

freedom over power. 'Her insignificance is her wildness.'[60] Therru, even more so, embodies transformative potential: '[T]he child who is our care, the child we have betrayed, is our guide. She leads us to the dragon. She is the dragon.'[61] Women can take to the air, with flame and fire.

Mills suggests that if Le Guin's aim was to restore balance between masculine and feminine in *Tehanu*, she has failed; the issues remain unresolved, and outside help is required to save Tenar and Therru.[62] This is despite the reversal of traditional mythic patterns at the end of *Tehanu*. The dragon comes not to threaten but to save, the maiden on the cliff emerges into true, clear sight, and she and the dragon rescue her adoptive parents, Ged and Tenar. Tenar is bound, muted and forced to eat dirt, as Therru transforms into Tehanu, epitomizing freedom and vision. Yet, Mills argues that although Le Guin does not gender her dragons, the identification of the dragon Kalessin with the Maker, Segoy, implicitly genders him male: there is a reference to Segoy in *The Farthest Shore* as masculine. This being the case, says Mills, Kalessin represents the Father of Fathers (and he also, of course claims Therru as his actual daughter), so arguably what we see is the female calling for paternal help.[63] This comes with the fire of the (male) dragon, destroying the evil wizard. All this leads Mills to a somewhat critical conclusion:

> Le Guin's analysis of women's power is least satisfactory when Kalessin is understood as a father and Therru as his daughter stuck between human and dragon. Not only does Tenar lose all her power in the final ordeal to grovel as an animal on the ground; not only does Therru call on her father for rescue when she comes to self-knowledge; but Therru's own dragon nature is initiated by men's abuse of her body as a helpless child. *Tehanu* thus gives a peculiarly nasty twist to a corruptly patriarchal order . . . the benefit seems to reside in the scarring and charring themselves. This is an extraordinary position for a feminist author to take.[64]

The question of Therru's wounds is considered below. With respect to the issue of balance between masculine and feminine, does the reading change if we 'ungender' Kalessin? Le Guin says firmly that 'the dragon defies gender entirely. There are male and female dragons in the earlier

---

60 Le Guin, *Earthsea Revisioned*, 23.
61 Ibid., 26.
62 Mills, 'Burning Women in Ursula K. Le Guin's *Tehanu*', 3.
63 Ibid., 5.
64 Ibid., 6.

books, but I don't know if Kalessin, the eldest, is male or female or both or something else.'[65] Within the narrative-world, the human reference to Segoy as masculine could be taken as a human assumption that power equates to masculinity. If Kalessin is not a male rescuer, we do not have a reiteration of the patriarchal myth form. Mills does consider this possibility, suggesting that if Kalessin is figured as female, the dragon would then represent the 'negative mother', 'lethal and devouring' – Tenar's shadowside, since she represents mother as nurturer. Kalessin, then, would embody all that Tenar, and women, had lost.[66] However, Mills considers this to be a difficult reading – not only because of Kalessin's title as Maker and Segoy, but also because female power would then become simply another manifestation of superior power, and indistinguishable from male power. 'Thus the dragon, if male, confirms Earthsea's patriarchal order; if female, does not transform it.' The better reading, it seems to me, is to stay with Le Guin's own reading of the dragon as transcendent of gender categories, which may thereby be disrupted.

Keller, similarly, is dismissive of *Tehanu* as myth of feminist consciousness. She notes how well the initial trilogy maps onto the Jungian model and documented Indo-European archetypes – light/male/yang/sun/activity balanced by dark/female/yin/moon/intuition. However, in the 'traditional' mythic of fairy-tale template, Yang does not abandon Yin; the prince and princess do not part ways at the conclusion of the quest. This, according to Keller, is just what has happened by the conclusion of *The Tombs of Atuan*:

> And so the tale of Tenar becomes, not simply (as some feminists have complained) 'a passive maiden rescue story,' but a significantly more exploitational echo of Theseus' abandonment of Ariadne, or Jason's (eventual) repudiation of Medea.[67]

Keller thinks it no coincidence that Tenar, Ariadne and Medea were all women of power hailing from matriarchal religious traditions. As can be seen in Chapter Three, I take a different line on that and see Tenar's departure from Atuan as a moment of self-actualization, and her parting with Ged as an opportunity for her further independent growth.

Keller is also scathing about Le Guin's portrayal of magic, even in her

65   Le Guin, *Earthsea Revisioned*, 24.
66   Mills, 'Burning Women in Ursula K. Le Guin's *Tehanu*', 6.
67   Tatiana Keller, 'Feminist Issues in Earthsea: *Tehanu: the Last Book of Earthsea*', The New York Review of Science Fiction 28 (December 1990): 14–16 (14).

attempt to revision *Earthsea* from a feminist point of view: Moss, the village witch, is the only female user of magic and 'the embodiment of every caricature drawn from medieval Christian tradition.'[68] Keller assumes that Le Guin, in completing the story of Tenar, cannot have a female mage because it would challenge the social, magical and political foundations of the world of Earthsea. Such a comment is strangely incognizant of the number of hints that the next Archmage will be female. Keller sees in Tenar's abdication from studies with Ogion and public life more generally a 'quietly devastating way for Le Guin to simultaneously support and endorse every poisonous myth fed to young girls about Real Womanhood . . . and trash her own carefully conceived secondary world.'[69]

However, it must also be said that *Tehanu* does not lock down the possibilities for the future. At the time of Le Guin's writing and Mills's and Keller's critiques, *Tehanu* was to be the last book of *Earthsea*. And it is true that at the end of the book, Therru/Tehanu cannot fly, nor breathe fire. However, there is a clear hint that Tehanu is at the beginning of her dragonly journey. She asks Kalessin if she is to accompany him to the others, on 'the other wind', but decides she does not wish to if it means leaving Tenar and Ged. Furthermore, she has work to do.[70] But Kalessin will come back for her; as he gives Tehanu into Tenar and Ged's care now, he expects them to return her to him in time. This need not be seen as a patronymic 'ownership' of Tehanu but an acknowledgement of her identity and an affirmation of her double participation in both human and dragon realms: the dragon future is an open possibility yet to come. Tehanu asks Tenar about the peaches; they are small and green now, Tenar tells her, but they will ripen. Tehanu at this stage is a promise, a hope, an anticipatory sign.

What of her wounds? Does the transformation of the burned child into dragon-child legitimate her abuse? I would argue that the dynamic can be read entirely differently, as an affirmation of survival, and more, of her own potentiality and self-transformation. Lindow also takes a similar line at this point: 'In a perfect world, child abuse and incest would not exist. . . . For an abuse victim to become a dragon is to transcend victimization and in so doing become an agent for social change, a being powerful enough to stop the victimization of others.'[71] At the same time, the learning of wisdom through pain can be discerned elsewhere in the cycle; one need

---

68 Ibid., 15.
69 Ibid., 16.
70 Le Guin, *Tehanu*, 202.
71 Sandra J. Lindow, *Becoming Dragon: The Transcendence of the Damaged Child in the Fiction of Ursula K. Le Guin* (Brownsville, TX: The University of Texas, 2003), 35.

only look at Ged's own initial 'coming of age' in his defeat of the shadow. Likewise, his 'spiritual son', Arren, knows how to listen and how to use his power with judgement because he, too, has 'been through the fire.'[72]

In some senses, dragonkind are Le Guin's response to the problem of theodicy. It is well known that Le Guin has drawn deeply upon Zen Buddhism and Taoism in her metaphysics of 'balance'. In a corollary to the Christian myth of the Fall, we learn in *The Farthest Shore* that only humans 'can destroy the balance of the world'; evil transpires when power is craved over life, and desire turns to greed; allied with knowledge, 'the balance of the world is swayed, and ruin weighs heavily in the scale.'[73]

Dragons, then, are Le Guin's ultimate response to evil. As Lindow points out, dragons in *Earthsea* are a moving target; in *The Wizard of Earthsea*, the Dragon of Pendor bears resemblance to the dragon of folklore and legend – or Smaug in *The Hobbit*. He is tricky, he likes jewels, he is ancient. By *The Farthest Shore*, the representation of dragons more closely allies with the trajectory taking us to *Tehanu* and then *The Other Wind*. Dragons symbolize 'life, ultimately generative, and function as an antithesis to the dry lands of death where all the potters' wheels are still, all looms empty and all creativity has died.'[74]

What is dragon-being? It is different from human-being. Ged instructs Arren in this regard. It is not only that dragons are wiser than humanity, and more ancient; dragons '. . . do not dream. They are dreams. They do not work magic: it is their substance, their being. They do not do, they are.'[75] Dragons, then, inhabit the timeless 'now', in contrast to humans 'who are constantly preoccupied with past mistakes, future goals.'[76]

McLean points out that Le Guin's indictment of patriarchy in *Tehanu* begins with the 'death of fathers, both literal and metaphoric.'[77] This is three-fold: the death of Ogion, wise and peaceful mentor to both Ged and Tenar; the death three years previously of Flint, Tenar's husband and father of her biological children; and the symbolic death of Ged, the Archmage, with the utter loss of his magic. The new king and 'father-to-be', Arren, is yet too young – and himself represents the evolution of *Earthsea* into a new time. After long ages, there is a King in Havnor, and one who will rule at last under the Rune of Peace. The search for a new

72 Le Guin, *Tehanu*.
73 Le Guin, *The Farthest Shore*, 334.
74 Lindow, *Becoming Dragon*, 33.
75 Le Guin, *The Farthest Shore*, 335.
76 Lindow, *Becoming Dragon*, 33.
77 Susan McLean, 'The Power of Women in Ursula K. Le Guin's *Tehanu*', *Extrapolation* 38, no. 2 (1997): 110–18 (111).

Archmage is unsuccessful; as McLean notes, little heed is paid to the
Master Patterner's statement that the pattern of the future centres on a
'woman on Gont.'[78]

Thus, already, the traditional hero-mould is broken. Tenar, and Ged also,
must find their own way. They are protectors and mentors of Therru; they
themselves have no guide. Nor are they the rescuers; in all the dangerous
situations in which they find themselves, help comes from external sources
– from the King, from the King's men, from the dragon Kalessin called
by Therru/Tehanu. The nature of power is recalibrated; this is typified by
Ged, who is initially convinced that his worth and self-identity have disap-
peared with his magical power. Ged learns, with difficulty, a different kind
of power. McLean considers Carol Gilligan's observation to be pertinent
here: Gilligan argued that male identity is primarily defined by 'separation and individuality', while women's identity 'is defined in a context of
relationship and judged by a standard of responsibility and care.'[79] Tenar,
the maternal figure par excellence, embodies strongly this kind of power.

As intimated earlier, I will continue the tale of Tehanu and the nature
of dragons by jumping forward to the conclusion of *The Other Wind*, as
this offers yet a further metaphysical revision and elucidation of the nature
of dragons. In *The Other Wind*, the barrier with the world of the dead had
appeared to be thinning once more; a young mender, Alder, is tormented
by dreams of his dead wife Lily calling to him over the wall. At the same
time, young dragons are encroaching on human territories and burning
farms in the West Reach. It transpires that the current imbalance has
ancient roots and is profoundly tied to the history of humans and of dragons. Once dragons and humans were one race. Then came the *Verdurnan*,
or division: basically a choice between possessions and settlement, and
flight and magic. The elder dragon Kalessin explains:

> Long ago we chose. We chose freedom. Men chose the yoke. We chose fire
> and wind. They chose water and earth. We chose the west, and they the east
> . . . in every generation of men, one or two are born who are dragons also. And
> in every generation of our people . . . one of us is born who is human.[80]

Tehanu is a human who is also a dragon; Irian is a dragon who is also a

78 Ibid.
79 McLean, 'The Power of Women in Ursula K. Le Guin's *Tehanu*', 113, citing
    Carol Gilligan, *In a Different Voice: Psychological Theory and Women's Development*
    (Cambridge, MA: Harvard University Press, 1990), 161.
80 Ursula K. Le Guin, *The Other Wind* (San Diego, CA: Harcourt & Brace): 152–53.

human. They are the last, the messengers, the bringers of choice. Irian goes on to explain why the dragons are angry with humankind. The folk of the Archipelago broke their promise. In return for possessions and ownership, those staying in the east were supposed to give up the Old Speech. Instead, the mages in the Archipelago captured the Old Speech in runic form and, having lost it as birthright, were thus able to acquire and transmit it as a learned language. Retaining power in this way, they were also able to steal half of the dragons' realm in the west, wall it off and weave a net of spells around it to catch the spirits of those humans with true names as they died. This was supposed to ensure human immortality after bodily death in the paradisiacal realm of the dead.

However, this went horribly wrong. Walled off, no winds blew in the land and no waters flowed. It became a land of dryness, of dust, and darkness and pain. The Summoner supposes that this is why the dead are now reaching out: they are anxious to come back to the realm of the living. No, says Alder: and explains that what the dead want is death, true death. This is granted to them by knocking down the walls around the realm of the dead.

What, then, to make of all this in terms of Le Guin's aim to revision *Earthsea*? With Tenar and Ged, we see a radical reorientation towards the world and how to live in it. It is a model based on care, community and networks of relations. Furthermore, Tenar has now built up a 'matrilineal' community in relations with other women. Ged is learning to live as a man of ordinary power and sexuality. Indeed, the revelations in *The Other Wind* expose the whole wizardly exercise of magic as one based on betrayal and a grasping after illegitimate power. On the one hand, this is a revaluing of a different mode of being; on the other it is simply an exposure of it. Tenar and Therru both suffer abuse. By turning her fictional historiographical eye onto the 'local' and domestic level of affairs in Earthsea, Le Guin is indicting patriarchal systems and refusing to accept that only 'public' spaces are of importance and worthy of narrative. In that respect, it can be seen as an act of solidarity, as can Tenar's own choice to abdicate from possible public prominence and live her quiet life. However, the startling element in *Tehanu* and *The Other Wind* is Tehanu herself. She represents a radical transcendence. The otherness, wildness and potentiality of dragons are inscribed on the body of a woman. Her flights on the 'Other Winds' open up gulfs of glimpsed possibilities, of spaces only yet imagined but not actualized. The symbolism of dragons resists closure, and it is precisely this wild irruption of possibility into the surfaces of patriarchy that is Tehanu's gift. She, and her dragon-sister Irian: the messengers, the bringers of choice.

TRANSFORMING WORLDS

BUFFY THE VAMPIRE SLAYER: 'BITE ME'

THE WRITER JOSS WHEDON's inspiration for *Buffy the Vampire Slayer* was the classic Hollywood formula:

> [T]he little blonde girl who goes into a dark alley and gets killed in every horror movie. The idea of *Buffy* was to subvert that idea, that image, and create someone who was a hero where she had always been a victim.[1]

His concept was originally aired as a film, and Whedon was disappointed: the approach taken by the film's director did not actualize his vision of female empowerment. When asked to turn *Buffy* into a television show, Whedon developed his original notion to include the metaphorical context of 'high school as hell', with the supernatural elements and conflicts acting as metaphors for the problems and anxieties of adolescence and young adulthood. Power, its distribution and circulations, is a central plot element, as one would expect from the angles of both gender and adolescence. These power dynamics are explored both in relation to the overarching good-versus-evil narrative, and with respect to particular individuals and their social, moral and psychological development. Questions then arise as to the extent to which *Buffy* is actually subversive of authorities, or to what extent it reinforces existing power structures and/or traditions. *Buffy* has been critiqued for failing to escape traditional models of self and

---

1   Joss Whedon, *Audio Commentary: Buffy the Vampire Slayer, Season One*, DVD, 'Welcome to the Hellmouth' and 'The Harvest', 2001.

society, and in consequence representing only a superficial potential for transformation and renewal. I argue here that *Buffy* does, in fact, embody a subversive attitude towards tradition, hierarchy and power structures. This has implications for models of self and self-in-relation; the nature of such models is central to philosophies and spiritualities of existence.

The playful and postmodern style of *Buffy* lends itself very well to a recoding and subversion of traditional constructs. It is a deliberate pastiche and is self-referential about its status as TV show; for example, it makes frequent allusion to fictional popular culture products within the real world such as James Bond, Harry Potter, Spiderman, Superman and the like. This shared referentiality casts an interrogatory eye at the boundaries between reality and fiction and thereby destabilizes markers of truth and certainty.[2] It could be said that this whole parodic structure of *Buffy* is intrinsically anti-authoritarian and subversive of tradition because it plays with established categories and norms. This is reminiscent of the carnivalesque. Mikhail Bakhtin theorized this as a literary tendency drawing its energy from the reversals and chaos of the carnival, in which established norms and hierarchies are suspended, mocked and overturned. It should be noted that the carnivalesque can be used to reinforce dominant ideologies and social structures, as well as to subvert them; furthermore, subversions may themselves ultimately act to shore up existing orders by permitting cathartic release. However, in *Buffy*, the decisive change in the Slayer tradition and the closing of the Hellmouth in the final episodes point towards a more genuinely transformational subversive dynamic which offers the potential to break apart oppressive thought patterns and clear space for emancipatory impulses.[3]

The world of institutional authority in *Buffy* is frequently presented as oppressive or corrupt, if not actively allied with dark forces, like Mayor Wilkins. School principal Snyder is in collusion with Wilkins. Former Watcher Gwendolyn Post is a user of black magic. Professor Maggie Walsh, leader of the military's research project into supernatural beings (the 'Initiative'), becomes obsessed with power and control and tries to have Buffy killed. Even the 'good' Watchers' Council, which oversees the Slayers, is presented with increasing ambivalence, as will

2 One notable episode in this respect is the episode 'Normal Again', where Buffy is hallucinating that she is in a mental institution, supposedly hallucinating about her life in Sunnydale.

3 See Mikhail Bakhtin, *Problems of Dostoevsky's Poetics*, trans. Caryl Emerson (Minneapolis, MN: University of Minnesota Press, 1984); Mikhail Bakhtin, *Rabelais and His World*, trans. Hélène Iswolsky (Bloomington, IN: Indiana University Press, 1984).

be seen below. Parental authority is not immune from the excesses of the 'insomniac rationality', which, according to Deleuze and Guattari, 'engenders monsters'.[4]

The third season's 'Gingerbread' episode is a fine example of this, in which 'Mothers Opposed to the Occult' (MOO) begin by wanting to take Sunnydale back from 'the monsters and the witches and the slayers', and end by trying to burn Buffy, Willow and Amy at the stake. MOO veers increasingly towards extremism, fascism and an organized programme of extermination. As Breton and McMaster comment:

> Confronted with an alien subculture [that of the monsters], which under-mines all they took for granted about reality, the adult response is a violent reinscription of the world order they are ideologically wedded to. The teenagers, on the other hand, have arguably less allegiance to the rules of a reality which seldom worked to their advantage anyway.[5]

The sub-culture of monsters and the sub-culture of youth are thus brought into alignment in the interstices of organized systems. Both occupy liminal spaces. *Buffy*, indeed, is brimming with themes of marginaliza-tion and sub-culturalism. The Scooby Gang is liminal within the liminal space of youth. It is so from its establishment in the first Season: Willow and Xander – geek, nerd, and the first 'Slayerettes' – occupy high school positions as 'losers'. Buffy chooses to locate herself in their space, which overlays her own marginal position as the Slayer.

Bieszk, offering an analysis of *Buffy* in terms of sub-cultures, makes a number of important points. She identifies at play the sub-cultural aesthetics of goth, punk and camp. Angel is the epitome of Gothic hero – a tormented, brooding figure of illicit desire. Spike, rebellious and hedonistic, is more a figure of goth punk:

> Punk is an offensive and violent aesthetic, translated literally in the show, which allowed Spike the luxury of covering his clothes in real human blood, instead of fake . . . Punk's agenda drenched in Apocalpytic imagery, profanity

---

4 Gilles Deleuze and Félix Guattari, *Anti-Oedipus: Capitalism and Schizophrenia* (London and New York, NY: Continuum International Publishing Group, 2004), 122. This quotation forms the epigraph for Rob Breton and Lindsey McMaster, 'Dissing the Age of MOO: Initiatives, Alternatives, and Rationality', *Slayage: The Online International Journal of Buffy Studies* 1, no. 1 (2001). Online: http://www.slayageonline.com/essays/slayage1/bretonmcmaster.htm

5 Breton and McMaster, 'Dissing the Age of MOO: Initiatives, Alternatives, and Rationality'.

and nihilism, encouraging perverse sexuality and obsessive individualism, suited Spike's image of contestation perfectly.[6]

Camp, in postmodern mode, is evident in the self-referential, self-mocking and playfully ironic use of classic themes and characters which simultaneously undercut and subvert each other: stylistic excess; a kitsch aesthetic; gender ambivalences and ambiguities. As Bieszk goes on to comment, this is not simply a matter of superficial gloss or vacuous style: 'Style however reflects attitude, which is another word for politics, without it, it is just a masquerade.'[7]

Sub-cultures function to provoke and subvert, and puncture pretensions towards monoculturalism in ways that dominant cultures may find unsettling or even dangerous. At the same time sub-culture sits within the interstices of the mainstream, not wholly apart from it, and forms of meaning are assimilated, diffused and transformed in both directions. It is the unfolding of another order within the normalized.

Buffy, then, works with sub-cultural worlds and motifs in a number of ways, including its aesthetics and its focus on youth, the monstrous, and the transgressive. Other transgressive elements include the Slayer's female identity, a feature examined later in this chapter, and the 'coming out' of Willow: *Buffy* is famous for being the first network television series in America to feature a lesbian sex scene, when Kennedy seduces Willow in Season Seven. While the relationship between Tara and Willow was overtly gay, magic frequently acted as sexual metaphor: the musical episode 'Once More with Feeling' is a prime example of this. Later in Season Six, Tara and Willow are shown in bed together, in what is clearly a post-sexual scene. This was a controversial move, and doubly so: on the one hand, it appears to push positively the envelope of lesbian visibility and representation; but on the other, it is also the episode in which Tara dies. Whedon thus came in for heavy criticism with the charge that this reinforced the association between lesbianism and a transgression which can only be dealt with by the effacement of death. This, of course, is a historically literal penalty for sub-cultures which dominant culture cannot contain or accommodate.

Another important factor in the show's representation of power and

6   Patricia Bieszk, 'Vampire Hip: Style as Subcultural Expression in Buffy the Vampire Slayer', *Refractory: A Journal of Entertainment Media* (4 February 2005). Online: http://blogs.arts.unimelb.edu.au/refractory/2005/02/04/vampire-hip-style-as-subcultural-expression-in-buffy-the-vampire-slayer-patricia-bieszk/
7   Ibid.

authority is its orientation towards traditional norms and structures. The next area examined here is aspects of the show's relation to religiosity, both overt and diluted. The world of the characters in *Buffy*, both vampiric and human, is not determined by traditional or institutional theologies. This is not, however, to say that the show's philosophy is divorced from theological themes and concerns. Rather, it is situated consciously and eclectically within a 'detraditioned' religious space. Despite this, it can be argued that *Buffy* remains dominated by Christian mythologies. For some commentators, such as Alderman and Seidel-Arpaci,[8] this undermines *Buffy*'s potential to point towards a genuinely alternative and inclusive model of spirituality, for it retains a covert commitment to Christian models which is ultimately both Western and conservative.

The vampire of traditional European mythology was constructed in part in relation to Christian thought-fields. This is particularly explicit with its advent in the literary realm. Bram Stoker's *Dracula* of 1897 has exerted enormous and iconic influence here in subsequent concepts of the vampiric. This includes the importance of crucifixes and holy water in the armoury for battle with the undead. These religious artefacts remain within the mythology of the Buffyverse. Buffy herself wears a crucifix, and it burns vampires to touch it. This might seem to imply at least a residual investment within Christian frameworks of meaning and power, despite Joss Whedon's own professed atheism; this is one of the factors leading to the complaint that *Buffy* retains Christianity as a privileged symbolic and mythological field. For example, Alderman and Seidel-Arpaci argue that choosing to keep the protective qualities of crosses and holy water in the Buffyverse erases the history of non-Christians in the 'West' and erodes the possibility of fully assimilating into the 'white Christian world represented by Buffy.'[9]

This does, however, seem to presuppose the possibility of a view from nowhere. Whedon accepts that his thinking and symbolism are influenced by Jewish and Christian cultures:

I do use Christian mythology. Buffy, resurrected much? She pretty much died for all of us by spreading her arms wide and . . . well, I won't go into it. That's what I was raised with. As much as I learned Greek myths and

---

8   Naomi Alderman and Annette Seidel-Arpaci, 'Imaginary Para-Sites of the Soul: Vampires and Representations of "Blackness" and "Jewishness" in the Buffy/ Angelverse', *Slayage: The Online International Journal of Buffy Studies* 3, no. 2 (2003). Online: http://www.slayageonline.com/essays/slayage10/Alderman_&_Seidel-Arpaci.htm

9   Ibid.

as much as I read Marvel Comics and watched 'The Prisoner,' I grew up around Christianity and Judaism and those are the prevalent myths and mythic structures of my brain.[10]

Thus, *Buffy* does make overt use of traditional Christian symbols, thought-structures and themes. It can also be argued, though, that these are relocated into a frame whereby their potency is cultural rather than confessionally religious. For example, it is undeniable that the crucifix and holy water are associated with the Christian religion. However, it is less clear to what extent they truly operate in *Buffy* as religious items. Abbott suggests they are better understood as 'another weapon to be used by the Slayer like a wooden stake, a quarter staff, a cross bow and even a rocket launcher';[11] Erickson describes the cross as 'neither Christian nor non-Christian'.[12] There is certainly no evidence of divine invocation or prayer accompanying use of the cross or holy water, which is what one would expect within an actively Christian framework. Playdon, in fact, puts the case that the Christian artefacts should be understood to operate in archetypal fashion. The cross has become translucent to a host of symbols, including the Tree of Life, the pine-tree of Attis, and Odin's world-ash; the holy water represents the generative power of the natural world, the tears of Christ, the Flood and the blood of the Grail.[13] Indeed, it is the symbolic rather than religious connotations which are voiced by the Master:

We are defined by the things we fear. This symbol, those two planks of wood, it confounds me. Suffuses me with mortal dread. But fear is in the mind. Like pain, it can be controlled. If I can face my fear, it cannot master me.

('Nightmares')

10 Joss Whedon, 'Joss Whedon – The Man behind the Slayer', interview by Laura Miller, *Salon.com*, 23 May 2003. Online: http://www.salon.com/entertainment/tv/int/2003/05/20/whedon/index.html
11 Stacey Abbott, 'A Little Less Ritual and a Little More Fun: The Modern Vampire in *Buffy the Vampire Slayer*', *Slayage: The Online International Journal of Buffy Studies* 1, no. 3 (2001). Online: http://www.slayageonline.com/essays/slayage3/sabbott.htm
12 Gregory Erickson, '"Sometimes You Need a Story": American Christianity, Vampires and *Buffy*', in Rhonda V. Wilcox and David Lavery (eds), *Fighting the Forces: What's at Stake in* Buffy the Vampire Slayer (Lanham, MD: Rowman & Littlefield, 2002), 108–19 (114).
13 Zoe-Jane Playdon, 'What you are, what's to come: Feminisms, citizenship and the divine in *Buffy*', in Roz Kaveney (ed.), *Reading the Vampire Slayer: The New, Updated, Unofficial Guide to* Buffy *and* Angel (London: Tauris Parke, 2004), 156–94 (171).

And, in fact, in 'Who Are You?', the limited power of Christian symbols and spaces is powerfully expressed by a vampire following the taking of hostages in a church:

> It's hard to believe. I've been avoiding this place for so many years, and it's nothing. It's nice! It's got the pretty windows, the pillars . . . lots of folks to eat. Where's the thing I was so afraid of? You know, the Lord? He was supposed to be here. He gave us this address. Well, we'll just have to start killing off His people, see if He shows up.

Of course, it is the Slayer who shows up – in duplicate, in the shape of a body-swapped Buffy and Faith. The piece of dialogue above is perhaps a commentary on secularization, and the declining power of religious institutions as people lose faith in their authority and doctrines. It is interesting that it is, specifically, the church as building – representing the institution – that is here represented as the place of an absence of God. On the other hand, it could be said that the symbolic and mythic power of Christianity is paradoxically affirmed in *Buffy*, through for example the continuing albeit not always efficacious use of the cross,[14] Buffy's substitutionary and sacrificial death in 'The Gift', and the potency of the resurrection motif. Other aspects of the *Buffy* narrative are specifically contrapuntal to Christian narratives (for example, Maggie Walsh's creation of the artificial monster Adam, which has shades both of Mary Shelley's *Frankenstein* and the Christian creation myth, and the revision of the origin of good and evil discussed below in Chapter Nine). As will be seen in the discussion of Pullman in Chapter Eight, such reversals or rewritings may constitute a rebuttal of the traditional Christian mythos, but it is still one that continues to acknowledge its foundational significance in Western culture. Indeed, any drama involving self-sacrifice is prone to be interpreted as Christological in kind, without authorial commentary to suggest or reinforce the interpretation. Given the intimate interconnections between Christian theology, Greek philosophy and the history of Western thought, it is also not surprising that many well-established models for ethics and knowledge can be both discerned in *Buffy* and seen to be resonant with Christianity.[15]

---

14 In 'Doppelgangland', a vampire's response to a cross and a vial of holy water is to say 'Whatever', and walk away.

15 There are many books, chapters and articles exploring religion and ethics in *Buffy the Vampire Slayer*. Popular examples include: Jana Riess, *What Would Buffy Do?* (San Francisco, CA: Jossey-Bass, 2004); Gregory Stevenson, *Televised Morality* (Lanham, MD: Hamilton Books, 2003). In Erickson, '"Sometimes You Need a

Buffy's own attitude towards institutional religion is pithily expressed in Season Three ('What's My Line, Part I') – 'Note to self: religion freaky.' This follows Giles's explanation to her of the nature of a reliquary during their search of a mausoleum. For the Slayer to find ossified holy remains 'freaky' is slyly ironic and invites contemplation of cultural attitudes towards the dead. Possibly it is the implied fetishization of the corpse fragments that Buffy finds disturbing; it is hardly the fragmented corpse as such. Or possibly Joss Whedon is taking the opportunity to turn a mirror back onto religious communities and invite reflection on how cultural practices that are normal or even prescribed in one group are absurd, or even 'freaky', to another.

In Season Seven, a vampire asks Buffy whether there is any word on the existence of God: 'nothing solid', she responds ('Conversations with Dead People'). It is interesting, as Erickson points out, that it is a vampire who asks Buffy this question, as if she might have special insight. Erickson also takes the two words 'nothing solid' as dialectically marking out a space where the theology of *Buffy the Vampire Slayer* might be located – a theology which is neither nothing, nor solid.[16] To be nothing solid, or a solid nothing, is appropriate to the way in which religion occupies a place of both tension and ambivalence in *Buffy*. It is not difficult to discern religion motifs and theological elements. Demons there are in plenty. There are also hell dimensions; persistence after death; and what Buffy believes to have been experience of heaven after her second death. Most art-forms which are built on battles between 'good' and 'evil' are readily relatable to religious schema of various kinds, not only Christian ones. The series draws eclectically upon a stock of predominantly Western mythic and neopagan motifs, without presenting any such systematically or coherently. Religion in *Buffy* can thus aptly be described as 'detraditioned'. As indicated, there is reference to religious symbols, rituals, myths and ceremonies, but this is part of the cultural milieu. Riley is a churchgoer; but of the main protagonists, only Willow, a Jewish Wiccan, is presented as having any formal religious location, and she is not presented as engaging in specifically religious dimensions of practice in either case (unless one exempts her placing stones on Tara's grave, a Jewish ritual of

Story": American Christianity, Vampires and *Buffy*', the cultural location of the relationship between the two is also explored; he draws parallels between the way in which both Christ and the vampire translated from a European context to an American one.

16   Greg Erickson, '"Religion Freaky" or a "Bunch of Men Who Died?" The (A)theology of *Buffy*', *Slayage: The Online International Journal of Buffy Studies* 4, no. 1–2 (2004). Online: http://www.slayageonline.com/Numbers/slayage13_14.htm

remembrance). There is no divine presence. If there is any divine authority, it is well obscured.

It is not only religion that is said to be 'detraditioned'; Abbott argues that this is true of the vampire, too, in a parallel move of demystification.[17] The vampire has become more physical: can feel pain, be ill, be injured and have sex. She uses the significance of blood exchange as part of an argument that *Buffy*'s vampirism is grounded less in mysticism and more in materiality. Blood is historically overdetermined in symbolic terms, connoting life, death, fecundity, miscegenation, pollution, femaleness and materiality, while in Stoker's *Dracula* 'the exchange of blood is ripe with symbolic and holy significance evoking or suggesting taboo forms of sexuality, holy communion, birth and death, as well as the creation of a psychic link between vampire and victim.'[18] Abbott argues that, in *Buffy*, blood exchange is presented simply as the mechanic through which 'turning' is accomplished, and as a source of food rather than immortality. If sustainable, this would contribute to a demystification of the vampiric state, turning it simply into a quasi-biological alternative mode of being, stripped of occultic, holy or symbolic force.

It can certainly be argued that the vampire in *Buffy* is not situated as unholy, but simply undead; its 'unnatural' existence is not presented as an infraction against God or the sacred, but rather as a material danger threatening the boundaries and integrity of mortal existence. This is what constitutes the vampire as pollutant. The vampires and demons of *Buffy* are not presented as a cosmic 'other' oppositional to a Creator God, but more as a different type of being which is often but not invariably hostile to humanity. Blood exchange in this context is indeed a mechanic of miscegenation and food sourcing rather than an occultic act. However, this cannot be read outside of a context which gives due importance to the power of the vampiric body as cultural symbol, a theme explored in more detail in Chapter Nine. Blood exchange in *Buffy* also retains significance in the field of psychosexuality, taking on in this context a particular but not merely mechanistic set of meanings. Therefore, blood exchange in *Buffy* may still be considered to hold symbolic if not holy power, which places both it and the vampiric body in networks of meaning and power that are not 'only' material. This does not undermine Abbott's point that the significance is not the same as in earlier folklore, and that it has

---

17 Stacey Abbott, "A Little Less Ritual and a Little More Fun: The Modern Vampire in *Buffy the Vampire Slayer*," *Slayage: The Online International Journal of Buffy Studies* 1, no. 3, http://www.slayageonline.com/essays/slayage3/sabbott.htm

18 Ibid.

been dislocated from the religious or superstitious. Indeed, she shows how *Buffy* chronicles the shift from a pre-modern to modern vampire, with a move away from a ritualized world which is an analogue both of secular developments and the changes in the characteristics of the Slayer introduced in the person of Buffy.

The series starts with an institutionalized opposition between the Brethren of Aurelius and the Watchers' Council on the other, the two bodies being the hierarchical structures for vampires and slayers respectively. 'Defined as the antithesis to Christianity, the vampires of the Brethren of Aurelius are like the vampires of 19th century folklore and much of its fiction', writes Abbott. The arrival of Spike then functions as a crucial pivot point in the detraditionalization process.[19] An excellent illustration of this is in the following speech:

> *Spike*: You were there? Oh, please! If every vampire who said he was at the crucifixion was actually there, it would have been like Woodstock . . . I was actually at Woodstock. That was a weird gig. I fed off a flowerperson, and I spent the next six hours watchin' my hand move.
>
> ('School Hard')

If we look at the Vampire Slayer herself, Buffy's iconoclastic attitude and inability to stick to the traditional model of the Slayer are themselves powerful statements about changing cultural modalities in terms of the individual's relationship to powers and authorities. In this she is supported by her network of friends, who enable her to operate in a different way from the traditional one. Again, this is ironically picked up on by Spike: 'A slayer with family and friends. That sure as hell wasn't in the brochure' ('School Hard').

The Scooby Gang comes to stand for an alternative organizational dynamic. On the one hand, the Council of the Watchers is increasingly shown up as an overly hierarchical, hidebound and patriarchal body with clear implicit parallels to religious groupings ordered by rituals, prophecies, superstitions and 'priestly' leaders. A pivotal episode is 'Helpless' (Season Three). Buffy is turning 18, and it transpires this means the Council will set her a test whereby she fights a vampire without her powers. To this end, Giles drugs her without her knowledge. The test is appropriately entitled 'Cruciamentum', which is Latin for 'torture'. The plan goes wrong when the vampire escapes and kidnaps Buffy's mother. As Barbaccia says, the episode becomes 'an unnerving allegory of a newly adult woman who

19 Ibid.

discovers that a patriarchy exists, that it authorizes her own power, and that female normalcy within that system equals helplessness.'[20] In the end, Buffy rescues Joyce by tricking the vampire into drinking holy water. This is symbolically significant in that water is traditionally associated with the feminine, over against the phallicism of a stake; the victory is also achieved through deception, which is likewise associated with the feminine mode. The incident sours her relationship with the Council. 'Bite me', she throws at Council member Quentin when he congratulates her upon passing the test.

By contrast, the Scooby Gang model is, albeit imperfectly, a far more democratic style of management. Each member has particular expertise or qualities to contribute. This change in organizational dynamics both reflects and enables different models of personal relations and priorities. In Season One, it is prophesied that Buffy will die in defeating the Master. Her friends refuse to accept this; Xander finds her with the help of Angel. She is then resuscitated from drowning face-down in a pool of water, marking a rupture in the 'normal' Slayer life cycle, actively expressed in the conferment of Slayerhood on Kendra. So then there are two. The singular, monolithic line of Slayer descent under the control of the Watchers' Council is already being disturbed through multiplication.

There are a number of stages in the journey through which Buffy and the Scooby Gang withdraw their allegiance from the Watchers' Council, and Slayer 'mythology' more generally. At the outset it is less a matter of ideological rejection of the Watchers, and more Buffy's own way of working. Three exchanges with Kendra illustrate this ('What's My Line, Part II'). First, Kendra refers to a Slayer Handbook, causing Buffy great surprise as she had not heard of it. Giles tells her he had thought it would be of no use in her case. Second, Buffy tells Kendra flatly: 'I don't take orders. I do things my way.' Kendra responds: 'No wonder you died.' However, it is exactly because of dissidence that Buffy lives (after having died!), as her friends try to help her rather than bow to the necessity and inevitability of her prophesied death. Third, Buffy tries to explain: 'Kendra, my emotions give me power. They're total assets.'

Her encounter with the First Slayer at the end of Season Four represents a vigorous rejection of her 'fate':

Tara (*speaking for the First Slayer*): The Slayer does not walk in this world.

---

20   Holly G. Barbaccia, 'Buffy in the "Terrible House"', *Slayage: The Online International Journal of Buffy Studies* 1, no. 4 (2001). Online: http://www.slayageonline.com/essays/slayage4/barbaccia.htm

Buffy: I walk. I talk. I shop. I sneeze. I'm gonna be a fireman when the floods roll back. There's trees in the desert since you moved out, and I don't sleep on a bed of bones.

('Restless')

It is not only archaic traditions that Buffy is rejecting, but a view of the Slayer as necessarily above or beyond this world. Buffy affirms the materiality and relationality of her own existence, enmeshed in 'normal' teenage life – talking, shopping – as well as Slayerhood. The First Slayer's response foreshadows the increasing challenges, uncertainties and alienations that Buffy will face – thinking that she knows who she is, what is to come, when in actuality she has not even begun to apprehend this.

Following on from this ominous foreshadowing, the transition from Season Four to Season Five marks a definitive transition in terms of Buffy's relationship to the Watchers' Council. In 'Checkpoint', the Council is subjecting her to a review to assess her fitness as Slayer, securing her compliance by threatening to have Giles deported. Finally, Buffy tires of the scenario and has an epiphany which she shares with the Council, uttering the phrase: 'Power. I have it. You want it.' This represents a rebuttal of her object-position, a tool wielded by the Council – they in fact exist to serve her. *She* is the Slayer. She goes on to set her terms.

An even more assertive Buffy is discernible in the later episode 'Graduation Day, Part I'. Angel is dying from a vampire-specific poison, and Buffy is wanting help from the Council of Watchers. They refuse. Try again, Buffy exhorts Wesley:

Wesley: Buffy, they're very firm. We're talking about laws that have existed longer than civilization.
Buffy: I'm talking about watching my lover die. I don't have a clue what you're talking about and I don't care . . .
Wesley: The Council's orders are to concentrate on . . .
Buffy: Orders? I don't think I'm going to be taking any more orders. Not from you, not from them. Wesley, go back to your Council and tell them until the next Slayer comes along, they can close up shop. I'm not working for them anymore.

This also reflects Buffy's tendency to privilege, or at least pay due attention to, matters in the emotional realm when making decisions – although her killing of Angel is a striking example of her capacity to put aside personal feelings where considered justified.

The rejection of traditional or institutional priorities and moralities could be said to signal a form of anarchy. In fact, Colonel McNamara of the Initiative labels the Scooby Gang not only a 'band of freaks', but also 'anarchists' who are too 'backwards' for the real world ('New Moon Rising'). This, of course, is not wholly true. Buffy is willing to co-operate with the legal system when she believes she has killed Katrina ('Dead Things'). As Bradney points out in one of a number of legal analyses of *Buffy*, her vocational aptitude test suggested she consider law enforcement as a career ('What's My Line, Part I'). She also heeds the law of the Watchers' Council until her breach with them. This is not gratuitous rebellion, but undertaken in the belief that their rules were sometimes wrong and unhelpful to Buffy's own priorities: fighting evil and saving the world (a lot). Fighting evil includes a more nuanced recognition of where evil resides than the Council guidelines allows, and a greater respect for the persons involved in combating it as individuals rather than functionaries. This does not signal anarchism in the popular sense of complete lack of regulatory framework, disorder and moral mayhem.

It could be argued, however, that the series moves towards an advocacy of anarchy in its stricter philosophical sense. Graeber identifies the principles of traditional anarchism as 'autonomy, voluntary association, self-organization, mutual aid, direct democracy';[21] Schantz finds that organization 'along anarchist lines' consists of 'small affinity groups that come together to work on specific actions or projects and which express a politics of direct action.'[22] This is the trajectory along which the Scooby Gang rather bumpily progresses as Buffy moves away from the control of the Watchers' Council and Giles's position becomes unofficial, and as the other members of the Scooby Gang take more of a co-responsibility role. This culminates in their temporary rejection of Buffy's leadership in Season Seven because they consider that she has become too authoritarian.

The spell through which the Scoobies defeat Adam, the Initiative's militaristic invention, is an example of their co-operative and participatory mode of working – it is collaborative, with Giles representing 'mind', Willow 'spirit', Xander 'heart', and Buffy 'hand' ('Primeval'). It is also an example of a primal, 'irrational' power over against the militaristic, mechanical predictability of the Initiative. In defeating Adam, Buffy tells him: 'You could never hope to grasp the source of our power.' This

21 David Graeber, *Fragments of an Anarchist Anthropology* (Chicago: Prickly Paradigm Press, 2004), 2.
22 Jeff Shantz, *Living Anarchy: Theory and Practice in Anarchist Movements* (Palo Alto, CA: Academica Press, 2008), 5.

is in direct opposition to the power that Adam, as the creation of the Army, represents: 'male, hierarchical, authoritarian'.[23] The opposition is not between adult/child, monster/human, or male/female, or even any straightforward account of good/evil – it is between modalities of power, and knowing, and being. The transgressive nature of *Buffy*'s construction of the 'monstrous' will be explored in Chapter Nine and is pertinent to this debate in that it confounds straightforward categorizations. Breton and McMaster tie this all together into an account whereby oppressive, binary rationalism is undercut by the fluidity of categories for Buffy and by the failure of traditional, rationally ordered power structures to contain her. In this way, 'youth culture' subverts organized society. The Initiative embodies rationalism, not just a repressive rationalism, manifesting 'the over-exaggerated application of formal rationality, formal method, into every area of knowledge.' This is supported by a 'calculating, instrumentalizing orientation to the outside world that thinks in term of domination.'[24]

Playdon identifies the principle of *Buffy* as inclusivity, whereby citizenship is outside of hierarchies, birth or money, and sees the constitution of the group as demonstrative of this – including, for example, a former vengeance demon (Anya), a being created from an energy-ball (Dawn), and a woman who believed she had demonic heritage (Tara).[25] However, it can be argued that Playdon's vision here is rather too utopic. Frictions and tensions perpetually exist in the group for a range of reasons; this is especially evident in Season Six and parts of Season Seven. Buffy works hard to exclude Dawn in order to protect her. Spike's affiliation is ambiguous at best. Faith's acceptance upon her return as a reformed character is tenuous because of mistrust. Anya 'falls off the wagon' and returns to vengeance-demon activities: an interesting moment in terms of leadership and authority, since Buffy wants to kill her and it is the others who argue for pursuit of an alternative way. The conditional nature of Anya's acceptance is demonstrated in the following exchange from 'Selfless':

> *Buffy*: She's not the Anya that you knew, Xander. She's a demon.
> *Xander*: That doesn't mean you have to kill her!
> *Buffy*: Don't act like this is easy for me. You know it's not.

---

23 Playdon, 'What you are, what's to come: Feminisms, citizenship and the divine in *Buffy*', 174.
24 Breton and McMaster, 'Dissing the Age of MOO: Initiatives, Alternatives, and Rationality'.
25 Playdon, 'What you are, what's to come: Feminisms, citizenship and the divine in *Buffy*', 180.

Xander: There are other options!

Buffy: I've considered them.

Xander: When? Just now? Took you all of ten seconds to decide to kill one of your best friends?

Buffy: The thought that it might come to this has occurred to me before. It's occurred to you, too.

Buffy's own position is always a negotiation between her status as one of a group and her ontological uniqueness. She is the Chosen One. The conversation above continues with Xander expostulating that this is a recurrent pattern, with Buffy cutting herself off from the others and 'everything human', and acting like she is 'the law'. Buffy responds:

It is always different! It's always complicated. And at some point, someone has to draw the line, and that is always going to be me! You get down on me for cutting myself off, but in the end the Slayer is always cut off. There's no mystical guidebook, no all-knowing council. Human rules don't apply! There's only me. I am the law.

This phraseology significantly points to the dangers faced by taking this route. Back in Season Three, Buffy rejected Faith's argument that Slayers embody the law and are not bound by rules ('Consequences'). This is leading in the direction of Faith's embrace of the 'dark side', and is specifically linked to a failure to recognize human boundaries. Angel tells her that she has a choice, and that to kill without remorse is to feel like a god, and that one shouldn't lose faith in humanity because people make mistakes. It is Buffy who tells Willow in Season Six ('Villains') that there are limits, and this is appropriate.

It is love, argues Bradney, that 'supplements and at times supplants the rigidities of state law and law of the Watchers' Council.'[26] It is love that prompts Xander and Willow to resist Buffy in her determination to kill Anya ('Selfless'), love that prompts Buffy to resist her friends when they want to kill Spike ('Lies My Parents Told Me'), and love that finally allows Dark Willow to be 'talked down' by Xander as she begins to initiate the apocalypse ('Grave'). It is also love, for Buffy, that causes Spike to withstand Glory's tortures and deny her the information that Dawn is 'the Key' ('Intervention'), and also to join the final battle against her believing

---

26 Anthony Bradney, '"I Made a Promise to a Lady": Law and Love in *BtVS*', *Slayage: The Online International Journal of Buffy Studies* 3, no. 2 (2003). Online: http://www.slayageonline.com/essays/slayage10/Bradney.htm

it will lead to his death ('The Gift'). This is a foreshadowing of Spike's self-sacrifice in the denouement of the whole show ('Chosen'). However, it should also be noted that personal love for individuals is not subordinated to the greater, agapeistic love for humanity's well-being as a whole. The paradigm example of this is Buffy's slaying of Angel ('Becoming, Part II'), and consequent condemnation of him to Hell.

Love as sacrifice is a recurrent theme. An especially potent climactic moment in this respect is the ending of Season Five, when Buffy chooses to die herself to save Dawn on the basis that they share the same blood and she can act as her substitute. The overt substitutionalism and her Christomorphic dive evoke strands of Christian theology in which Christ is understood to have redeemed the world through 'standing in' for the sins of humanity. Mary Alice Money points out that the importance of love is especially highlighted in the alternate-universe episode 'The Wish'. In this reality, Buffy never came to Sunnydale, which is overwhelmed by its demonic and vampiric inhabitants. Xander and Willow are sadistic vampires. Buffy is cold, uncaring and ultimately less effective: she dies. 'How does a human become less human?' asks Money. The answer is: 'By disregarding love, by becoming inflexible, by operating as a machine without choice, knowledge or wisdom.'[27] This Buffy has been moulded into obedi-ence to the Watchers' Council. The importance of love is here connected with models of social power which do not operate on blind and inflexible adherence to predefined rules. That care, that love, enables Buffy of the Scooby Gang to survive, not only because of the very real help her friends bring to her tasks, but because it inspires an adaptive model of action which is attentive to the particular other and thereby sensitive to its particular nature and needs. Bradney sums up these interconnections: 'This particular morality play rejects a centuries-old dominant tradition of law as patriarchy and power in favour of a notion of law as intimacy and discretion.'[28]

The extent to which the Slayer lineage is enmeshed in the law of patriarchy is further underscored when the means by which power was bestowed in the first place is uncovered in Season Seven ('Get It Done'). The precursors to the Watchers, the Shadow-Men, staked a woman out in the desert to be violated and thereby infused with demonic power. Thereafter, the power has passed from Slayer to Slayer under

---

27 Mary Alice Money, 'The Undemonization of Supporting Characters in *Buffy*', in Rhonda V. Wilcox and David Lavery (eds), *Fighting the Forces: What's at Stake in Buffy the Vampire Slayer* (Lanham, MD: Rowman and Littlefield, 2002), 98–120 (102).
28 Bradney, '"I Made a Promise to a Lady": Law and Love in *BtVS*'.

the Watchers' 'panoptic eye'.[29] There is an important structural moment here. Buffy, transported to the Shadow-Men through a portal, is likewise shackled in the desert to receive the 'gift' of further strength to fight the First. Buffy refuses this and breaks free, returning to Sunnydale through means of Willow's magic. This is paralleled by a sequence in 'End of Days', where a secret female group known as 'The Guardians' are found to exist, who have watched the Watchers since ancient days and guarded a weapon for the final battle: a scythe which Buffy had earlier pulled from rock in a manner reminiscent of Arthurian legend. (Spike also refers jokingly to the scythe as the 'Holy Grail'.) The refusal by Buffy of the patriarchs' gift and acceptance of the matriarchs' has an obvious symbolic valence. The scythe itself represents not only death, time and harvesting (the Grim Reaper; Father Time), but also the crescent moon: generally understood as a feminine symbol. The scythe is also associated with the feminine avatar of Mother Time, Rhea Kronia, and the mythical castration of gods. It is perhaps significant in this respect that Buffy kills Caleb by splicing him upwards through the groin.

Buffy's transformation of the Slayer heritage also radicalizes the distribution of power. At Buffy's request, Willow taps into the power of the Scythe and every Potential Slayer in the world is enabled to come into the actuality of power. This is Buffy's speech to those who are present:

> So here's the part where you make a choice. What if you could have that power, now? In every generation, one Slayer is born, because a bunch of men who died thousands of years ago made up that rule. They were powerful men. This woman is more powerful than all of them combined. So I say we change the rule. I say my power, should be *our* power. Tomorrow, Willow will use the essence of this scythe to change our destiny. From now on, every girl in the world who might be a Slayer, will be a Slayer. Every girl who could have the power, will have the power. Can stand up, will stand up. Slayers, every one of us. Make your choice. Are you ready to be strong?
>
> ('Chosen')

It is a recognition of the failure of the Council's strategy to control and conceal both power and truth in the name of the greater good – a strategy Buffy had to an extent been mimicking, hence the friction with her friends and then the Potentials who are being trained in Season Six and Season Seven.

---

29   Julie Sloan Brannon, '"It's About Power": Buffy, Foucault, and the Quest for Self', *Slayage: The Online International Journal of Buffy Studies* 6, no. 4 (2007). Online: http://slayageonline.com/essays/slayage24/Brannon.htm

Brannan argues that Buffy's actions amount to the establishment of a new economy of power, which, citing Foucault, allows 'the effects of power to circulate in a manner at once continuous, uninterrupted, adapted, and "individualized" throughout the entire social body.'[30] If one were to compare it to the Christian mythos, it is a moment of Pentecost: the pouring out of the 'Spirit' into the world. In this case, it is not 'followers' who receive the gift but 'every girl in the world who might be a slayer' ('Chosen'). It is a signifier of female empowerment through power-sharing.

This is especially significant if considered against the backcloth of the Slayer lineage. The violent nature of the conferment of power upon the First Slayer has already been revealed. In one of her previous visitations to Buffy, the spirit of the First Slayer says to her: 'I have no speech. No name. I live in the action of death. The blood cry. The penetrating wound. I am destruction. Absolute. Alone' ('Restless'). This is a potent image of a silenced female, the screen upon which male death drives have been projected and absorbed.

Power, then, emerges as a central dynamic across the whole of the *Buffy* seasons. This is related to the show's focus on teenagers navigating their way through to adulthood, and thereby learning about power, its limits and its appropriate uses. It is in that respect an example of the 'quest' narrative. In Chapters Two and Three, I considered the *Harry Potter* books and the *Earthsea* series respectively from the point of view of the hero's journey. It is equally possible to apply such an analysis to *Buffy*. This kind of reading focuses on the individual's own maturation and transformation, negotiation with surrounding powers, and growth into her own.

At the macro-level, one sees this pattern clearly in Buffy's maturation to the end of Season Five (including 'Meeting the Goddess' – the First Slayer – and 'Atonement with the Father', as she adjusts her relationship with Giles outside of Watcher constraints). Apotheosis comes with her sacrificial death, followed by her resurrection and return. The 'refusal to return' occupies most of Season Six. This has a post-resurrection Buffy suffering from profound alienation and struggling to adjust to life. In 'Once More with Feeling', in which Sunnydale is under a demonic spell making everybody behave as if they were in a musical, Buffy sings out the truth of her emptiness ('Give me something to sing about'). It is, ironically, the undead in the shape of Spike who tries to tell her the nature of living: that life is not in fact a song, but just this – living.

30 Julie Sloan Brannon, '"It's About Power": Buffy, Foucault, and the Quest for Self', citing Michel Foucault, 'Truth and Method', in *The Foucault Reader*, ed. Paul Rabinow (New York, NY: Pantheon Books, 1984), 61.

Dawn adds a spoken coda to this: 'The hardest thing in this world is to live in it', echoing Buffy's own words to Dawn in the 'The Gift' before she plunges to her death. The difficulty of this existence stands in contrast to Buffy's experience of what she thought was heaven until her friends pulled her out: a time when there had been no pain, no fear and no doubt.

The final season culminates with the granting of the 'boon' to the world by sharing Slayer power with all of the Potentials. Buffy's status as 'Master of Two Worlds' is assured by her simultaneous positioning both as Slayer and being no longer unique. This gives her 'Freedom to Live'.[31]

This 'hero-quest' analysis, then, emphasizes individuation and psychological development. Julie Sloan Brannon counterpoises this with a Foucauldian reading of Buffy's quest for self. Such a reading lays particular stress on the social and political context of subject formation. It also highlights the manner in which the Council acts as a 'surveilling body', in particular through impositions of disciplines upon the Slayer's own body which both increase its economic utility and diminish its power politically through subjection. It represents a dissociation of Buffy's body from her subjective autonomy.

On this reading Buffy's quest can then be seen as a drive to redefine the parameters of the power structure in which her subjectivity is constituted. South, similarly, compares the events of Season Seven to an emergence from Plato's cave and a radical fracturing of pre-existing teleologies.[32] The potency of this approach is demonstrated in the exchange between Xander and Willow in 'Chosen', the very final episode. 'We saved the world', says Xander. Willow replies: 'We *changed* the world.' This is an echo of Karl Marx's famous dictum that for philosophers to interpret the world is not enough: the point is to change it. Similarly, saving the world is not enough – it merely preserves it from whatever threat is at hand. Changing the world, though: that is a different type of legacy. As Brannon says:

> This exchange underscores the nature of the boon that Buffy bestows from her quest: power as shared phenomenon rather than power concentrated and controlled. In this way Buffy defeats the enemy she'd fought for seven

31   See, for example, analyses by Sofrina Hinton, 'Confluence: The Quest for Self in *Buffy the Vampire Slayer*', *Phase Five* 1, no. 2 (25 November 2002). Online: http://www.bibliora.com/P5_0302/html/confluence.html and Laurel Bowman, '*Buffy the Vampire Slayer*: The Greek Hero Revisited', 2002. Online: http://web.uvic.ca/~lbowman/buffy/buffythehero.html

32   James, B. South, 'Buffy the Concept Slayer', interview by Alan Saunders on *The Philosopher's Zone*, ABC Radio National, 29 March 2008. Online: http://www.abc.net.au/rn/philosopherszone/stories/2008/2198169.htm

years: an isolation enforced by a patriarchal structure that feared the power which it bestowed.[33]

The question of changing the world is also significant to the final area I shall discuss in this chapter, namely the representation of 'femininity'. This has attracted considerable critical debate: is Buffy a feminist icon or yet another image of patriarchal repression? So, yes, you can be a woman of super-strength, but only if you also wear skimpy halter-tops, lipstick, like shopping and generally act rather like a ditz. On the latter reading, Buffy's slaying activity is a castrating force, threatening to the dominant socio-cultural order, which must be compensated (or even overcompensated) by the representation of her in other respects as a 'girly' girl, which carefully contains her aggressive killing capacity in a fog of femininity. This leads to radically divergent accounts of her potential to represent a politically transgressive model of the female. There is, on the one hand, her identity as Slayer; on the other, as Pender says, 'she might justifiably be accused of subscribing to, and therefore reinscribing, commercial and patriarchal standards of feminine beauty.'[34] Putting both together leads Owen to conclude that 'political potency is both imagined and reduced to matters of consumer style.'[35] In fact, Buffy's 'dark double' Faith sums up this problematic in 'End of Days'. Discussing the loneliness of being a Slayer with Buffy, she says: 'Thank god we're hot chicks with superpowers.' 'Takes the edge off', Buffy agrees.

Pender explores some of the critical responses to Buffy's conflicted identity under the rubric of feminist camp, with its self-conscious parodying of gender roles and performances. This includes its male protagonists, with Xander being an 'archetype of a new 1990s embattled masculinity.'[36] On one occasion, Xander announces that: 'Cavalry's here; frightened guy with a rock, but it's here' ('Becoming, Part II'); on another he decides it's time to act like a man: 'And hide' (Bewitched, Bothered and Bewildered').[37] Pender draws out the recurrent chiastic movement between the sublime and the ridiculous, foundationally present in the high school/Hellmouth analogy, but argues that too little attention has been

33 Brannon, '"It's About Power": Buffy, Foucault, and the Quest for Self.'
34 Pender, '"I'm Buffy and You're . . . History": The Postmodern Politics of *Buffy*', 36.
35 Susan A. Owen, 'Vampires, Postmodernity and Postfeminism: *Buffy the Vampire Slayer*', *Journal of Popular Film and Television* 27, no. 2 (Summer 1999): 24–31 (30).
36 Pender, '"I'm Buffy and You're . . . History": The Postmodern Politics of *Buffy*', 39
37 Ibid., 39–40.

paid to a similar movement in the eponymous title of the show: 'Buffy', the 'Vampire Slayer'. While each element has received consideration, political commentary has not always followed through on the implications of the composite effect: 'The "joke" of the cheerleading demon hunter is not a one-line throwaway gag but the foundational myth and ongoing premise of the entire series.'[38] A similar chiastic movement is present in the location of Sunnydale at the Hellmouth.

Analyses which see a contradiction requiring separation into mutually opposing parts are perhaps not giving the postmodern cultural location of *Buffy* its due, wherein the 'archaic "either/or"' has given way to the 'anarchic "neither/nor"'.[39] The case can also be made that polarizing accounts of Buffy as feminist/non-feminist, patriarchal/non-patriarchal are insufficiently attentive to the politics of culture in the negotiation of identity. While the constructs of 'feminine' and 'masculine' stand, there is no place for a woman, or a man, to locate her/himself which does not take that as benchmark and gravitational centre. One is either assimilated into the stereotype, or one exceeds it and therefore becomes projected onto its other. A woman who is aggressive is deemed to be inhabiting a 'masculine paradigm'; a man who cries is showing his 'feminine side'. This is further complicated because one is not caught between two mirrors for identity of equal power. Instead, woman is herself the mirror for man: as Virginia Woolf put it, women are 'looking-glasses possessing the magic and delicious power of reflecting the figure of man at twice its natural size.'[40] In the analysis of Luce Irigaray, the feminine as such does not exist, but is merely appropriated by and subsumed into the masculine; the feminine, and feminine desire, remain unthought in the phallogocentric economy, and therefore woman as subject in her own right has yet to be. 'The maternal-feminine remains the *place separate from "its" own place*, deprived of "its" place. She is or ceaselessly becomes the place of the other who cannot separate himself from it [emphasis original].'[41]

Thus, the feminine, absorbed into the masculine imaginary which defines itself in relation to it, lacks a site to exist as a speaking subject. Since, within the phallogocentric economy, there is no space for her to constitute her own subjective life, she is required to adopt artificial strategies. Irigaray describes this thus: 'Her clothes, her makeup, and her

---

38 Ibid., 42.
39 Ibid., 43.
40 Virginia Woolf, *A Room of One's Own* (San Diego, CA: Harcourt & Brace, 1981), 35.
41 Luce Irigaray, *An Ethics of Sexual Difference*, trans. Carolyn Burke and Gillian C. Gill (Athlone Press: London, 1993), 10.

jewels are the things with which she tries to create her container(s), her envelope(s). She cannot make use of the envelope that she is, but must create artificial ones.'[42]

Irigaray's analysis follows a different route to arrive at the same point of 'neither/nor'. The subjectivity of women is not adequately manifested in the artificial envelope of patriarchal culture. But nor can women effect, *ex nihilo*, a complete transformation in the social and symbolic order such that an alternative site for feminine becoming might instantly be made present. This is one of the drivers behind parody as political transgression – and yet, it is always questionable whether parody will remain merely a mode of play, creating a superficial challenging of boundaries in ironic mode, while leaving those boundaries in place institutionally and in the socio-symbolic order. In this respect, one is reminded of models of the carnivalesque whereby the mocking and reversal of hierarchies is actually an outlet for repressed energies which ends up reinforcing those same hierarchies. Irigaray's own strategy for countering – or rather, negotiating – this 'neither/nor' double-bind is through mimesis. I would like now to consider this as a model for reading *Buffy*, since it combines the mimicry inherent in parody with a deliberate and self-conscious politicized framework.

Mimesis is a polysemic term. Its fundamental meaning is imitation, which can imply both reproduction of the same and parodic recapitulation. Irigaray employs both of these meanings in her use of it. The first stage is a deliberate occupation of the feminine role as marked out in the masculine economy:

> There is, in an initial phase, perhaps only one 'path', the one historically assigned to the feminine: that of *mimicry*. One must assume the feminine role deliberately. Which means already to convert a form of subordination into an affirmation, and thus begin to thwart it . . .[43]

This amounts to recovering the place of exploitation in discourse, while yet refusing to be simply reduced to it. There is a presupposition, Irigaray goes on to add, that one can copy anyone or anything without appropriating them to oneself or adding to it. Playing the mimetic role 'does not kill her, quite', because something continues to subsist elsewhere, even though the act of staging has 'probably metabolized' it so thoroughly she has forgotten

42 Ibid., 11.
43 Luce Irigaray, *This Sex Which Is Not One*, trans. Catherine Porter (Ithaca, NY: Cornell University Press, 1985), 76.

it. The 'something' is 'her own sex'.[44] Mounting a direct challenge to the feminine condition would amount to a demand to speak from the position of the masculine, and in fact constitute a sexual indifference. At the other end of the spectrum, hysteria is an amplification of feminine mimesis in an effort to inscribe identity and sexuality over against destruction, and an overcompliant parody.[45] The hysteric offers a glimpse of a subversive way forward through deliberate mimesis, which must yet avoid falling into the self-paralysis of the hysteric.

> It means to resubmit herself – inasmuch as she is on the side of the 'per-ceptible', of 'matter' – to ideas, in particular to ideas about herself, that are elaborated in/by a masculine logic, but so as to make 'visible', by an effect of playful repetition, what was supposed to remain invisible: the cover-up of a possible operation of the feminine in language.[46]

This kind of mimesis is politically understood and proceeds from a recognition of the 'cultural reserve yet to come', which prevents the mimesis becoming simply a repetition of and absorption into the same. This mimesis is instead a productive one, and allows women to 'revisit and repossess the discursive and material sites where "woman" was essential-ized, disqualified or quite simply excluded.'[47] This is not about restoring a lost origin to women, or constituting women in relation to origin (the maternal), but a collective negotiation of discursive constructs of the female, bringing about 'a mode of representation that would take the fact of being a woman as a positive, self-affirming political force.'[48]

An argument can be made, therefore, for a reading of *Buffy* in mimetic mode. Her parodic inscription of the Barbie-doll feminine is underlined by its chiastic relation to her Slayer identity, which casts it into sharp and apparently incongruous relief. At the same time, her miming of the feminine prevents her Slayer identity from becoming absorbed into a mere reproduction of the masculine same. By closing the gap between appar-ently non-complementary modalities of being, a gap is in fact opened,

---

44 Ibid., 151–52.
45 Elizabeth A. Grosz, *Sexual Subversions* (London and Sydney: Allen & Unwin, 1989), 135.
46 Hilary Robinson, *Reading Art, Reading Irigaray: the Politics of Art by Women* (London: I.B.Tauris, 2006), 76.
47 Rosi Braidotti, 'On the Feminist Female Subject or from She-self to She-other', in G. Bock and S. James (eds), *Beyond Equality and Difference: Citizenship, Feminist Politics and Female Subjectivity* (London: Routledge, 1992), 176–92 (187).
48 Ibid., 186.

in which alternative expressions of becoming-subject can be glimpsed. If mimetically reproducing the house of patriarchy as self-same merely adds further carceral layers for the feminine subject, perhaps mimetically replaying it will expose these cracks at its very foundations; and foundations, once exposed, are liable to weather into dust.

In conclusion, *Buffy* offers a slickly postmodern portrayal of young adult sub-cultures which challenge or subvert normative patterns of power and authority in a range of ways. *Buffy* is suffused with issues pertaining to power and identity. These issues are of relevance in both social and religious or spiritual contexts. Corporately – in the shape of the Scooby Gang – and individually, the show portrays a navigation of controlling structures of power and authority in order to construct alternative models which are more empowering to the self and more co-operative for the group. This is set against traditionally patriarchal and hierarchical modes of structuring organizations and relating to persons. It achieves this in a variety of ways, including its style of parody and pastiche. The power of love, friendship and compassion are endorsed. The show also subverts norms and expectations of the good and the monstrous, an aspect explored more fully in Chapter Nine. The vampire itself, representing the forbidden in both form and function, has been called the 'ultimate subculture';[49] this 'monstrous' vampiric body and its capacity for transgressing established cultural norms are likewise explored further in Chapter Nine. I have also argued that Buffy, 'hot chick with superpowers', navigates a fine line in resisting and encoding patriarchal regulatory modes. This can be related to Irigaray's theory of mimesis, as a way of parodically subverting the system from within to find a space for the female subject to speak. *Buffy* can also be likened to Bakhtin's concept of the carnivalesque, with dominant styles and assumptions disrupted by humour, chaos and excess. This analogy is especially appropriate given Bakhtin's argument that the de-privileging of the authoritative voice enables polyphonic dialogue to emerge. This is an apt metaphor for the decisive change brought about in the Buffyverse through the de-privileging of the authority of the Slayer as Chosen One when Buffy and Willow call all the Potentials to full Slayerhood: an ultimate act of power-sharing. Thus, understood holistically, the sub-cultural dynamics, parodic style and carnivalesque inversions in *Buffy* do not function merely to play superficially with established codes, nor to reinforce them, but to effect genuine transformation and change. This remains, of course, a moment in an ongoing navigation of oppression,

---

49 Bieszk, 'Vampire Hip: Style as Subcultural Expression in *Buffy the Vampire Slayer*'.

power and liberatory openings. As Dawn says to Buffy in the very final words of *Buffy the Vampire Slayer*: 'What do we do now?'

Buffy contemplates the question while gazing at the remains of Sunnydale, and smiles.

TRANSFORMING WORLDS

HARRY POTTER: 'TOUJOURS PUR'

THE *HARRY POTTER* SERIES has been extensively scrutinized from the point of view of its socio-political values and relations. Weisman comments on *Harry Potter and the Goblet of Fire*: 'The context of the book is magic, but its subject is society.'[1] This, I suggest, holds true for the series in its entirety. An incomplete list of areas suggesting themselves for consideration in this respect demonstrates the extent to which a wide range of socio-political concerns and issues are embedded in the fabric of the narratives. The following, for example, spring to mind: class, gender, family structures, ethnicities, sport, the media, technology, class, education, consumerism, political systems and nationalism. All fictional worlds can be subjected to ideological analysis, of course: I do not suggest that the *Harry Potter* series is unique in that respect, but the series does feature explicitly all of the potential areas for examination mentioned above. A further characteristic of the *Harry Potter* world is its occupancy within a (fictionalized) 'real' Britain: the fact that the Ministry of Magic has a formal but secret relation to the British Cabinet is a telling case in point. The combination lends itself to analysis which locates the *Harry*

---

1   Steven R. Weisman, 'Editorial Observer; A Novel That Is a Midsummer Night's Dream', *The New York Times: Opinion*, 11 July 2000. Online: http://www.nytimes.com/2000/07/11/opinion/editorial-observer-a-novel-that-is-a-midsummer-night-s-dream.html

Potter socio-political world in the context of 'real' British history and society. That will be an implicit backdrop rather than specific focus in the following critical reflections. From the multiple possible analytical routes that could be taken in considering the world of *Harry Potter* from a socio-political perspective, I concentrate in this chapter on selected areas relating to social stratification. This relates also to the question as to what extent *Harry Potter* can be said to present a consolationist and nostalgic world, embodying primarily traditionalist and conservative values. In addressing this point, I will be entering into sustained dialogue with the work of Farah Mendlesohn, who has made a significant contribution to the argument that the world of *Potter* is fundamentally one of privilege and elitism.[2]

Socio-political analysis is important to this project because, as intimated in the Introduction, one of the premises of the book is that spirituality is not simply an 'inward' orientation or journey, but unavoidably enmeshed in social, political and economic domains. Even varieties of spirituality which seek to establish themselves as world-renouncing can only do so from within the 'world', and by definition are deliberately constructing themselves in (renunciatory) relationship to it. What is being renounced and why? What is being embraced, or implicitly accepted, and why? It is the value-orientation contained within ideological expressions that connects it to spiritual concerns.

Religion itself does not appear here as a topic for consideration. That is because the *Potter* narratives are singularly silent on matters of institutional religion. Hogwarts has no school worship. No character engages in religious practice. No deities are invoked. The only residual religious dimensions are in the celebration of Christmas, in cultural terms such an embedded part of the rhythm of the British year that it is difficult to see how it could be avoided, and the presence of churchyard burial grounds. Indeed, so little reference is made to religion that it is jarring in a story which does weave in and out of a 'real' world setting. The absence is clearly deliberate on the part of Rowling, presumably to underline a complete disjunction between her invented world of magic and religious frameworks. She does not posit that her world of magic stands in any relation at all to religion, whether Christian or neopagan or anything else. This makes the religious storms and controversies over the series even more ironic.

---

2   Farah Mendlesohn, 'Crowning the King: Harry Potter and the Construction of Authority', in Lana A. Whited (ed.), *The Ivory Tower and Harry Potter: Perspectives on a Literary Phenomenon* (Columbia, DC and London: University of Missouri Press, 2004), 159–82.

None of this, of course, is to suggest that religious and spiritual themes are not present. Some of these were explored in Chapter Two, in relation to the 'hero-quest'. In this chapter, the spiritual themes are identified as social and political expressions of what and who are valuable in life, what aspirations and achievements are presented positively, and what models of relations between self and society are implicitly or explicitly endorsed.

As intimated, in terms of socio-political values and structures, Rowling's novels have been condemned as instilling a retrogressive nostalgia. A. S. Byatt, for example, concluded that the series was a 'derivative manipulation of past motifs'.[3] Nicholas Tucker described the books as 'looking back.'[4] Acocella suggests that the very success of the books lies in Rowling's 'utter traditionaliasm'.[5] The wizarding world is in some ways presented as a relic of Old England. Its primary educational institution is a boarding school (complete with feasts and house rivalry); there is an established aristocracy based on pure blood, which is connected with inherited wealth; and its technology is that of a prior age as magic is typically used as an alternative. There are steam trains which can navigate to 'unplottable' destinations, flying motorbikes and Ford Anglias, and space-expanding cars, but not telephones as standard. Computers and gaming technology are known of – they are referred to in relation to Dudley Dursley's leisure activities – but not used.

Farah Mendlesohn sees in all of this a nostalgia at work that actually bolsters real-world structures of authority, because it is 'hostile to the "real" world but not subversive of it.' It is, for her, a mode of the fantastic that functions as escapism and consolation, in which moral conflict is acted out between different types of authoritarianism and conservatism rather than offering a more genuinely liberal or radical vision.[6] She shows how class representations in *Harry Potter* can be related to 1980s British Tory politics: on the one hand, the bigotry of the aristocrat is rejected (as represented by, for example, the Malfoys); on the other hand, the Dursleys are a parody of the aspirational business family of middle-class suburbia

3   A. S. Byatt, 'Harry Potter and the Childish Adult', *The New York Times*, 7 July 2003, New York Edition, A13.
4   Nicholas Tucker, 'The Rise and Rise of Harry Potter', *Children's Literature in Education* 30, no. 4 (1999): 221–34 (233).
5   Joan Acocella, 'Under the Spell', *The New Yorker*, 31 July 2000: 74–78.
6   Mendlesohn, 'Crowning the King: Harry Potter and the Construction of Authority', 167. She relates this to a 'Tory' model of fantasy as found for example in Michael Moorcock, *Wizardry and Wild Romance: A Study of Epic Fantasy* (London: Gollancz, 2004); Diana Waggoner, *The Hills of Faraway: A Guide to Fantasy* (New York, NY: Atheneum, 1978); John Grant, 'Gulliver Unravels: Generic Fantasy and the Loss of Subversion', *Extrapolation* 41, no. 1 (Spring 2000): 21–27.

in Thatcherite Britain.[7] Both of these poles are rejected in the *Potter* narratives, but this is seen to remain in tension with the status location of the Dumbledores, Weasleys and Potters as 'old blood' families. This leads Mendlesohn to the conclusion that the real choice we are given is not between the 'aristocrat' and revolutionary change, but between two visions of aristocracy in competition.[8] One such would be based on power entitlement, and one on the historic ideal of service.

Thus, Mendlesohn discerns a fundamentally hierarchical structure of authority and status quo at work in the *Harry Potter* series, whereby justice depends not on making radical alterations to the system but on making sure that the '"proper" people are in charge.'[9] This is supported by a perceived dynamic of entitlement, whereby heredity grants one privileges within the system, 'whether this be assistance in the House Cup, excusal from punishment, or survival through the death of others.'[10] A philosophy of patronage extends the benefits of hereditary entitlement to those mantled in the cloak of friendship (such as Hermione or Hagrid). This leads her to a damning conclusion:

> The result is a muddled morality that cheats the reader: while the books argue superficially for fairness, they actually portray privilege and exception-alism, not in the sense of 'elitism' but in a specifically hereditarian context that protects some while exposing others; they argue for social mobility while making such mobility contingent on social connections, and they argue for tolerance and kindness toward the inferior while denying the oppressed the agency to change their own lives.[11]

Karin E. Westman also relates the world of *Potter* to contemporary British politics, but sees a more complex and nuanced exploration of socio-political moralities at work. This includes a 'sustained critique of ideologies based upon material differences',[12] which functions not simply as escapism, but as 'a radical way to explore very real issues in contemporary readers'

---

7   Mendlesohn, 'Crowning the King: Harry Potter and the Construction of Authority', 167.
8   Ibid., 169.
9   Ibid., 181.
10 Ibid.
11 Ibid.
12 Karin E. Westman, 'Specters of Thatcherism: Contemporary British Culture in J. K. Rowling's Harry Potter Novels', in Lana A. Whited (ed.) *The Ivory Tower and Harry Potter: Perspectives on a Literary Phenomenon* (Columbia, DC and London: University of Missouri Press, 2004), 305–28 (312).

lives.'[13] Here, Rowling's vision is seen to comprehend far more than simply varieties of conservatism and hereditarianism. Westman also relates the books to Tory politics, but argues that it is the *spectres* of Thatcherism with which the books deal, reflecting their location of production within the late capitalist and global consumer society of post-Thatcherite England. As such, the politics of New Labour haunt the books as much as the heritage of Thatcherism: 'the world Cornelius Fudge has inherited harbors social inequities and injustices that masquerade behind the draperies of democracy, much as they do in the time of John Major and Tony Blair.'[14] All in all, Westman sees the problems of the wizarding world as analogues for those of contemporary Britain, and Rowling as insistently questioning both the distribution and circulation of power in society, and materialist ideologies of difference.[15]

There are two obvious ways in which the world of *Potter* is socially stratified along lines of difference: according to magical blood heritage within the human world, from the pure-blooded wizard or witch at one end of the spectrum to non-magical Muggles at the other; and between human persons and magical non-human persons. Within the wizarding world, blood purity is a motif which emerges early on and intensifies in significance and explicitness. It is a marker of its importance that it emerges in Harry's very first encounter with a peer, who happens to be Draco Malfoy. Harry has just informed Draco that his parents are dead:

'But they were *our* kind, weren't they?'

'They were a witch and wizard, if that's what you mean.'

'I really don't think they should let the other sort in, do you? They're just not the same, they've never been brought up to know our ways. Some of them have never even heard of Hogwarts until they get the letter, imagine. I think they should keep it in the old wizarding families.'[16]

In *Chamber of Secrets*, blood heritage is a dominant plot driver. First, the term 'mudblood' is introduced as a 'really foul' name for those born to Muggle, i.e. non-magic, parents.[17] Then, writing on the dungeon walls announces that the Chamber of Secrets has been opened: 'ENEMIES OF

13 Ibid., 308.
14 Ibid., 307.
15 Ibid., 328.
16 J. K. Rowling, *Harry Potter and the Philosopher's Stone* (London: Bloomsbury, 1997), 60–61.
17 J. K. Rowling, *Harry Potter and the Chamber of Secrets* (London: Bloomsbury, 1998), 89.

THE HEIR, BEWARE.'[18] The heir in question is revealed to be the heir of Slytherin, who had wanted to restrict magical education to the pure-blooded.[19] It is significant that Rowling stated in an interview that: 'Key things happen in book two. No one knows how important those things are . . . yet.'[20] The introduction of the first Horcrux, Tom Riddle's diary, is clearly one of these; so also is the development of the character of Ginny, Harry's future wife. However, I suggest that the centrality of the argument around blood heritage is also one of those 'key things', and pivotal to the series as a whole. This dispute within the wizarding world is replayed throughout the books, and forms a major ideological demarcation between Voldemort and his followers, and his opponents. *Goblet of Fire* features the violent tormenting of Muggles at the Quidditch World Cup, and *Half-Blood Prince* introduces assaults upon Muggle as well as resistant magical communities. The theme is reprised in the domestic as well as political arenas: in *Order of the Phoenix*, we learn of the rupture in the 'Noble and Most Ancient House of Black' on this issue: 'Stains of dishonour, filthy half-breeds, blood traitors, children of filth . . .' screeches the portrait of Mrs Black in commentary upon the presence of Harry, Hermione and the Weasleys in her house.[21] 'Toujours pur' was the House of Black's motto, and traitors to this ideology such as Sirius and Andromeda were blasted off the family tapestry.

The contrasting viewpoint is also put, chiefly by Order members and affiliates. The irrelevance of blood purity in terms of magical heritage is asserted on a number of occasions – Hagrid tells Harry in *Philosopher's Stone* that it is not important, and exceptional talent can emerge from Muggle lineage;[22] he cites Lily as an example, as does Slughorn in *Half-Blood Prince*. Ron assures Harry in *Chamber of Secrets* that while families like the Malfoys hold that pure-bloods are superior, '. . . the rest of us know it doesn't make any difference at all'; Ron further notes that most wizards are half-blood anyway, for without marrying Muggles the line would have died out.[23] Dumbledore states to Fudge: 'You fail to recognize that what matters is not what someone is born.'[24]

18 Ibid., 106.
19 Ibid., 114.
20 J. K. Rowling, '*Harry Potter and the Chamber of Secrets*, Audio Interview: J. K. Rowling', interview by Steve Head, 13 November 2002. Online: http://ffmovies.ign.com/filmforce/audio/press_conf_jk.mp3
21 J. K. Rowling, *Harry Potter and the Order of the Phoenix* (London: Bloomsbury, 2003), 96.
22 Rowling, *Harry Potter and the Philosopher's Stone*, 61.
23 Rowling, *Harry Potter and the Chamber of Secrets*, 89.
24 J. K. Rowling, *Harry Potter and the Goblet of Fire* (London: Bloomsbury, 2000), 700.

These competing attitudes towards the significance of blood purity act as a metaphor for attitudes and prejudices in the 'real' world. This is under-scored by the date of Dumbledore's defeat of Grindelwald and his reign of terror across several European countries: 1945, which coincides with the downfall of the Nazi regime, a primary modern signifier for prejudice based on ethnic heritage. Modern scientific and medical developments had given impetus to the significance of blood in the early twentieth century, including its relationship to social and national identity, through developments in the study of blood and heredity – for example through advances in genetic understanding, and the identification and analysis of blood groupings. Interwar Europe saw a significant focus on the biological constitution of identity as a feature of nationalist politics. In the wizarding world, the form of belonging is social rather than national, but emphasis on blood heritage functions similarly to identify the 'insider' and 'outsider' (who is to be disenfranchised, expelled, or even eliminated), the 'pure' and the 'impure' (who is threatening).

The meta-narrative of the series clearly rejects the ethos of Voldemort and the Death Eaters, and promotes an inclusive ideology whereby blood heritage is immaterial. Choice, rather than any pre-given nature of being, is presented as the defining feature of a person. This is embedded at the very heart of the story arc. However, Mendlesohn argues that other ele-ments within the structure of the narrative run counter to this. One such emerges because the structure of the European fairy tale is encoded in *Harry Potter*. Exemplified by Hans Christian Anderson, in this tradition 'leadership is intrinsic, heroism born in the blood, and self-interest simply the manifestation of those powers that ensure a return to order.'[25] On the one hand, modern fantasy has shifted the emphasis from the finale to the journey itself, which charts the development of the hero into appropriate maturity and power. This model of the hero emphasizes the importance of growth, choice and becoming 'worthy' of honours subsequently bestowed. However, the concept of birthright, which is intrinsically linked to heredi-tarian assumptions, remains as a sub-text or even dominant note.

This resonates with the analysis in Chapter Two, whereby the hero of classical hero journeys is observed to be somehow 'chosen': a child of des-tiny growing up in exile or obscurity but returning to reclaim or establish their true inheritance. With respect to the *Harry Potter* series, it can be claimed that Rowling's narrative simultaneously asserts heroic structures emphasizing individual moral worth and choice, but also the significance

25 Mendlesohn, 'Crowning the King: Harry Potter and the Construction of Authority', 160.

134

of birthright. In support of this, the main plot of the *Harry Potter* books is summarized by Mendlesohn as 'that of the returning prince, deprived of his heritage by the actions of a usurper, who has come to reclaim his throne, and with it, herald a new age of happiness.'[26] This is shored up by Harry's patrilineage within the wizarding world, as a scion of the pure-blooded, talented and wealthy Potters. Mendlesohn also takes the view, on the basis of evidence up to the end of *Goblet of Fire*, that the Sorting Hat is a visible symbol of destinarian thinking, Dumbledore's rhetoric about moral choice and freedom notwithstanding. The Hat actually constructs social order, on this interpretation. This leads Mendlesohn to a strong claim regarding the 'loyal, hardworking and true'[27] members of Hufflepuff:

> But they can never be leaders because somehow they are not fully human, and it is perfectly acceptable to kill off Cedric Diggory, captain of the Hufflepuff Quidditch team, in order to provide our hero with a motive to hold out, and in order to allow Dumbledore to deliver his 'consolatory' speech, which closes *Goblet of Fire*.[28]

The theme of the 'Chosen Hero' would certainly appear to undercut Rowling's attempts to establish a non-hereditarian model for social being in *Harry Potter*. However, two points could be made against this. One is attentive to the significance of that liminal status, 'half-blood', within the story. The three most significant human half-bloods are Harry himself, Snape and Voldemort. Between them, these three represent a continuum of attitudes towards Muggles. Harry stands with the Order, who seek to protect and defend Muggle rights. Snape occupies an ambivalent position, encapsulated in his castigation of Lily, the woman whom he loved devotedly all his life, as a 'Mudblood'. Voldemort, of course, rejects violently his Muggle heritage and allies himself with the pure-blooded contingent. Of the whole concept of a community stratified in this way, Rowling commented:

> If you think this is far-fetched, look at some of the real charts the Nazis used to show what constituted 'Aryan' or 'Jewish' blood. I saw one in the Holocaust Museum in Washington when I had already devised the

---

26 Ibid., 162.
27 Rowling, *Harry Potter and the Philosopher's Stone*, 118.
28 Mendlesohn, 'Crowning the King: Harry Potter and the Construction of Authority', 171.

'pure-blood', 'half-blood' and 'Muggle-born' definitions, and was chilled to see that the Nazis used precisely the same warped logic as the Death Eaters. A single Jewish grandparent 'polluted' the blood, according to their propaganda.[29]

Thus, within the social structure of the wizarding world, Harry's location as simultaneously 'Chosen One' and 'half-blood' is itself a powerful critique of the notion that pure-blood is superior. The second reason why Harry's status as the 'Chosen One' does not reinforce hereditarian assumptions emerges in revelations made in *Order of the Phoenix* (appearing subsequent to the time of Mendlesohn's writing). In the concluding scene between Dumbledore and Harry, it is revealed that Harry's 'chosen' status is contingent: it was, in fact, Voldemort who chose him, by deciding that he was the child of the prophecy.[30] Furthermore, in *Half-Blood Prince* Dumbledore explains to Harry that the prophecy itself is simply that: it does not constrain free will: '. . . you are free to choose your way, quite free to turn your back on the prophecy!'[31]

So, social stratification of the human world by blood heritage, and the various accompanying bigotries and social intolerances, is a major and sustained structuring theme in the *Harry Potter* series. It is an analogue for class distinctions. The pure-blood/Muggle continuum is an obvious dimension of this, but there are others. Class is not only an aspect of the human world, but also draws in the non-human sentient beings, all of whom are differently positioned within the social, economic and political strata. The linking of class and blood, whether human or non-human, unites considerations of class with considerations of ethnicity. While Rowling does unobtrusively include persons of differing ethnicities within the magical world, this is liable to be perceived as tokenism. However, it could be said that racism is actually explored in a more metaphorical manner, through the divisions between the various beings.

The magical world is deeply stratified. Only humans are permitted wands.[32] There is prejudice and hostility between the various groups. The treatment of Lupin as a werewolf, and Hagrid's fear of stigmatization as a half-Giant, indicates a narratorial finger pointing in disapproval at intolerant attitudes; this is particularly so since it is sympathetic characters

29 J. K. Rowling, 'J. K. Rowling Official Site. Section: F. A. Q.'. Online: http://www. jkrowling.com/textonly/en/faq_view.cfm?id=58
30 Rowling, *Harry Potter and the Order of the Phoenix*, 742.
31 J. K. Rowling, *Harry Potter and the Half-Blood Prince* (London: Bloomsbury, 2005), 479.
32 Rowling, *Harry Potter and the Goblet of Fire*, 132.

whom Rowling has placed in positions of persecution. The most extended consideration in the narrative of racial prejudice and social stratification is in the treatment of house-elves. This raises significant questions regarding the acceptance of slavery in the magical world, which only Hermione appears genuinely shocked and concerned by. It includes the portrayal of house-elves as actively happiest in their servitude, with no desire to be freed:[33] Dobby is presented as a maverick in this respect – a 'weirdo', in Hagrid's words. Mendlesohn makes a damning case here:

> The slaves are presented as happy, simple souls who merely wish to serve their families to the best of their ability. No one who has seen *Birth of a Nation* (1915) or *Gone with the Wind* (1939) could fail to recognize the resemblance of the relationship between the relationship of Scarlett O'Hara and Mammy, and of 'Master Barty' and Winky (*Goblet of Fire*, 683).[34]

Dobby's troubles do not end when he attains freedom – he cannot get work because he wants to be paid, and the other house-elves do not fully accept him: he is considered mad, or dangerous.[35] The arguments of Rowling's characters do indeed sound straight from the American antebellum South, as Mendlesohn states: Ron thinks the house-elves are happy,[36] Mr Weasley considers the timing wrong to discuss the matter,[37] Percy Weasley believes that house-elf loyalty to their masters is more of an issue than house-elves.[38] Dumbledore, it is true, willingly pays Dobby, but does not consider it appropriate to move forward to mass liberation, at least of the Hogwarts elves. Mendlesohn is well aware that Rowling is not advocating slavery, and may well be seeking to educate children through confrontation with the issue, but 'the fact that house-elves absolutely cannot free themselves, but must be freed by others, creates a dynamic in which all justice must be offered from above, rather than taken from below.'[39]

Once more, Westman has a different perspective to offer, observing the patronizing dynamic but viewing it as a satire on left-wing middle-class

---

33   Ibid., 178.
34   Mendlesohn, 'Crowning the King: Harry Potter and the Construction of Authority', 179.
35   Ibid., 377, 381.
36   Ibid., 125.
37   Ibid., 139.
38   Ibid., 154.
39   Mendlesohn, 'Crowning the King: Harry Potter and the Construction of Authority', 181.

liberals speaking on behalf of the lower classes, whom they have never met.[40] In fact, Hermione in this respect is representative of J. K. Rowling herself, and what we see here is also self-satire. Rowling used to work as a research assistant for Amnesty International in Francophone Africa in the field of human rights abuses, and was drawing on her own experiences as an enthusiastic teenager. As she says in an interview with Evan Solomon:

> Well, she's fun to write because Hermione, with the best of intentions, becomes quite self-righteous. My heart is entirely with her as she goes through this. She develops her political conscience. . . . But . . . in fact she blunders towards the very people she's trying to help. She offends them. . . . Hermione thinks she's going to lead them to glorious rebellion in one afternoon and then finds out the reality is very different . . .[41]

Thus, the issue of house-elf rights appears to highlight the intersection between class, ethnicity and oppression in social stratification, and how class on the basis of ethnicity becomes institutionalized.

Taking a somewhat different tack, McDaniel argues that the house-elves are more suitably compared to housewives confined by their domestic roles, rather than to slaves embracing their own oppression. Parallel to many twentieth-century housewives, many house-elves 'derive enjoyment, a sense of purpose, the very core of their identity from their service to home and family, and so have no wish to be "liberated."'[42] This point is reinforced by the fate of Winky, sinking into despair over her freedom, which she does not experience as liberating in the least. The strength of the house-elves' magical power renders their situation ironic; it also demonstrates the critical blindness of the elite to the talents and skills of those beneath them. It was the help of Kreacher that enabled Regulus Black to steal one of Voldemort's Horcruxes: as Hermione points out, it '. . . would never have occurred to him that they might have magic that he didn't.'[43] Dobby's

40 Karin E. Westman, 'Specters of Thatcherism: Contemporary British Culture in J. K. Rowling's Harry Potter Novels', 328.
41 J. K. Rowling, interview by Evan Solomon, CBCNewsWorld: *Hot Type*, 13 July 2000.
42 Kathryn N. McDaniel, 'The Elfin Mystique: Fantasy and Feminism in J. K. Rowling's Harry Potter Series', in Amy H. Sturgis (ed.), *Past Warchful Dragons: Fantasy and Faith in the World of C. S. Lewis* (Altadena, CA: Mythopoeic Press, 2007), 183–207 (186).
43 J. K. Rowling, *Harry Potter and the Deathly Hallows* (London: Bloomsbury, 2007), 194–96.

death underscores the heroic capacity of house-elves; his life is a symbol for the fact that house-elf enslavement is not a necessary condition, and that house-elves are not constitutionally unable to embrace freedom.

The treatment of gender in the *Harry Potter* series is another area receiving considerable critical consideration. One route is to analyse gender in the series from a role-portrayal point of view: what are the functional locations of male and female characters respectively? How are stereotypes of 'feminine' and 'masculine' models of behaviour reinforced or destabilized? Who is active, who passive? Who speaks, and with what authority? It can be argued that presentation of gender is not infrequently stereotypical – with groups of girls who whisper and giggle and shriek, Tonks losing her focus when she is heartsick for Lupin, and Hermione only becoming more generally socially acceptable when she improves her appearance. The action favours the male protagonists: Hermione spends much of *Chamber of Secrets* in hospital (either furry or frozen); Fleur appears ineffectual in *Goblet of Fire*, although presumably must have been a talented witch to be selected for the competition; in *Half-Blood Prince*, the climactic action favours Dumbledore, Harry, Snape and Draco. In *Deathly Hallows*, one of the strongest female characters, Ginny, is barely present. Based on the earlier books, Schoefer stirred up controversy with the following claim:

> Girls, when they are not downright silly or unreliable, are helpers, enablers and instruments. No girl is brilliantly heroic in the way Harry is, no woman is experienced and wise like Professor Dumbledore.[44]

However, the case can also be made in the opposite direction. If looking at the portrayal of girls, we might, for example, focus on the way in which Hermione is portrayed as purveyor of knowledge. She is also outspoken, justice-seeking, and frequently the voice of reason. Girls in the *Harry Potter* series are presented as competing on equal terms at Quidditch – except in Slytherin House, whose team is an all-male preserve. Witches occupy positions of authority in public life, and the teaching staff at Hogwarts appears relatively gender-balanced. Based on decisions to show women in positions of power and authority and for Harry to have a visible cohort of

44   Christine Schoefer, 'Harry Potter's Girl Trouble', *Salon.com*, 13 January 2000. Online: http://www.salon.com/books/feature/2000/01/13/potter/index1.html. See also Elizabeth E. Heilman (ed.), *Critical Perspectives on Harry Potter*, 2nd edn (Routledge, 2008). The latter book benefits from its later date in terms of being in a position to offer an evaluation based on the whole series.

important female friends (Hermione, Ginny, Luna), it can be postulated that Rowling, from a liberal feminist perspective, has endeavoured to present a picture of female equality. At the same time, it could also be said that nuances of behaviours and symbolisms betray the continuing enmeshment of the female in a patriarchal socio-symbolic order.

By way of example, let us consider an instance of gender representation from a symbolic point of view. In relation to the film of *Chamber of Secrets*, Michelle Yeo believes it is possible to discern an underlying symbolic representation of women as connected to evil and dark magic, as well as in traditional passive and naïve roles.[45] The contours of her analysis can also be applied to the text version. One theme that Yeo explores is the mythopoetical significance of blood.[46] As understood in relation to women, blood has historically been seen as a form of pollution, impurity and danger in the contexts of menstruation and childbirth. This is in contradistinction to accounts of male blood; for example, in Judaism circumcision as a ritual is related to the covenant, and in Christianity the blood of Christ is redemptive. *The Chamber of Secrets* has Ginny, on the threshold of puberty, writing three messages in blood on the walls while possessed by Voldemort; Yeo argues that 'the blood becomes a feminine symbol of dangerous power, female puberty initiation, the life-force and death, and Christ and the foreshadowed redemption.'[47]

In *Chamber of Secrets*, Riddle vampirizes Ginny's soul through the medium of the diary: 'Ginny poured out her soul to me, and her soul happened to be just what I wanted . . . I grew stronger and stronger on a diet of her deepest fears, her darkest secrets . . . '[48] Having made her write her own farewell on the wall, Riddle takes her down to the Chamber of Secrets – where she '. . . struggled and cried and became *very* boring.'[49] Yeo notes how reminiscent of sexual assault this description is; a spiritual assault has certainly taken place, as Riddle/Voldemort has fed off her energy until she is so depleted she can barely sustain her own life. Yeo sees this as metaphorical of the relationship between masculinity and femininity within traditional patriarchy, with the male gaining in power through violence against and exploitation of the female. This interpretation is reinforced for Yeo by the parallel with *Philosopher's Stone*, where

45   Michelle Yeo, 'Harry Potter and the Chamber of Secrets: Feminist interpretations/
     Jungian dreams', *Studies in Media and Information Literacy Education* 4, no. 1 (2004).
     Online: http://www.utpjournals.com/simile
46   Ibid.
47   Ibid.
48   Rowling, *Harry Potter and the Chamber of Secrets*, 228.
49   Ibid., 231.

Voldemort feeds off the blood of the unicorn, also a symbol of purity and virginity.[50]

A sexualized reading is further justified when one considers a set of factors supplementary to Voldemort's predation of a young girl. The basilisk itself is a serpent, and thus a phallic symbol. The girl, on the threshold of puberty, has been writing on the walls in blood. Furthermore, the entrance to the Chamber of Secrets is through the fountain in the girls' bathroom, into which adolescent boys must trespass to gain access to it; this is achieved through Harry whispering in the tongue of snakes, whereupon entrance into the dark and wet cavern is gained. Having rescued the girl, he emerges from the Chamber covered in muck, slime and blood. For Yeo the symbolism surrounding all of this justified a reading whereby:

> Women's bodies – and in particular, women's sexuality – is represented as the literal location of danger and evil, a place of darkness and fear, where the young male child redeemer must wage battle, extricate himself, and then return to the world of light and air above.[51]

A similar and parallel analysis could be made with respect to masculinities. Schoefer's account above regarding the portrayal of girls and women as stereotypically feminine implicitly assumes the presentation of boys and men as stereotypically masculine. However, when it comes to the presentation of masculinities, Wannamaker argues that the *Harry Potter* series undermines traditional stereotyping:

> The varied depictions of Harry, Hagrid, Neville, Ron, Dumbledore, Malfoy, and other male characters in the *Harry Potter* novels show us that unconventional versions of masculinity are quite prevalent . . . and these depictions show boys they are not alone in their difficult negotiations with, on the margins of, and against hegemonic masculinity.[52]

---

50 Granger suggested that 'Ginny' should be read here as 'Virginia', i.e. 'virgin'; see John Granger, *Looking for God in Harry Potter* (Carol Stream, IL: Tyndale House Publishers, 2006), 139. However, Ginny's full name is revealed by J. K. Rowling as 'Ginevra'. See 'J. K. Rowling Official Site. Section: Characters'. Online: http://www.jkrowling.com/en/index.cfm

51 Yeo, 'Harry Potter and the Chamber of Secrets: Feminist interpretations/Jungian dreams'.

52 Annette Wannamaker, 'Men in Cloaks and High-heeled Boots, Men Wielding Pink Umbrellas: Witchy Masculinities in the Harry Potter Novels', *The Looking Glass: New Perspectives on Children's Literature* 10, no. 1 (2006). Online: http://www.lib.latrobe.edu.au/ojs/index.php/tlg/article/view/96/81

Examples cited by Wannamaker of such non-hegemonic masculinity include Hagrid's nurturing devotion to various creatures and his pink umbrella; Dumbledore's high-heeled boots and floor length purple cloak; Harry and Ron having a girl as a best friend; the revelation by Myrtle of Draco's sensitive and vulnerable side as a boy not afraid to show his feelings. It is also important, as Wannamaker points out, that when non-conventional modes of masculinity are presented, they are not presented as 'feminine', but as a legitimate alternative way of being masculine.[53]

In summary, views on the presentation of gender in *Harry Potter* are notable for their contradictory nature. This may well reflect complex and contradictory gender-codings embedded in the text. However, this should perhaps not be surprising. Rowling's world navigates the fantastic and the mimetic: if novels are to bear any resemblance to the world of ordinary experience, it would hardly be believable if the cultural coding of phenomena such as gender accorded entirely with utopic aspiration.

The final area to be explored in relation to social stratification is the relationship between success, heredity and wealth as personified in the character of Harry. This, Mendlesohn believes, supports her contention that – protestations within the text to the contrary – who you are in terms of birth and wealth is of more importance than what you are in terms of actual talent and application of it. For example, she claims:

> Put bluntly, Harry is set up as the gentleman scholar: he works enough that his natural talent will take him through, but he is never shown at the top of the class, as this, a position occupied by Hermione, is despised as too showy for a gentleman . . . The structure of the books around a school year and examinations may disguise this, but all of Harry's important magical adventures focus on his talents and not his learning.[54]

Thus, the implication is that Harry does not cultivate his talents and earn his achievements, but relies on natural abilities. At the same time, she also holds that Harry's talents are actually rather limited. Despite the emphasis on heredity and the recurrent claim that James and Lily Potter were both outstanding in magical power, Harry is not presented as superlatively gifted in this respect. His school success is modest, with

---

53   Ibid. Wannamaker is drawing on points made by Sharon R. Bird, 'Welcome to the Men's Club: Homosociality and the Maintenance of Hegemonic Masculinity', *Gender and Society* 10, no. 2 (April 1996): 120–32.
54   Mendlesohn, 'Crowning the King: Harry Potter and the Construction of Authority', 169.

his best achievements in the field in which he had most opportunity to practice – Defence Against the Dark Arts. Mendlesohn also points out an interesting materialist dimension to Harry's achievements, based on 'gifts' which are external and bestowed rather than innate, and charts this through the corpus at the time of her writing to *Goblet of Fire*. For example, while Harry is presented as having inherited James's talent at Quidditch, this is underpinned by his possession of exceptionally good and expensive broomsticks, notably the Firebolt. Quidditch, indeed, is the only sporting activity in evidence, and it is clear that money does matter here as well as ability. Students are allowed to ride their own broomsticks, which vary markedly in quality and performance. Mendlesohn also cites the Invisibility Cloak, Marauder's map, Harry's ability to withstand Voldemort's curse, and, 'the best touch of all, he has "inherited" part of Voldemort, which is crucial in the wand selection that helps him to withstand the villain.'[55] This is all of key significance because it leads her to the conclusion that Harry does not act with what he can call his own, or with gifts earned through learning, hard work and application. Thus, Mendlesohn suggests that magic does not encourage Harry in self-development, but instead acts as a metaphor for it.

Similar arguments are made when considering the relationship between Harry and his friends. It is traditional in fairy tales and fantasy for the hero to operate with a circle of supportive companions: this is classically evident in the whole concept of Tolkien's *The Fellowship of the Ring*; thus, it is no surprise to find in the *Harry Potter* series that those surrounding him possess qualities and attributes which contribute to his success. Mendlesohn goes further and says that Harry's success actually rests on his companions' ingenuity, intelligence and courage, and that (at least up the time of writing) Harry does not show evidence of learning from his companions' strengths and wisdom.[56] What is more, it is Harry to whom the credit accrues. Once more, all of this leads, for Mendlesohn, to a rather passive hero, who is nevertheless presented as a 'shining prince' and avoids the normal consequences of his actions (such as expulsion for use of underage magic in the Muggle world).[57]

Various points could be made in mitigation of some of these arguments. For example, there is no evidence that it is a 'gentlemanly' dynamic which causes Harry to work less hard at knowledge acquisition than, say,

---

55 Ibid., 163.
56 Ibid., 164. She also here identifies the companion as 'teacher' to be a functional role in fantasy, but not fairy tale.
57 Ibid., 165.

Hermione. He is presented as simply less interested in scholastic attainment, which is not untypical for persons of his portrayed age. It is true that Harry is not shown as outstandingly powerful in magical terms. However, this is surely exactly to reinforce the point that character traits and qualities matter more than raw power. The texts emphasize Harry's capacity to love, his courage, and purity of heart over and above his magical talent. A similar point could be made in respect of Harry's use of supporting 'props' to assist him in reaching his goals – and indeed, the extent to which his friends act to help him. Harry is not portrayed as solitary, self-contained and sufficient unto himself. The fact does remain that Harry is privileged in terms of wealth, and has access to resources that Ron, for example, does not. However, this is presented self-consciously within the text as a difficult issue between himself and Ron, which one could say reflects the realities of existence in contexts of unequal wealth distribution, but one that Rowling does not leave unproblematized. Furthermore, it must not be forgotten that a number of those material gifts are not 'just' material: as discussed in Chapter Two, some of the objects (such as the Invisibility Cloak) are symbolically important in connecting Harry to his absent antecedents.

This survey has shown a number of ways in which the *Harry Potter* series presents a world deeply socially stratified – along lines of blood heritage, of species, of class, of gender, and on individual wealth and status. It is argued that these divisions are metaphorical representations of parallel contexts within 'real' Britain. More controversial is the question of how this should be interpreted. One school of thought – largely represented in this study through the voice of Mendlesohn – holds that the world of *Potter* is inscribed with traditional, conservative and elitist values which run counter to the articulated philosophy of liberal humanism, emphasizing personal capacity and choice rather than social standing. Over against that, critics such as Westman argue that these material differentiations are deliberate ideological statements which are satirical in nature and intended to expose the systemic flaws in contemporary society.

This difference in opinion is played out in evaluation of the *Harry Potter* series as a work of fantasy. Pennington, for example, condemns it for being too close to the consensus reality 'from which [Rowling] simultaneously wants to escape', and thereby failing as a work of fantasy.[58] Byatt argues in a similar vein:

---

58 John Pennington, 'From Elfland to Hogwarts, or the Aesthetic Trouble with Harry Potter', *The Lion and the Unicorn* 26, no. 1 (2002): 78–97 (79).

Ms. Rowling's magic world has no place for the numinous. It is written for people whose imaginative lives are confined to TV cartoons, and the exaggerated (more exciting, not threatening) mirror-worlds of soaps, reality TV and celebrity gossip. Its values, and everything in it, are, as Gatsby said of his own world when the light had gone out of his dream, 'only personal.' Nobody is trying to save or destroy anything beyond Harry Potter and his friends and family.[59]

She complains also about the banality of the evil, which apart from Voldemort, is 'caused by newspaper gossip columnists' and 'bureaucratic interference in educational affairs'.[60]

Such critiques mirror the debate about whether the *Harry Potter* series is to be understood as nostalgic and traditional. In both cases, reading the texts as parody and as satire casts a very different light on the dynamics of the worlds presented. The novels undoubtedly 'mime' contemporary concerns – a far greater range of them than it has been possible to make mention of here. For example, Voldemort's campaign is strikingly reminiscent of terrorism, both in terms of tactics and consequences. The nationalistic scenes at the Quidditch World Cup also find their analogue in sporting contexts. Percy's concerns over cauldron-bottom thickness and Ali Bashir's carpets can be related to current European co-operation in commercial regulation. The removal of the technological paraphernalia of the 'real' world only serves to reveal the persistence of social and political problems – rather than, as Chevalier notes, stemming from 'nostalgia for cultural stability'.[61]

With respect to generic evaluation, Falconer suggests: 'rather than seeing her as failed high fantasist, we would understand Rowling better if we approached her as a writer who systematically and playfully hybridizes different genres.'[62] She, and Barfield,[63] take the line that I follow myself, namely that these are works of satiric fantasy. As such, they are calling for the reader to develop a critical eye and turn it back upon their own contexts. In this respect, it can be deemed subversive fantasy along the

59 A. S. Byatt, 'Harry Potter and the Childish Adult'.
60 Ibid.
61 Noel Chevalier, 'The Liberty Tree and the Whomping Willow: Political Justice, Magical Science, and Harry Potter', *The Lion and the Unicorn* 29, no. 3 (2005): 397–415 (402).
62 Rachel Falconer, *The Crossover Novel: Contemporary Children's Fiction and its Adult Readership* (London: Taylor & Francis, 2008), 44.
63 Steven Barfield, 'Fantasy and the Interpretation of Fantasy in Harry Potter', *The Washington and Jefferson College Review* 54 (Fall 2004): 24–32.

lines outlined by Rosemary Jackson: by redirecting attention to suppressed and repressed areas which are normalized and covered over.[64] What is particularly of interest here, however, is that there are no pat answers. This is a mirror of striving for change in real life. The problems are identified, but few are solved. Markers of progress along the way are shown through the slow process of negotiation and reform. Barfield contends that the ambiguous politics reflects a loss of faith in political narratives on the part of children and young adults, such that there is no clear metaphysical or political framing to point the way ahead. However, in Rowling's world, we are encouraged to look at things aslant. Things are not always what they seem. Perhaps that is how we locate the path to social justice and transformation. Enter through Diagon Alley, and find the world, again: diagonally.

---

64 Rosemary Jackson, *Fantasy: Literature of Subversion* (London: Routledge, 1981).

THE GOOD AND THE MONSTROUS

HIS DARK MATERIALS: '. . . AND YE SHALL BE AS GODS'

PULLMAN'S PANORAMIC RECASTING OF Milton's *Paradise Lost* involves an inversion of traditional Christian theological ideas concerning goodness and sin: the Fall is not in fact a 'fall', but an accession of a fuller mode of being and becoming through enhanced consciousness and sexual awareness. It is, according to Pullman, 'the best thing, the most important thing that ever happened to us.'[1] This is somewhat reminiscent of Friedrich Nietzsche's view of Christian values as pervasively toxic to humanity – Christianity is seen as a life-negating religion of pity appealing to those in states of subjugation, but ultimately condemnatory of the world and flesh as sinful.

> Wherever the influence of theologians is felt there is a transvaluation of values, and the concepts 'true' and 'false' are forced to change places. Whatever is most damaging to life is there called 'true,' and whatever exalts it, intensifies it, approves it, justifies it and makes it triumphant is there called 'false' . . .[2]

---

1   Wendy Parsons and Catriona Nicholson, 'Talking to Philip Pullman: An Interview', *The Lion and the Unicorn* 23, no. 1 (January 1999): 116–34 (119).
2   Friedrich Wilhelm Nietzsche, *The Antichrist*, trans. H. L. Mencken (Whitefish, MT: Kessinger Publishing, 2004), 6.

From similar premises with respect to a turning 'upside-down' of the traditional Fall narrative, Pullman charts a humanistic course in a post-Christian reconstruction of the democratic, non-theistic Republic of Heaven. He moves in rewriting the theology of the Fall to an account of an alternative moral framework. Good and evil are not powers with independent existence, but simply, in Mary Malone's words, 'names for what people do.' A deed is good if it helps someone, or evil if it hurts them, and individuals are too complex to be designated as one or the other.[3] Pullman's concept of the Republic of Heaven was discussed in detail in Chapter Four, primarily by way of heuristic comparison with certain Buddhist concepts and traditions. This chapter concentrates on elucidating related themes pertaining to the nature of good and evil, with allusion to some of the ways in which Pullman references, subverts or recasts mythological and Christian themes and symbols in pursuit of his ends.

The Church in Lyra's world is a distorted echo of Christianity in our own, complete with its own (variant) Adam and Eve founding myth. The clear similarities have fuelled the controversies over Pullman's representation of the Church, his protestations that it is simply a story notwithstanding. This Church is a clericalized and corrupt mass of competing power-bases, limiting knowledge and stamping out all challenge to its authority. The witch-queen Ruta Skadi declares '. . . every church is the same: control, destroy, obliterate every good feeling';[4] Stanislaus Grumman puts it thus to Will:

> There are two great powers . . . and they've been fighting since time began. . . . Every little increase in human freedom has been fought over ferociously between those who want us to know more and be wiser and stronger, and those who want us to obey and be humble and submit.[5]

The Church body the General Oblation Board is responsible for one of the central abominations represented in *His Dark Materials*, namely intercision. This is the deliberate sundering of the dæmon from its human counterpart. It is explicitly compared in the texts with practices of genital mutilation also known in this world. In *Northern Lights*, Asriel compares intercision to the practice of castrating boys to maintain their treble

---

3   Philip Pullman, *The Amber Spyglass* (London: Scholastic, 2001), 470–71.
4   Philip Pullman, *The Subtle Knife* (London: Scholastic, 2007), 50.
5   Ibid., 319.

singing voices ('so useful in Church music').[6] In *Subtle Knife*, the witch Ruta Skadi declaims of their southern lands:

> There are churches . . . that cut their children too, as the people of Bolvangar did – not in the same way, but just as horribly – they cut their sexual organs, yes, both boys and girls – they cut them with knives so that they shan't feel. That is what the church does . . .[7]

Intercision in Lyra's world is performed by the General Oblation Board for three purposes. First, there are those in the Church who believe that Dust is original sin, that Dust settles on humanity when the dæmon reaches its settled form at puberty, and therefore that the way to avoid original sin is to separate (and thereby destroy) the dæmon. This is the purpose of the General Oblation Board's experimental station at Bolvangar, and it kidnaps children through the agency of Mrs Coulter for use there. The children, thus, are a hideous analogue of the mediaeval Church's practice of oblation, which involved parents irrevocably giving their offspring over to monastic life as gift and sacrifice. Second, some of the staff workers at Bolvangar are intercised: producing the perfectly passive and biddable worker, incurious and blank.[8] Mrs Coulter's bodyguards have also undergone the process, and thus have no fear, imagination or free agency, and will '. . . fight till they are torn apart.'[9] Third, the process of intercision generates phenomenal power. The President of the Consistorial Court of Discipline commits self-intercision in an act of martrydom to fuel the bomb which is intended to kill an absent Lyra through resonance with her stolen strand of hair. This act opens the unnatural abyss into which Dust begins to haemorrhage, thereby initiating an apocalypse of consciousness.

Northern Lights establishes the horror of the intercision process through graphic accounts of the effect it has. Confronted with the outcome of it in the shape of a severed boy, Lyra's first impulse was to turn and run, or to be sick. A human being with no dæmon was like someone without a face, 'or with their ribs laid open and their heart torn out: something unnatural and uncanny that belonged to the world of night-ghasts, not the waking world of sense.'[10] In *Subtle Knife*, Spectres perform a similar function:

6   Philip Pullman, *Northern Lights* (London: Scholastic, 2005), 374.
7   Pullman, *The Subtle Knife*, 50.
8   Pullman, *Northern Lights*, 284.
9   Pullman, *The Subtle Knife*, 199.
10 Pullman, *Northern Lights*, 215.

they are dæmon-eaters which have for 300 years preyed on the world of Cittàgazze. They target adults rather than children because their food is attention: a 'conscious and informed interest in the world.'[11] Mrs Coulter learns to dominate them and press them into her service. Through use of a Spectre she wrings the truth of Lyra's identity as the new Eve out of the witch Lena Feldt, who suffers 'a hideous and sickening despair', before sinking into death in life.[12]

The use of intercision is not confined to the Church. Besides mention of the African *zombi*,[13] simple boundary lines between the forces of 'good' and 'evil' are confounded for Lyra when Lord Asriel, in opposition to the Church, sacrifices Roger in this way to generate the power to open the bridge to another world. Lyra's devastation prompts her to consider the possibility that if all those adults who acted in such a way thought Dust was bad, perhaps they were wrong; perhaps Dust was to be 'sought and welcome and cherished.'[14] Inspired by this possibility, Lyra and her dæmon leave the world of their birth in quest of Dust: they 'looked towards the sun, and walked into the sky.'[15]

The 'North', in the first book of the trilogy, is the theatre for playing out the initial stages in the grand battle for all three main groupings to whom we are introduced: the forces of the Church, the rebel leader Lord Asriel, and those (such as the gyptians, witches of the same mind as Serafina Pekkala, and the armoured bear Iorek Byrnison) who would give their loyalty to Lyra – the child prophesied by the witches as she without whom all would die, but who must fulfil her destiny in ignorance.[16] The spatial convergence on the polar regions of the North is important here. The idea of the North is richly textured as a place of danger, strangeness and grandeur.

To Lyra in Oxford, the North is a source of glamour and fascination; tales of polar explorers stir her heart with admiration.[17] By contrast, the priest Semyon Borisovitch finds the North horrifying: 'All things from the north are devilish. Like the witches – daughters of evil! The church

---

11 Pullman, *The Subtle Knife*, 280.
12 Ibid., 314.
13 Lord Asriel informs Lyra about the African way of separating body and dæmon to make a *zombi* slave, with no will and who will work ceaselessly without complaint. (Pullman, *Northern Lights*, 375).
14 Ibid., 398.
15 Ibid., 399.
16 Ibid., 175–76. Lyra, we learn in *Subtle Knife*, is also she who will *end* destiny in the witches' prophecy (Pullman, *The Subtle Knife*, 274).
17 Pullman, *Northern Lights*, 78.

should have put them all to death many years ago.'[18] The polar regions have profound symbolic resonance for those to whom they are alien. Wilson suggests that the 'frozen continent of the south – a land of white denial, empty as air and full as the void – has spawned a history of negative discovery, a hermeneutics of despair';[19] David suggests that the Arctic region had a hold on the British imagination in Victorian times no less significant than 'the exoticism of the Orient or the darkness at the heart of Africa.'[20] The poles are interfaces with the heavens, or portals to the centre of the earth. They are mysterious and dangerous, fascinating and hostile, unearthly and surreal. The glamour and heroism of exploratory expeditions lends a sense of romance; the popular image of ice-blasted, desolate wastes with strange sounds and eerie light lends a sense of the uncanny. The Poles conjure the feeling of boundaries, of the end of the world, of the limit of what is known and mastered. In these days of polar melting, the images seem sadder and frailer, but still remain in the consciousness. as an immense other.

Leane identifies a number of features in polar mythology (although with an interest in establishing the specificity of Antarctic and Arctic symbolisms). Citing Victoria Nelson,[21] she points to the fact that the poles were 'initially celestial rather than terrestrial features', around which the stars seemed to revolve; it was here, at the apex and nadir of the zodiac, that souls departed and returned at death and rebirth respectively. However, in the Renaissance, 'the poles were transferred to the Earth', and the 'mythological holes in the heavens thus became holes in the earth.'[22] The poles then have been endowed with a quasi-mystical significance. The notion of the poles as terrestrial/celestial portals is especially relevant to Pullman's presentation of the aurora borealis in *Northern Lights*:

> Streams and veils of light hung like curtains, looped and festooned on invisible hooks hundreds of miles high or blowing out sideways in the streams of some unimaginable wind. . . . As [Lyra] gazed, her wonder grew, because

18 Pullman, *The Amber Spyglass*, 105.
19 Eric G. Wilson, 'Polar Apocalypse in Coleridge and Poe', *Wordsworth Circle* 35, no. 1 (Winter 2004): 37–44 (37).
20 Robert G. David, *The Arctic in the British Imagination, 1818–1914* (Manchester: Manchester University Press, 2000), 6.
21 Victoria Nelson, 'Symmes Hole, or The South Polar Romance', *Raritan: A Quarterly Review* 17, no. 2 (Fall 1997): 136–66.
22 Elizabeth Leane, 'Locating the Thing: The Antarctic as Alien Space in John W. Campbell's "Who Goes There?"', *Science Fiction Studies* 32, no. 2 (July 2005): 225–39 (230).

there in the sky was the unmistakeable outline of a city: towers, domes walls
. . . buildings and streets, suspended in the air![23]

Later, seeing it for herself rather than in Asriel's photogram, she is moved
to tears and finds the experience 'so beautiful it was almost holy', giving
her a trance-feeling akin to when she reads the alethiometer.[24] Later still,
when Asriel succeeds in piercing the vault of heaven, he speaks ecstatically
of the feel of the sun and wind from another world.[25] In a listserv posting
cited by Lenz, Pullman writes that the wording here is a deliberate echo
of the Stefan George poem 'Entrueckung' [Transcendence]: '*Ich fühle luft
von anderen planeten*" [I feel an air from other planets blowing]'.[26] The
launching pad of the North, then, establishes a suitably epic context from
which the war in heaven can proceed, as the remote and alien site of both
monstrosity and the sublime.

Across the bridge, Asriel constructs a massive fortress in the mountains
at the edge of the world, as bastion for the rebel forces.[27] It is from here
that he proposes to launch his war against heaven: not merely against the
Church, but 'the highest power of all', as his manservant informs Serafina
Pekkala: Asriel, he believes, has 'gone a-searching for the dwelling place
of the Authority Himself, and he's a-going to destroy Him.'[28]

God, the Authority, appears, therefore, to have been set up as the
highest opposing principle, the real power behind the corrosive activities
of the church. In fact, Pullman's narrative deconstructs such a theology.
There is no god to be force for either good or evil. Metatron, the regent
angel, is the real opponent of Asriel, and is defeated by Asriel and Mrs
Coulter following her maternal change in both heart and allegiance. The
Authority is revealed to be the first angel, now ancient, decrepit and senile.
His ending is not made in cataclysmic climax, but almost incidentally, as
an act of passing compassion on the part of Lyra and Will. They come
across the Authority in his crystal litter, his escort eaten by cliff-ghasts; he
is demented, mumbling and frightened. They help him out of the cask; his
eyes blinking in 'innocent wonder', he responds to their 'simple kindness
like a flower in the sun', but in the open air he begins to dissolve:

23   Pullman, *Northern Lights*, 23–24.
24   Ibid., 183.
25   Ibid., 394.
26   Millicent Lenz and Peter Hunt, *Alternative Worlds in Fantasy Fiction* (London and
      New York, NY: Continuum, 2001), 129. The posting in question is to <child_lit_
      serv>, 27 July 2000.
27   Pullman, *The Subtle Knife*, 143.
28   Ibid., 46.

Only a few moments later he had vanished completely, and their last impression was of those eyes, blinking in wonder, and a sigh of the most profound and exhausted relief.[29]

As Russell observes, this is not murder, not deicide; rather, it signals the transition between an ancient age of deceit in the shape of a false god, and a new age of knowledge in the person of Lyra.[30] A central symbolism within *His Dark Materials* is the role of Lyra as 'Eve! Mother of all! Eve, again! Mother Eve!', who will be life, and who will disobey: a designation stammered out by the unfortunate tortured witch Lena Feldt.[31]

Lyra, Will and Mary Malone offer us a range of alternative mythological and theological symbolisms and resonances from those represented by the opposing powers fronted by the Authority on the one hand, and led by Asriel on the other. These representations of the mythological and theological are reinforced by nomenclature. While such connotations of the name 'Mary' spring easily to mind, and are unpacked in more detail below, the set of symbolisms around 'Lyra' is less obvious. The name itself means 'lyre', a small harp-like instrument. 'Lyra' is also the name of a constellation, allegedly called so in honour of the shape of the harp of Orpheus. This is especially appropriate. In myth, Orpheus descends to the Underworld to rescue his wife, Eurydice. Singing and playing his lyre, he charms the King and Queen of Hades into permitting her to leave with him (although in some versions of the myth, by disobeying the injunction not to look back, he loses her again). This is strikingly reminiscent of Lyra and Will's journey to the world of the dead in search of Roger, where Lyra uses her own gift of the silver tongue to secure the passage of the dead past the warding Harpies and into the true death of dissolution. As discussed in Chapter Four, it is the telling of *true* stories which makes this possible; when she offers lies, the harpy No-Name screams 'Liar! Liar! Liar!' at her, the words echoing such that 'she seemed to be screaming Lyra's name, so that *Lyra* and *liar* were one and the same thing.'[32] Thus, Pullman's analogue for Orpheus' compelling and transformative artistry of song and music is the compelling and transformative artistry of telling stories – but stories which are nevertheless *true*. Orpheus – interestingly in view of the union between Will and Lyra – is also symbolic of the

29 Pullman, *The Amber Spyglass*, 432.
30 Mary Harris Russell, 'Eve, Again! Mother Eve!', in Millicent Lenz and Carole Scott (eds), *His Dark Materials Illuminated: Critical Essays on Philip Pullman's Trilogy* (Detroit, MI: Wayne State University Press, 2005), 212–22 (220–21).
31 Pullman, *The Subtle Knife*, 313.
32 Pullman, *The Amber Spyglass*, 308.

'sacred marriage', and conjoining of feminine and masculine principles. Furthermore, Jane Harrison's description of the religion ascribed to the teaching of Orpheus is as follows:

> The religion of Orpheus *is* religious in that it is the worship of the real mysteries of life, of potencies [*daimones*] rather than personal gods [*theoi*]; it is the worship of life itself in its supreme ecstasies of life and love.[33]

The similarities between this paradigm of religiosity and the materialist, humanistic but nevertheless vitalized Republic of Heaven described in Chapter Four are notable.

Lyra's name also evokes the Lyca of Blake's *Songs of Experience*. Lyca is the little girl who will herald the awakening of earth from sleep and the transformation of wild desert to mild garden. Lyca, according to Kathleen Raine, is also Earth, and Ahania – the consort and emanation of Urizen. She goes on to say:

> *The Book of Ahania* describes the outcast condition of Earth by a morality that regards the body as evil. . . . Earth cast out from Heaven becomes one of those Newtonian 'globes rolling through voidness,' a dark shadow circling the sky, more like the dead and sterile moon than the living and happy earth.[34]

Ahania is 'immortal' not in the sense of undying, but of the perpetually renewed, and constant generation. Again, the resemblances with Pullman's positive account of materiality and view of death as natural renewal are evident.

Another name for Lyra is, of course, Pantalaimon. As the name of her dæmon, it is the name of her soul. Again, there are a range of evocations here. In Greek, the derivation is from *panta* (all) and *eleimon* (merciful; compassionate). This is a common designator for the divine.[35] In Orthodox Christianity and Catholicism in particular, mercy is also commonly associated with Mary: Mother of God, Mother of Mercy. Mercy is closely allied theologically to grace, and like Mary in the Ave Maria, Pantalaimon in his settled form of a polecat is 'full of grace'.[36]

33 Jane Ellen Harrison, *Prolegomena to the Study of Greek Religion* (Princeton, NJ: Princeton University Press, 1991), 657.
34 Kathleen Raine, *Blake and Tradition*, vol. 1 (London: Taylor & Francis, 2002), 155.
35 It is also the name of an Orthodox Christian saint associated with healing.
36 Pullman, *The Amber Spyglass*, 527.

Pantalaimon is known most frequently and familiarly as Pan: this also brings with it a set of symbolisms. In Greek mythology Pan is a nature demigod, associated with woods and fields, sensuality and fertility, music and dancing. Pan came to be associated with nature itself, since the word also means 'all'. Given his part-goat form, and associations with both untrammelled sexuality and the wilderness, it is perhaps not surprising that Pan became identified with the Christian archetype of evil, Satan.[37] In the context of Pullman's reversals of certain Christian traditions and concepts, particularly the anti-worldly and anti-bodily strains, 'Pan' appropriately conjures up images of the natural, the material, the free and the sensual. Pan, the diminutive nickname, is the spirit of anarchy characterizing the younger Lyra: 'In many ways Lyra was a barbarian.'[38] Pantalaimon, the all-merciful, is the spirit of responsible compassion guiding the older Lyra at the close of the trilogy: if they had gone with Will and Kirjava, they would not have been able to build the Republic of Heaven: 'No one could, if they put themselves first', says Lyra.[39]

Lauren Shohet, seeing Lyra as figuring 'lyric/narrative/art', views Will as figuring 'human will/desire/agency' within the trilogy's symbolic field:

> 'Will' is similar to art in its negotiations between individual self-determination and the complex web of agency that enables it to act. . . . Will's surname, 'Parry,' suggests the ways the will must flexibly deflect and engage the challenges it meets.[40]

Will is also the bearer of the subtle knife. Subtle energy is an animating, etheric life force found within alternative metaphysics, often likened to the ancient concepts of *prana*, *chi* and *mana* in Ayurveda, traditional Chinese and Hawaiian medicines respectively; it is also associated with 'spirit' or *pneuma* in Jewish and Christian traditions. One sees in this a reference to the function of the knife in cutting windows between worlds. Will himself is also associated with the subtle in a different sense. The name of his dæmon, Kirjava, means 'multi-coloured' in Finnish. Settling into the form of a cat, her fur is described in lush terms, 'lustrous and rich', glinting with a thousand different shades:

---

37 See, for example, Toni Reed, *Demon-lovers and their Victims in British Fiction* (Lexington, KY: University Press of Kentucky, 1988), 23–24.
38 Pullman, *Northern Lights*, 35.
39 Pullman, *The Amber Spyglass*, 548.
40 Lauren Shohet, 'Reading Dark Materials', in Millicent Lenz and Carole Scott (eds), *His Dark Materials Illuminated: Critical Essays on Philip Pullman's Trilogy* (Detroit, MI: Wayne State University Press, 2005), 22–36 (26).

[I]nk black, shadow-grey, the blue of a deep lake under a noon sky, mist-lavender, moonlight-fog . . . To see the meaning of the word *subtlety* you had only to look at her fur.[41]

Shohet also points out that in Milton's *Paradise Lost*, it is for its subtlety that Satan chooses the form of a serpent.[42] This subtlety in Will is married to an insistence upon indetermination. As he ultimately declares to the angel Xaphania: 'Whatever I do, I will choose it, no one else.'[43]

All this points to a manner in which the symbolic valence of the name 'Will' sits in appropriate partnership with the symbolism of 'Eve, Mother Eve': for, theologically, the nature and understanding of human will are deeply imbricated in interpretations of Genesis 2–3. As has been seen, the second creation account in Genesis is traditionally understood as the 'Fall' of humanity into original sin; the perfect relation between God and humans was disrupted by a choice to disobey the will of God. In this manner, sin, death and suffering entered into the world. Furthermore, human will is itself contaminated. While free will remains, it is like weighted scales: there is a bias towards choosing the wrong. Augustine has this to say on the matter:

Human nature was certainly originally created blameless and without any fault; but the human nature by which each one of us is now born of Adam requires a physician, because it is not healthy. All the good things, which it has by its conception, life, senses, and mind, it has from God, its creator and maker. But the weakness which darkens and disables these good natural qualities, as a result of which that nature needs enlightenment and healing, did not come from the blameless maker but from original sin, which was committed by free will. . . . For all sinned, whether in Adam or in themselves, and have fallen short of the glory of God.[44]

Thus the free choice of humanity caused evil, sin and suffering to enter the world. This is theologically significant, because it justifies their existence. It has long been a theological conundrum: how do you reconcile the existence of evil and suffering in the world with the existence of God, who is both perfectly good and all-powerful? Paraphrasing Epicurus,

41 Pullman, *The Amber Spyglass*, 527.
42 Shohet, 'Reading Dark Materials', 26–27.
43 Pullman, *The Amber Spyglass*, 525.
44 Augustine, de natura and gratia iii,3-iv,4, in Alister E. McGrath (ed.), *The Christian Theology Reader* (Oxford: Wiley-Blackwell, 2006), 416.

David Hume puts the problem in this way: 'Is he willing to prevent evil, but not able? Then he is impotent. Is he able, but not willing? Then he is malevolent. Is he both able and willing? Whence then evil?'[45] Philosophers such as Alvin Plantinga appeal to the Free Will Defence in answer to this challenge. This rests on the argument that it is possible that certain 'good' states of being which do not per se include evil, nor require its existence, nevertheless must permit its existence in order for that same good state of being to be brought about. A world containing creatures who have moral freedom, and 'freely perform more good than evil actions', may be 'more valuable, all else being equal, than a world containing no free creatures at all.' To create creatures capable of freely choosing moral good, it is necessary that creatures be capable of freely choosing moral evil. To intervene and prevent immoral actions would contravene the very freedom at stake.[46]

Pullman adapts Genesis 3 for the church of Lyra's world, but maintains its primary contours. A key particularization is that innocence is figured by the mutability of dæmons, representing a state akin to childhood. The serpent asserts to the woman that eating the fruit of the tree in the midst of the garden will not, as God claims, cause death; rather, '. . . your eyes shall be opened, and your dæmons shall assume their true forms, and ye shall be as gods, knowing good and evil.'[47] There is an implication that dæmons, until the eating of the fruit, did not communicate with the man and the woman: 'And the eyes of them both were opened, and they saw the true form of their dæmons, and spoke with them.'[48] In 'knowing' their dæmons, they knew their difference from other creatures, and they knew good and evil. Thus, Lord Asriel tells Lyra, that is the point of origin for sin: the moment their dæmons became fixed.

Pullman's retelling of Genesis 3 lays a particular slant on the question of what 'knowing good and evil' actually entails. In traditional Christianity, it has been understood as sexual knowledge. Pullman's version by no means excludes this, indeed the reverse: awareness and shame of nakedness as a result of the 'sin' remain; the 'fixing' of dæmons is understood throughout the series to occur at puberty; and this is reinforced in *The Amber Spyglass* when Pantalaimon and Kirjava take their permanent shapes after the love exchange between Lyra and Will. However, a further dimension is made

45 David Hume, *Dialogues concerning Natural Religion and Other Writings*, ed. Dorothy Coleman (Cambridge: Cambridge University Press, 2007), 74.
46 Alvin Plantinga, *God, Freedom, and Evil* (Grand Rapids, MI: Eerdmans, 1977), 30.
47 Pullman, *Northern Lights*, 372.
48 Ibid.

explicit here through the consequence of speaking to and knowing their own dæmons, which equates to knowledge and consciousness of self.

Consciousness establishes identity, by allowing perception of the self as separate and different from everything else. According to John Locke:

> [A person] is a thinking intelligent being, that has reason and reflection, and can consider itself as itself, the same thinking thing, in different times and places; which it does only by that consciousness which is inseparable from thinking, and, as it seems to me, essential to it: it being impossible for any one to perceive without *perceiving* that he does perceive.[49]

Therefore, 'knowledge of good and evil' fundamentally is knowledge of self: this leads to self-consciousness in a dual sense, both in terms of awareness of self as self, but also in consequence as a self capable of shame. Thus, alongside the emergence of self-awareness is the development of moral awareness and responsibility, and hence agency. In traditional Christian theology, the human endeavour should be to act in ways in accordance with the will of God. The divine will is sovereign (and incidentally leads to considerable debate regarding the interplay between divine will as eternal and immutable and human will as free). Writers such as Feuerbach insisted that this kind of dynamic disempowered the human, projecting all that was great onto an illusory divine and leaving humanity degraded. By contrast, an agnostic or atheist humanism posits human action and choice in a world which is not underpinned, ordered or, as some might say, overshadowed by a divine will. In light of this, human will becomes fully autonomous – autonomous, that is, within the conditions and limitations of material and communal existence and relations. Granted the caveat that human will differs from the theological positing of a divine will within monotheistic religions, being neither unconditioned nor immutable, human will still in this scenario takes on a more fundamental role. There is no divine 'thy will' to be done. In this respect, the significance of human will is elevated, at least within its own framework of existence. Thus, human will occupies a central position within humanist philosophies. In this respect, the naming of 'Will' and his emphasis on choice offers us a symbol of the humanist human, the citizen of the Republic of Heaven.

The *subtlety* of Will/will is important here. In terms of making judgements, subtlety is the capacity for discernment; it is the ability to make fine distinctions and operate through skill rather than force. Discernment

---

49 John Locke, *An Essay Concerning Human Understanding* (Stilwell, KS: Digireads. com Publishing, 2008), 204.

is a central theological category within Christian and Jewish traditions, as exemplified in the following passages: 'And this is my prayer: that your love may abound more and more in knowledge and depth of insight, so that you may be able to discern what is best' (Phil. 9.10); 'So give your servant a discerning heart to govern your people and to distinguish between right and wrong' (1 Kgs 3.9). Will's subtlety resides also in his preference for acting quietly, and not drawing attention to himself: 'He could make himself inconspicuous; it was his greatest talent.'[50] This is in sharp distinction to that other central protagonist of the humanist rebellion, Lord Asriel: he is flamboyant, ambitious to a fault, and willing to commit the murder of a child in pursuit of his perceived 'higher good'.

Mary's role is to act the serpent, as disclosed to her by the angel Xaphania. This is another example of Pullman's revaluation of Christian mythologies. On the world of the mulefa, they have their own mythology regarding the acquisition of the knowledge of good and evil. In this, a snake instructed a creature with no name to place her foot through the hole in a seed-pod; this enabled oil, and thus sraf/Dust, to be absorbed into her body. Then 'they discovered that they knew who they were, they knew they were mulefa and not grazers. They gave each other names.'[51] The parallels are plainly drawn; the female identity of the first creature to initiate the process is emphasized through repetition of the feminine pronoun, as the mulefa Atal tells the story to Mary:

[A]s she played she –
She?
She, yes.[52]

It is a snake whose comments induce the female creature to act, promising that wisdom will ensue. There follows naming, of each other and of 'all the creatures and plants',[53] in recognition that their species is different, having acquired the sraf, and thus 'memory and wakefulness'.[54]

There are also what appear to be deliberate inverse parallels to the Genesis story. Mary questions Atal: 'The snake spoke to her?' Atal responds impatiently: 'No! no! It is a make-like.'[55] Thus, Pullman inserts an ironic dig at those who take mythologically transmitted 'truths' as

50 Pullman, *The Amber Spyglass*, 101.
51 Ibid., 237.
52 Ibid., 236.
53 Ibid., 237.
54 Ibid., 236.
55 Ibid.

strictly literal in point of historical fact. Snakes themselves are considered positively on the world of the mulefa. Further, the culmination of the mulefa's mythological story is a symbiotic and harmonious relationship between the animal, mineral and vegetable worlds: riding on wheels, the mulefa break down the seed-pods, which enables more seed-pod trees to grow, which generates the oil imbued with sraf. This is in stark contrast to the Genesis story, which ends with violent rupture between all three domains. God pronounces enmity between the serpent and the woman, asymmetry between the woman and the man (who will rule over her), and a relationship of grim toil between the man and the earth. A further conspicuous contrast is the absence in the mulefa's story of either a deity or a prohibition: it is a wholly naturalistic mythology.

Mary's role as serpent is also interesting because of Pullman's choice of name for her. In the Christian biblical tradition, there are four Marys of note. Miriam – the equivalent name – is the first female prophet (Exod. 15.20). Mary of Bethany is praised by Jesus (in contradistinction to her sister Martha) for listening to his words rather than being distracted by household tasks (Lk. 10.38-42). The Virgin Mary is the mother of Jesus. And Mary Magdalene is a prominent disciple, held by dissident tradition to have been Jesus' wife, and by mainstream tradition to have been a former prostitute (neither case is attested in the New Testament texts). Thus, the name 'Mary' represents multiple central female identities in Christianity. Mary Malone in Pullman's text is one who has consciously rejected the Christian tradition. From being a nun, she moves to the position of perceiving Christianity as a 'very powerful and convincing mistake.'[56]

So, Mary Malone represents post-Christianity. There is an interesting irony here. In *His Dark Materials*, Lyra is quite explicitly pronounced to be Eve – 'again'. However, in Christian tradition, it is Mary the Mother of Jesus who is the new Eve. The church father Irenaeus wrote in the second century:

> And thus also it was that the knot of Eve's disobedience was loosed by the obedience of Mary. For what the virgin Eve had bound fast through unbelief, this did the virgin Mary set free through faith.[57]

This theme was taken up in *Lumen Gentium*, one of the principal documents of the Second Vatican Council, where we find:

---

56 Ibid., 464.
57 Irenaeus, *Against Heresies*, 3.22.

By her belief and obedience, not knowing man but overshadowed by the Holy Spirit, as the new Eve she brought forth on earth the very Son of the Father, showing an undefiled faith, not in the word of the ancient serpent, but in that of God's messenger.[58]

Pullman's Mary, instead of rejecting the word of the serpent, is asked to speak the words of the serpent. In doing so, she does not herself become the 'new Eve', but sets Lyra's steps on the path to doing so.

What does acting the part of the serpent entail? One of the ghosts emerging from the land of the dead, an old woman, is speaking to Mary of the need to tell the harpies true stories. Then she is gone, and Mary suddenly remembers her conversation with Xaphania; dreamlike, it dissolves and is gone: 'All that was left was the sweetness of that feeling, and the injunction to *tell them stories*.'[59] This is exactly what Mary does. She tells Will and Lyra of the experiences which led her to renounce her vows as a nun. Conversing with an attractive man at a conference, the taste of marzipan reminds her of an encounter with a boy as a young girl, who had given her marzipan to eat: '. . . and I fell in love with him just for that, for the gentle way he touched my lips with the marzipan.'[60] The memory inspires her decision to open herself to such experiences again and leave her order.

Mary's words have a profound effect on Lyra, who feels unaccountably both excited and frightened by the sensations provoked. 'She felt as if she had been handed the key to a great house she hadn't known was there.'[61] She is wakened to an awareness of sexual desire and love. This precipitates the pivotal scene with Will:

Then Lyra took one of those little red fruits. With a fast-beating heart, she turned to him and said, 'Will . . .'

And she lifted the fruit gently to his mouth. . . . 'I love you, Will, I love you –'

The word *love* set his nerves ablaze. All his body thrilled with it . . .[62]

The intensity of their love acts as a magnet for Dust. By the serendipity

---

58 'Dogmatic Constitution on the Church – Lumen Gentium', chap. 8. Online: http://www.vatican.va/archive/hist_councils/ii_vatican_council/documents/vat-ii_const_19641121_lumen-gentium_en.html

59 Pullman, *The Amber Spyglass*, 456.

60 Ibid., 467.

61 Ibid., 468.

62 Ibid., 492.

of timing and placing, they created a powerful attractive force which reversed the flow of Dust. This had been flooding out of the universe with the creation of the abyss, but was now cascading back: 'and these children-no-longer-children, saturated with love, were the cause of it all.'[63] As Russell says, Mary Malone might be deemed a 'serpent mother' to Lyra, 'the initiator into knowledge – rational knowledge and sensual knowledge.'[64]

Thus Pullman's narrative rejects the interpretation of Genesis 3 in the Church of Lyra's world: namely, that the fixing of the dæmon (representing both self-knowledge and sexuality) is a negative event. Concomitantly, the onset of Dust in the movement from innocence to experience is likewise to be celebrated, and not feared and condemned in the way of the Church. The result is the fulfilment of humanity. In traditional theological anthropology, humanity is in the image of God (Gen. 1.27) – albeit, since the 'Fall', in a blurred and somewhat defaced way. Pullman revalues this too. Mary Malone is watching Lyra and Will returning, holding hands, following their love interlude:

> There was no need for the [spy]glass; she knew what she would see; they would seem to be made of living gold. They would seem the true image of what human beings always could be, once they had come into their inheritance.[65]

The 'true image' of the human is located in the fulfilment of humanity's own potential. Again, this recalls Feuerbach's thesis that human alienation is generated in the relinquishing to God of humanity's own self: 'Man propels his own nature from himself, he throws himself outward.' However, this is a moment in a dialectic, following which '[man] receives the rejected nature into his heart again.'[66] Similarly, Pullman is seeing humanity, represented by Will and Lyra, come of age.

Dust, as was seen in Chapter Four, is the wellspring of love, wisdom, rationality and compassion. These are all traditionally qualities associated with what it means to be in the 'image of God', now decisively reclaimed in Pullman's narrative as what it means to be in the image of the 'true human'. Pullman's story does not reserve these qualities for the human,

63 Ibid., 497.
64 Russell, 'Eve, Again! Mother Eve!', 217.
65 Pullman, *The Amber Spyglass*, 497.
66 Ludwig Feuerbach, *The Essence of Christianity*, trans. Marian Evans (New York, NY: Calvin Blanchard, 1855), 54.

of course: his universe is richly populated with beings who are imbued with Dust. One particularly significant figure is the angel Xaphania, who is associated by a number of commentators, including Pinsent and Lenz, with the Wisdom figure of Judaism and Christianity.[67] Xaphania is the leader of the rebel angels and is probably to be identified with the female angel who was banished by the Authority, for she was 'wiser than he was, and she found out the truth':[68] i.e. that the Authority is not in fact God but simply the first angel.

Divine Wisdom – *sophia* in the Greek, *hochmah* in the Hebrew – is personified as a feminine figure in the Jewish and later Christian traditions (see, for example, Proverbs 1–9, and apocryphal texts such as the Wisdom of Solomon and Sirach). *Sophia* is identified with the Holy Spirit in the New Testament (as in the Prologue of John). *Sophia* can also be identified with the *Logos* – the Word of God.[69] The *sophia* traditions continued to be of importance in Gnostic circles and in the Eastern churches, and have been enthusiastically embraced by feminist theologians in recent decades as a basis for refiguring patriarchal imagery and structures.[70] The Gnostics represent a strand of early Christian development which came to be deemed heretical, some of whose writings survive in non-canonical form (notably in the Nag Hammadi Library, discovered in Egypt in 1945 and containing over 50 texts). Gnostic writings do not form a cohesive whole, but point to the existence of a range of alternative readings and theologies, a number of which are well known for forefronting the feminine (for example, 'The Thunder, Perfect Mind'; 'The Sophia of Jesus Christ').

67 Pat Pinsent, 'Unexpected Allies? Pullman and the Feminist Theologies', in Millicent Lenz and Carole Scott (eds), *His Dark Materials Illuminated: Critical Essays on Philip Pullman's Trilogy* (Detroit, MI: Wayne State University Press, 2005), 199–211; Lenz and Hunt, *Alternative Worlds in Fantasy Fiction*, 122–69.
68 Pullman, *The Amber Spyglass*, 34.
69 As Ruether says: 'The roots of the Logos concept in the Wisdom tradition are evident at many points. Paul says, "We are preaching a crucified Christ . . . who is . . . the Wisdom of God"' (1 Cor. 1:23-24). Several of the Christological hymns substitute the word Logos for the word Sophia. Theologically, Logos plays the same cosmological roles as Sophia as ground of creation, revealer of the mind of God, and reconciler of humanity to God' (Rosemary Radford Ruether, *Sexism and God-talk: Toward a Feminist Theology* [Boston, MA: Beacon Press, 1983], 54).
70 Feminist theologians such as Elizabeth Schüssler Fiorenza and Elizabeth A. Johnson take the divine *Sophia* as a primary means of revisioning the Christian God in ways more hospitable to the feminine. See Elisabeth Schüssler Fiorenza, *Jesus: Miriam's Child, Sophia's Prophet* (London and New York, NY: Continuum, 1995) and Elizabeth A. Johnson, *She Who Is: The Mystery of God in Feminist Theological Discourse* (New York, NY: Crossroad, 1992).

Xaphania speaks of wisdom in terms reminiscent of these alternative traditions. As the witch Serafina recounts to Mary Malone, after meeting her:

> 'She told me many things . . . She said that all the history of human life has been a struggle between wisdom and stupidity. She and the rebel angels, the followers of wisdom, have always tried to open minds; the Authority and his churches have always tried to keep them closed . . . And for most of that time wisdom has had to work in secret, whispering her words, moving like a spy through the humble places of the world while the courts and palaces are occupied by her enemies.'[71]

Pullman is not presenting Xaphania as a goddess, but she is probably the one who most embodies the divine qualities of wisdom, compassion, grace and knowledge in *His Dark Materials*. It is significant that she is a feminine figure, and equally so that she, and the followers of wisdom, are presented as marginal and suppressed voices. Pullman's account here evokes the history of alternative theological traditions – which also often gave more prominent roles to women and feminine imagery – that were rejected as heretical in the development of the Church.

As Russell's analysis of 'Pullman's Eve Variations' points out, citing Elaine Pagel's seminal work in this area,[72] the presentation of Lyra in *His Dark Materials* resonates with alternative accounts of Eve also to be found in certain Gnostic traditions.[73] In some accounts, Eve is associated with a female spiritual principle, the serpent, and the instruction in or seeking of knowledge. Russell summarizes:

> While Eve's knowledge seeking is eventually conflated with Hesiod's negative vision of Pandora in the works of Origen and Tertullian and bolstered by the pseudo-Pauline epistles, these early Christian and Hebrew traditions valued an Eve who, 'mother of us all' in some way, sought knowledge like the serpent.[74]

Lyra is presented at the outset as possessed of both an insatiable curiosity

---

71 Pullman, *The Amber Spyglass*, 506.
72 See, for example, Elaine H. Pagels, *Adam, Eve, and the Serpent* (New York, NY: Vintage Books, 1989); Elaine H. Pagels, *The Gnostic Gospels* (New York, NY: Vintage Books, 1989); Elaine H. Pagels, *The Origin of Satan* (New York, NY: Vintage Books, 1996).
73 Russell, 'Eve, Again! Mother Eve!'.
74 Ibid., 214.

and a certain lack of respect for boundaries. The childlike quest for knowledge which leads her to hide in the Retiring Room or explore rooftops and vaults gives way to a genuine interest in experimental theology: in due course, 'she would know more about Dust than anyone in the world.'[75] That Lyra is the keeper of the alethiometer is in itself a potent symbol of her status as truth-seeker.

Hence, Pullman's rewriting of Genesis 2–3 as a 'fortunate fall' comes down heavily on the side of promoting human freedom, knowledge and potentiality for both male and female. He does not, however, suggest that human action should be unlimited, but rather tempered by qualities such as compassion, wisdom and duty. Asriel stands as a paramount symbol in this respect. Asriel, like Milton's Satan in *Paradise Lost*, is a Prometheus figure. (Asriel's name is also reminiscent both of Milton's rebel angel Ariel, and of Azrael, mythologically the angel of death.) According to Greek legend, Prometheus hubristically stole fire from Zeus for mortal benefit; he was punished by being bound to a rock and having his liver eaten by an eagle, only for it to regenerate for the following day's aquiline delectation. The boundaries transgressed by Asriel were not divine in origin, but offences against the moral foundations of society (through child murder), and against the very integrity of the universe. The leaking of Dust is one manifestation of the latter, but so also is the ecological catastrophe precipitated by Asriel's actions in tearing the passage to another world, thereby ripping a 'great opening out of his own world':[76] as noted in Chapter Four, looking down at the 'melting ice-cap, the flooded lowland forests, the swollen sea', the witch Serafina Pekkala was sick to her heart.[77] The ecologically balanced world of the mulefa is similarly presented as suffering damaging imbalances. These situations are paralleled with real-world global warming: as Will says to Lyra: '. . . people have been interfering with the atmosphere by putting chemicals in it and the weather's going out of control.'[78] Asriel, again like Milton's Satan, therefore functions ambivalently: on the one hand, as leader of the rebel forces he is a sympathetic figure; on the other, as one ruthlessly indifferent to consequences to others in pursuit of his ends, he is a disturbing one. His sacrificial death, cast down into the abyss with Mrs Coulter is, once more, reminiscent of the fate of Satan both in Milton and Revelation 12.

The concern with appropriate limitation can also be seen if we turn to

75 Pullman, *Northern Lights*, 218.
76 Pullman, *The Amber Spyglass*, 523.
77 Ibid., 39.
78 Pullman, *The Subtle Knife*, 322.

consider the seeking and acquisition of knowledge. As has been argued, both here and in Chapter Four, this is positively valued in Pullman's world. However, in this respect a note of caution is sounded regarding the need to respect boundaries and use knowledge wisely. The subtle knife – 'æsahættr', the 'god destroyer' – is a primary example of this. Made 300 years previously by the Guild of Torre degli Angeli, the armoured bear Iorek recognizes its capacity for unlimited harm. The intentions of a tool are what it does; as Iorek points out to Will, he is unable to know everything that the knife does, and therefore follows not only his own intentions but those of the knife without meaning to do so.[79] It transpires, as Will's dæmon Kirjava tells him and Lyra, that an unknown intention of the knife is to cut into the 'emptiness outside', the same emptiness as that of the abyss created by the bomb, into which Dust is pouring. Nobody knew: 'the edge was too fine to see.' Not all the windows between worlds had been closed; this was the cause of the heightened leakage of Dust out of the worlds and into nothingness over the preceding three centuries. Furthermore, the act of cutting a window allows a Spectre to float out from the abyss and enter the world.[80] The story of the subtle knife is, then, a cautionary tale about the dangers in utilizing scientific and technical knowledge without full awareness of what the consequences might be, and a warning that the consequences might be both wholly unlooked for and catastrophically dangerous. Pullman's advocacy of knowledge is balanced with an advocacy of wisdom. Again, one returns to the significance of discernment.

The final limitation I shall allude to is that of ethical action. The ethical system promoted in *His Dark Materials* respects both rights and duties. Lyra tells Pan as she sits in the Botanic Gardens at the conclusion of the series:

> We have to be all those difficult things like cheerful and kind and curious and brave and patient, and we've got to study and think, and work hard, all of us, in all our different worlds . . .[81]

The ethical impetus of the Republic of Heaven is actually then rather similar to traditional values. Gooderham sees in this a major failing of the new order; for little has changed. Instead, we have an order 'powered by young people who, after the first blush of sexual experience, settle for

---

79 Ibid., 190–91.
80 Pullman, *The Amber Spyglass*, 512–15.
81 Ibid., 548.

the realism of their mentor's single, sublimated, socially responsible and hardworking way of life.'[82] What is more, he points out that the 'sudden, absolute and emotionally crucifying'[83] separation of Lyra and Will only serves to highlight alienation: 'Their situations are certainly very far from the promise of libidinal social transformation implied by the *felix culpa* as type and model for all personal relationships.'[84] In this respect, the limitations imposed by this particular manifestation of an ethic of duty may actually narrow the potential spaciousness of the horizons glimpsed at in the notion of the Republic of Heaven.

All told, however, it can be said that human knowledge, responsibility and potentiality are valorized in *His Dark Materials*. The central signifi-cance of female imagery and symbols also sets Pullman's vision counter to traditional patriarchal and hierarchical systems and further emphasizes the democratic nature of the Republic of Heaven. The male/female pairings of human and dæmon, and of Will and Lyra, point to a gender model of partnership, harmony and balance – although as Gooderham has pointed out, this happy state may in fact be undermined by the separation of Will and Lyra at the conclusion of the series. The presentation of such limita-tions in *His Dark Materials* means that, notwithstanding his high view of humanity and dismissal of the divine, humans, male and female, cannot be said to have become 'as gods'. Recognition of boundaries is, indeed, an important theme: in *His Dark Materials*, human striving and achievement neither can nor should be untrammelled.

82 David Gooderham, 'Fantasizing It as It Is: Religious Language in Philip Pullman's Trilogy, His Dark Materials', *Children's Literature* 31, no. 1 (2003): 155–75 (172).
83 Ibid., 169.
84 Ibid.

THE GOOD AND THE MONSTROUS

BUFFY THE VAMPIRE SLAYER: 'FROM BENEATH YOU, IT DEVOURS'

As ONE WOULD ANTICIPATE, monsters and heroes abound in *Buffy the Vampire Slayer*. Conceptually speaking, the good and the monstrous are inextricably interlinked, with the one securing the identity of the other. Both, of course, are significant features in religious and spiritual landscapes and may be variously understood in terms of both nature and ground. Determining which is which is a re-iterative task, a systematization and classification which is never done with. The monstrous represents that which is ejected, feared, reviled: it is a screen upon which cultural fears are projected, made animate and particular in the fantastic worlds of fictions. Monstrosity can thus be seen to be culturally specific. The monstrous may be human in form – an abyssal moment explored in a range of literary and visual genres – or it may emerge from the realms of supernatural horror, science fiction and fantasy in a dizzying array of shapes and natures. Despite this diversity, it can be argued that the monstrous, howsoever con-stituted, in some way serves to 'reflect and critique human existence.'[1]

Monsters mark out moral and metaphysical contours of being human, but also topographical ones:

---

1   Niall Scott (ed.), *Monsters and the Monstrous: Myths and Metaphors of Enduring Evil* (Amsterdam: Rodopi, 2007), 1.

From classical times onward, the monster inhabited geographical extremities, as travellers' tales furnished the occidental imagination with visions of strange beasts whose epiphany into the ordered certainties of the known social and natural order signalled the radical reconceptualizations occasioned by new conquests and territories.[2]

Monstrosity can thus also be deeply political, representing spatial and genealogical accounts of difference which fund xenophobic, oppressive, exclusionary or even genocidal discourses. The monster may be an intra-societal pathologized other too, whereby 'women, racial and sexual minorities, political radicals or those with physical or mental impairments' are deemed less than human, or inhuman.[3] Monstrosity is also linked to fear of miscegenation, contamination and assimilation: it projects fear of the loss of identity, or a debasement of identity through pollution.

Monsters both reinforce established cultural classifications and confound them by prowling the boundaries. The monstrous can transmute into the good and vice versa, exposing the fragility of such borders, and the interpenetration between the two. In what follows, I examine the borders of the monstrous in relation not only to the figure of the vampire in *Buffy*, but also to the figure of the Vampire Slayer. It is argued that inasmuch as the vampire in *Buffy* can be deemed an inassimilable other, it is humanity's refusal and externalization of its own 'shadow' that is represented. The vampire is also a potent figure of both transgressive desire and of alienation. *Buffy the Vampire Slayer* further problematizes the good/monstrous divide through the presence of ostensible hybrids such as ensouled vampires – Angel and Spike – which highlights the complex, shifting and multiple nature of identity. Ultimately this points towards an identity model based on existential choice rather than essentialism, but one which grounds choice in bodily and social particularity. This is within a universe where religious absolutes are lacking, as discussed in Chapter Six.

There may be no religious absolutes, but there remain powers, for both good and evil. There is the First Evil, Buffy's greatest adversary, discussed in more detail towards the end of the chapter. There are gods – Glory is one, but her godhood is not equivalent to the divinity expressed in monotheistic religions. She is, besides, a being of evil. There are demons, who came before humans. Giles explains this to Buffy in 'The Harvest':

---

2   Elaine L. Graham, *Representations of the Post/human: Monsters, Aliens and Others in Popular Culture* (Manchester: Manchester University Press, 2002), 53.
3   Ibid., 53.

This world is older than any of you know. Contrary to popular mythology, it did not begin as a paradise. For untold eons demons walked the Earth. They made it their home, their . . . their Hell. But in time they lost their purchase on this reality. The way was made for mortal animals, for man. All that remains of the old ones are vestiges, certain magicks, certain creatures.

In the Buffyverse, the vampire is one of those remnants from the time of the demonic Old Ones: it is formed from the miscegenation of demon and human, infusing the human body with demonic spirit through the mixing of bloods. The vampire is located wholly outside of religious mythologies. As Erickson puts it, the vampires on *Buffy* are 'not participants in a cosmic war, not "arrows in the side of Christ," not chosen or damned, they just *are*.'[4]

There are also benevolent powers and guides. Buffy meets her spirit guide in the 'Intervention' episode, and learns of the ancient female Guardians in 'End of Days'. The spin-off series *Angel* introduces the mysterious 'Powers That Be', who resisted the demonic Old Ones, left the earth, but continued to be watchful ('Shiny Happy People'). Even these are ambivalent in certain respects: in *Angel*, 'Deep Down', Fred refers to them as the 'Powers that Screw You'. There is also the naturalistic power of the universe itself. Willow, following her turn to and return from the dark side, is rehabilitating in the care of Giles. She and he have the following conversation about power ('Lessons'):

> *Willow*: It's all connected. The root system, the molecules . . . the energy. Everything's connected . . .
>
> *Giles*: Everything's connected. You're connected to a great power whether you feel it or not.
>
> *Willow*: Well you should just take it from me.
>
> *Giles*: This isn't a hobby or an addiction. It's inside you now. You're responsible for it.

Even here, the 'great power' is not explicated, but the strong inference is that it emanates from cosmic interconnections. Willow is presented in the series as a Wiccan, and is undoubtedly a magic practitioner – although, as mentioned in Chapter Six, the lack of a religious framework for her practice makes her identity as a Wiccan less clear.

---

4   Greg Erickson, '"Religion Freaky" or a "Bunch of Men Who Died?" The (A)theology of *Buffy*', *Slayage: The Online International Journal of Buffy Studies* 4, nos 1–2 (2004). Online: http://www.slayageonline.com/Numbers/slayage13_14.htm

Within this panoply of forces and powers, we have the vampire. It could be argued that, as its uncanny double, the 'vampire' interrogates the whole conception of the 'human' at a time of uncertainty about humanity's nature, limits and inherent worth. This returns us to theology; in a religiously constituted universe, humanity has a place, a purpose, an identity. Post-Enlightenment times in the West also famously enthroned the human subject – only to be later deconstructed as actually signifying the (male) 'man of reason',[5] and further to this, the (white) man of reason. As Winnubst argues, the vampire trope 'unravels how whiteness, maleness, and heterosexuality feed on the same set of disavowals – of the body, of the Other, of fluidity, of dependency itself.'[6]

The decentering and fragmentation of the human subject is one of the key features typically identified as 'postmodern'; at the same time, humanity's centrality has also been displaced by environmentalist critiques of anthropocentricism. The deep ecology movement, for example, radically diminishes the importance and significance of the human species by locating it simply as an element in the ecosphere as whole. The large-scale atrocities committed by human beings in the twentieth and twenty-first centuries render problematic any easy equation of the 'human' with the 'morally conscious'. Therefore, as William Patrick Day says, 'we can no longer be sure about the line between the human and monster.'[7] The 'vamp face', appearing just as a vampire is about to feed, is a reminder to the viewer both of the boundary between human and vampire and that the vampire serves as a monstrous double of the human.

Vampiric bodies are liminal, betwixt and between two terms of oppositions by which human culture is organized: dead/not-dead; human/not-human; civilized/not-civilized; subject/not-subject. To collapse these oppositions is to disintegrate the means by which cultures make sense of the world. Vampires are the ultimate death-in-life and life-in-death. As such, the vampiric ought to be a figure of ultimate abjection. According to Julia Kristeva, the abject is 'death infecting life.'[8] It is associated with '[t]he repugnance, the retching that thrusts me to the side and turns me away

---

5   Genevieve Lloyd, *The Man of Reason: 'Male' and 'Female' in Western Philosophy* (London: Routledge, 1993).
6   Shannon Winnubst, 'Vampires, Anxieties and Dreams: Race and Sex in the Contemporary United States', *Hypatia* 18, no. 3 (2003): 1–20 (1).
7   William Patrick Day, *Vampire Legends in Contemporary American Culture* (Lexington, KY: University Press of Kentucky, 2002), 6.
8   Julia Kristeva, *Powers of Horror*, trans. Leon S. Roudiez (New York, NY: Columbia University Press, 1982), 4.

from defilement, sewage, and muck';[9] it is 'something rejected from which one does not part.'[10] The corpse is the primary example of the abject, confronting us with the trauma of our own mortality and showing us what is 'permanently thrust aside in order to live.'[11] The abject marks a border of separation in identity constructions which remains always threatened – not only by death, but by what is 'double, fuzzy, heterogeneous, animal, metamorphosed.'[12] The vampire, as living projection of human death, as the metamorphosed, doubled and animalized human, evokes the abject. This is the more so because the vampire brings with it the threat and fear of identity-effacement. Kristeva comments that abjection is experienced 'only if an Other has settled in place and stead of what will be "me"'; it is an Other that can be neither incorporated nor identified with.[13] The vampire, with its power of 'turning', threatens not only death but metamorphosis into an Other who is not-me.

However, if the vampire is supposed to elicit feelings of fear, disgust or loathing, this does not seem borne out in the general reported experience of watching *Buffy the Vampire Slayer* – at least with respect to the vampire itself; demons such as the 'The Gentlemen' in the 'Hush' episode might be deemed far more unsettling. I suggest this is for two reasons: the first is that 'laughter palliates the abject condition.'[14] Kristeva says:

> The worlds of illusions, now dead and buried, have given way to our dreams and deliriums, if not to politics or science – the religions of modern times. Lacking illusions, lacking shelter, today's universe is divided between boredom . . . or (when the spark of the symbolic is maintained and the desire to speak explodes) abjection and piercing laughter.[15]

Thus, in a godless postmodernity, the subject is shelterless. On the one hand lies enervation, on the other, desire may explode into speech: facing abjection, into laughter. The source of this is what Freud glimpsed – the unconscious, 'repressed, suppressed pleasure, be it sex or death.'[16] In this way, the comedic may render the abject bearable. Or, it may subvert the

9   Ibid., 2.
10   Ibid., 4.
11   Ibid., 3.
12   Ibid., 207.
13   Ibid., 20.
14   John Limon, *Stand-up Comedy in Theory, or, Abjection in America* (Durham, NC: Duke University Press, 2000), 74.
15   Kristeva, *Powers of Horror*, 133.
16   Ibid., 206.

experience of abjection precisely by rendering laughable the possibility of the boundary breaches with which the subject is faced. In this respect, comedy defuses horror, or refuses horror. The self-parodying nature, wit and amusing irony of *Buffy* forestall it acting as a vehicle for abjection for the viewer.

So that is the first reason why the vampires in *Buffy* may not fully offer a confrontation with the abject. A second reason may lie in the changing manner in which the contemporary vampiric symbolic is constructed. Put bluntly, vampires are hot. Vampire symbols have long been associated with the sexual, but current popular vampires are actively promoted and adulated as sexual icons. From Anne Rice's suave vampire Lestat, to sparkly Edward in *Twilight*, to the popular television show *True Blood*: the vampire is a sex object. More: the vampire is now a figure of romance, not only as in the high romantic dark and brooding tradition, but as the male or female protagonist of love stories. The same trend is very evident in the genre publishing industry, with a rapidly developing sub-genre of 'vampire' chick-lit. One publisher's 'Undead' series includes titles such as: *Undead and Unwed* ('Betsy Taylor finds out that not only is she Queen of the Vampires, she's been buried in cheap shoes. The horror!');[17] *Tall, Dark and Dead* ('Carnet's got her hands full running a bookstore. She doesn't need a vampire lover, too. Or does she?').[18]

Love, sex and death are clearly interlinked in the Buffyverse. In 'Fool for Love', Spike points out to Buffy that 'Every Slayer has a death wish – even you', and goes on to say that when that desire overtakes her, there he will be: he will 'slip in'. As Wilcox comments, this 'unquestionably joins visions of sex and death.'[19] So, too, do Buffy's interactions with Angel and Riley. She tells the former that 'When I kiss you, I want to die' ('Reptile Boy'), and the latter 'When I kiss you, it'll make the sun go down' ('Hush').

The intertwining of love, sex and death is especially evident in that necrophilia is part of the sexual texture of *Buffy the Vampire Slayer*. The necrophiliac aspects, however, pass almost unnoticed: Buffy's vampire lovers Angel and Spike make such very lively cadavers. When Buffy finally consummates her relationship with Angel, it seems like a natural, desirable culmination which is tragically doomed because of the nature

17 MaryJanice Davidson, *Undead and Unwed* (New York, NY: Berkley Books, 2004).
18 Tate Hallaway, *Tall, Dark and Dead* (New York, NY: Berkley Books, 2006).
19 Rhonda Wilcox, '"Every Night I Save You": Buffy, Spike, Sex, and Redemption', in Rhonda Wilcox, *Why Buffy Matters: The Art of Buffy the Vampire Slayer* (London: I. B. Tauris, 2005), 79–89 (83).

of the gypsy curse that restored his soul: if Angel experiences a moment of true happiness, he will lose it again. As Spaise points out, so natural does the sexual encounter between Buffy and Angel appear, 'that she was technically making love with a corpse was overlooked entirely by the audience.'[20] Vampire lovers, of course, breach the normal boundaries of necrophiliac categorization. They are dead, but not dead: they are the nullification of death (they are un-dead), but also its confirmation (they are un-alive). Day argues that the vampire has now become just one more image of sexuality in a society increasingly open to all forms of sexual representation.[21] He goes on to ask:

> What does the vampire offer us? In transcending death, time and space, un-bound by the laws of God, nature or society, the vampire is a figure of freedom and the gratification of all desire, the ultimate affirmation of the individual and, in one line of contemporary stories, an image of the true human.[22]

Day is thinking here of vampires such as Anne Rice's Louis and Lestat, and Yarbro's Saint-Germain. Such vampires represent the 'true human' exactly in their existential problematic, as outsiders seeking to come to terms with a divided self struggling for self-acceptance and self-expression. This variety of vampire protagonist is a figure 'not only of sexual freedom but of transcendent individuality', embodying 'aspirations to psychological and spiritual freedom', which are also the basis of various self-help movements and New Age religions offering alternatives to normative Christian traditions. In accepting our 'inner vampire', dualities such as sacred/profane, life/death and good/evil are unified and the self is integrated. These 'hero vampires' represent dreams not only of freedom, but also of belonging, of community, and of love.[23]

Ironically, it is partly through the experience of alienation that vampires of this kind become the authentically human. The alienation in question speaks to all manner of estrangements. Rice has this to say of her famous *Interview with the Vampire*:

> [It] is about the near despair of an alienated being who searches the world for some hope that his existence can have meaning. His vampire nature is

20 Terry L. Spaise, 'Necrophilia and SM: The Deviant Side of *Buffy the Vampire Slayer*', *Journal of Popular Culture* 38, no. 4 (May 2005): 744–62 (744).
21 Day, *Vampire Legends in Contemporary American Culture*, 5.
22 Ibid., 6.
23 Ibid., 34.

clearly a metaphor for human consciousness or moral awareness. . . . It is an expression of grief for a lost religious heritage . . . [M]any of the young 'Goth' readers who write to me are hungering for transcendence. They gravitate to these books because they find their environment sterile, secular, and materialistic and to a large extent unsatisfying.[24]

The estrangement within the self is marked by the struggle to deal with monstrosity, which is featured in the presentation of characters such as Angel and Oz, who feel guilt and self-loathing for their actions as vampire and werewolf respectively, and seek to manage their conditions through ethical commitments. As Callander puts this:

> To a large extent, Angel and Oz are marked as more human than human, for their angst isn't concealed or repressed, but exquisitely conscious. Consequently, we are able to see very clearly just how their moral crises direct their behaviour; in this, Whedon presents Angel and Oz as, in many ways, more admirable than most of his human characters.[25]

The latter represents an alternative, heroic account of the vampire.

Another irony of the vampiric body is its bodily integrity. It is supposed to be the hero's body which represents the impermeable ideal. Again, with reference to Kristeva's theory of abjection, the infant conceptualizes a secure boundary between inside and outside as part of the development of awareness of individuality; reminders that this boundary is *not* secure, but permeable and leaky, are sources of horror (such as, for example, blood and bodily wastes).[26] The vampiric body in *Buffy* is not, in fact, wholly 'closed'; vampires bleed; but they do not breathe (see 'Prophecy Girl') and are not subject to the normal biological processes of mortal existence; wounds reseal themselves. Abrogation of the vampire's boundary through staking, however, leads to complete dissolution. In *Buffy*, this is emphasized by the staked vampire's disappearance into a cloud of dust – a non-corporeal form of extinction.

Another stream of contemporary stories does, though, draw out the pathological nature of the vampire, its unnatural, parasitic and need-driven existence. The quintessential figure combining both of these strands of

---

24 Anne Rice, 'Essay on Earlier Works', *Anne's Bookshelf*, 15 August 2007. Online: http://www.annerice.com/Bookshelf-EarlierWorks.html
25 Michelle Callander, 'Bram Stoker's *Buffy*: Traditional Gothic and Contemporary Culture', *Slayage: The Online International Journal of Buffy Studies* 1, no. 3 (2001). Online: http://slayageonline.com/essays/slayage3/callander.html
26 Kristeva, *Powers of Horror*, 65.

thought in *Buffy* is Spike, Buffy's second vampire lover. Judging from fanfiction and related sites, Spike figured as an object of sexual desire to viewers long before he held any attraction for Buffy within the narrative. Spike, a vampire who like Angel enters into extended interaction with the Scooby Gang, is reviled by the Scoobies not only after the Initiative implant the chip which makes it impossible for him to harm humans, but also after he has undergone trials and had his soul restored. He continues to be an object of revulsion to Buffy even while she is sleeping with him. More on the question of this, and of Spike's soul will be said below. First, let us pause to consider Spike's simultaneous positioning as object to Buffy of both desire and horror in terms of abjection. For it can be argued that even though this may not be the viewing experience, it is abjection that he represents to Buffy.

The abject, it is recalled, is an unassimilable impossible: but another feature of the abject is that this is not only rejected; it 'beseeches, worries, and fascinates desire'.[27] This is an apprehensive desire, which turns aside, and a sickened desire, which rejects. A certainty 'protects [desire] from the shameful'.[28] But at the same time, 'that impetus, that spasm, that leap, is drawn toward an elsewhere as tempting as it is condemned.'[29] This is a maelstrom, a vortex, of 'summons and repulsion.'[30]

When Buffy finally turns to Spike it is symptomatic of psychological trauma. Following her resurrection, she is profoundly alienated from her normal existence and her friends. She is simply 'going through the motions' ('Once More with Feeling'). In this dislocated state, it is the dead with whom she feels most connection. Her relationship with Spike is character-ized by exactly that admixture of summons and repulsion described by Kristeva. She cannot keep away from him, but she is disgusted with herself at the same time – so ashamed, in fact, that she hides her behaviour from her friends. This is a desire which is simultaneously turned aside or rejected, and embraced: the 'certainty' which Kristeva suggests protects desire from the shameful is assaulted in the face of a radical uncertainty – about mean-ing, purpose, and her own identity. Her liaison with Spike is a facet of her own repressed fear that she 'came back wrong' ('Dead Things').

If Spike represents what Buffy abjects, this can be related dialectically to his function as her shadow-side or double, and a concomitant dialectic between repression and revelation. The abjected is a repression that inspires

27 Ibid., 1.
28 Ibid.
29 Ibid.
30 Ibid.

nausea; the shadow-double confronts us with that part of us we seek to repress, thereby bringing it to light. As Wilcox argues, both Faith and Spike act as Buffy's 'dark doubles'.[31] With Faith, the doubling is overt. She is a Slayer herself, a multiplication of the 'Chosen One' made possible because of Buffy's own death. In that sense Buffy 'mothered' both Kendra and Faith. She is dark to Buffy's fair. She even occupies Buffy's own body, and takes on her life ('This Year's Girl'; 'Who Are You?'). And as she says to Buffy: '[You] kill me, you become me' ('Enemies'). Caleb actually says to Faith in 'Dirty Girls': 'Well, you're the other one, aren't you. You're Cain to her Abel. No offense meant to Cain, of course.'

That Spike also acts as a 'dark double' to Buffy is less obvious. In Jungian terms, as seen earlier in this text, the 'shadow' is a repressed and unacknowledged aspect of the self, the integration of which is a move towards psychic expansion and wholeness. In terms of psychoanalytic theory, it is not identifiable with the abject, which is by definition excluded. I juxtapose the two here as a hermeneutical tool to draw out Spike's multiple narrative functions in the identity construction of Buffy's persona, as Buffy's perception of both himself and herself develops. Spike is constantly forcing Buffy to acknowledge her own shadow-side, by exposing to her the similarities and affinities between them. Wilcox notes also that for Jung, the 'shadow' is the same sex as the subject and considers whether Spike might then be more properly deemed to represent Buffy's animus.[32] This is particularly appropriate since 'Spike' is a phallic name, and Spike's whole personality seems predicated on 'a highly masculinized compensation for the relatively feminized poet William [Spike's human precursor].' At the same time, Wilcox does not feel bound by Jungian gender-typing and remains willing to call Spike Buffy's Shadow.[33] As she goes on to say, Spike can also be seen as Buffy's id, in contrast to Angel (who must exercise total control around Buffy or lose his soul), and is thus in the position of the superego.

Given the role that Spike plays in doubling Buffy's darker side, violence and death-drives, it is not surprising that sadomasochism is part and parcel of their interactions. Indeed, when her mother asks whether she has given Spike any encouragement to fall for her, she responds: 'I do beat him up a lot. For Spike, that's like third base' ('Crush'). The 'super-powered' bodies of both Buffy and Spike allow for a dynamic of violence in sexuality which transcends the ordinary limitations of fragile

---

31 Wilcox, '"Every Night I Save You": Buffy, Spike, Sex, and Redemption', 81.
32 Ibid., 82.
33 Ibid., 83.

human flesh. Jenny Alexander notes the ambivalence of the presentation of their relationship. On the one hand, the story arc clearly positions it as unhealthy, and Buffy is ashamed of herself for her erotic games with Spike. However, 'the camera tells a different story. It continually lingers on the unzipping and re-buckling of black leather.'[34] Alexander also argues that the show's pornographic elements are part of a post-feminist cultural moment in which it is almost exclusively the women who are on top, and the men whose tortured, dominated bodies are eroticized. She observes of Angel and Spike that:

> Over the course of the show, our vampire heroes have been, between them, in deliberated torture scenes; chained up, staked, amputated, run through with iron bars, cut with knives, turned inside out, beaten to bloody pulps, stabbed with scissors, and burnt with matches, holy water and crosses.[35]

This is part of the subverted power dynamics discussed at greater length in Chapter Six. The kinky dimensions to *Buffy* not only make it an astonishingly risqué teen television show, but are part of a deconstruction of established understandings of personal and social being. The sadomasochistic sexualities are another forum both for mocking the imposition of narrow normativities, and for exposing identities as threaded through with elements coded as dark or transgressive by conventional culture.

It is a fear of Buffy that she, herself, is monstrous. This self-questioning begins even before her return from death and her relationship with Spike. At the outset of Season Five, Dracula challenges her to consider the darkness within her own power, and to come to terms with it: indeed, he identifies finding that darkness as her finding her 'true nature' ('Buffy vs. Dracula'). Buffy is restless throughout this season: 'Restless', of course, was the title of the last episode in Season Four, which ended with the First Slayer telling Buffy that she has not even begun to know who she is, and what is to come – a dictum echoed by Dracula. The restlessness about her own nature is what prompts the encounter with her spirit guide in 'Intervention'. She admits that she fears losing her ability to love, and the guide confronts her with her fear that being the Slayer means losing her humanity. Her existential questioning continues right through to the end of the season, in 'The Gift', as she confides in Giles:

---

34 Jenny Alexander, 'A Vampire is being Beaten: DeSade through the Looking Glass in *Buffy* and *Angel*', *Slayage: The Online International Journal of Buffy Studies* 4, no. 3 (2004). Online: http://www.slayageonline.com/essays/slayage15/Alexander.htm

35 Ibid.

I sacrificed Angel to save the world. I loved him so much. But I knew . . . what was right. I don't have that any more. I don't understand. I don't know how to live in this world if these are the choices . . . The spirit guide told me . . . that death is my gift. Guess that means a Slayer really is just a killer after all.

Buffy interprets her 'gift' of death as confirming her nature as a killer; in fact, the gift is given in the last episode of Season Five, when she leaps sacrificially to her death in place of Dawn to save the universe. After she is resurrected in Season Six by Willow, not only is she scared that she 'came back wrong', she is experiencing deep alienation. Her sadomasochistic relationship with Spike appears in this context to be fuelled by two factors. One is self-disgust. Another is a desire for some, any, kind of feeling and connection to the world.

The boundaries between reality and unreality are played with again and again in the love-relationship between Buffy and Spike, underlining its liminal and knife-edge nature. On the one hand, their actual relationship is prefigured by unrealities. In 'Something Blue', they become engaged under the influence of a spell. In Season Five, Spike consoles himself with a robotic artificial Buffy, the Buffybot. However, this segues towards the real when Spike withstands the tortures of Glory in order to protect Buffy and Dawn. 'What you did for me and Dawn, that was real', Buffy tells Spike ('Intervention'). Once they are in a relationship, Buffy consistently denies the reality of Spike's feelings for her. Spike's response to her attitude towards him is that while he may be dirt, she is the one who likes to roll in it ('Wrecked').

Buffy herself is a liminal figure, poised between dark and light.[36] Dracula quotes Nietzsche to her: 'Whoever fights monsters should see to it that in the process he does not become a monster. And if you gaze long enough into an abyss, the abyss will gaze back into you.'[37] Her relationship with Spike as her double reinforces this, for it is this which plays out most fully Buffy's own affinity with death, darkness and destruction. As discussed in Chapter Six, it is revealed during the course of the programme that the source of Buffy's own powers is actually demonic. Buffy battles with this. When Faith is in Buffy's body, she batters her own, calling it 'disgusting, murderous' ('Who Are You?'); this represents Faith's self-hatred, but as

36 For this argument, see also Wilcox, '"Every Night I Save You": Buffy, Spike, Sex, and Redemption'.
37 Friedrich Wilhelm Nietzsche, *Beyond Good and Evil*, trans. Walter Kaufmann (New York, NY: Vintage Books, 1966), 89.

Buffy's double, it also represents Buffy's hatred for the darker side of her own self. She batters Spike in 'Dead Things', insisting that he cannot love her: 'You don't have a soul. There is nothing good or clean in you. You are dead inside. You can't feel anything real. I could never be your girl.' This is evidently projection; Spike, the soulless vampire, *does* feel: it is Buffy whose emotions have been deadening.

In 'Seeing Red', Buffy rejects Spike, who then attempts to rape her. This is an encounter fraught with complexity, however. Spike, intent on getting Buffy to admit that she loves him, forces himself upon her and is oblivious to the wrongness of his actions until Buffy has stopped him: realizing what he has done, or nearly done, he is appalled. It is this action which launches Spike on the road of trials which eventually leads to the restoration of his soul. Spike says himself in 'Seeing Red' that the chip makes him neither monster nor man, a state he believes makes him 'nothing'. Xander, before the rape scene, castigates Spike as, basically, a leashed but soulless evil. If this is the case, it does raise the question of whether Spike can even be considered morally responsible. It is surely, in fact, the amoral bloodlust of vampires and lack of true personhood which makes 'dusting' them an act of necessary execution rather than simply mass murder – a genocide, in fact, a form of species cleansing. And yet, when it comes to post-resurrection Buffy, Spike's chip is inoperative because something has changed slightly in her. His actions to her are *his* actions, and even in his soulless state, throughout Season Six this includes acts of compassion, protection and – following the attempted rape – even remorse. So, lacking a soul, he may be less than a man, but he is not unequivocally a monster. He willingly undergoes ordeals to remove himself from this impasse: '. . . make me what I was so that Buffy can get what she deserves', he asks in 'Grave'. The anger he is feeling towards Buffy and the language he chooses in relation to her – 'Bitch is gonna see a change' ('Villains') – suggest it is the removal of the chip that he is seeking, but it is the restoration of his soul that he receives. The viewer is left with ambiguity: was that what he *really* wanted all along? Has the demon granted what Spike was truly seeking? Certainly, Spike makes a number of statements in Season Seven indicating that he has in fact gone through all that to receive his soul 'for her'.

Progressively, Buffy comes to realize she is mistaken about Spike, especially after he has regained his soul for her. In 'Never Leave Me', she says to him: 'You faced the monster inside of you and you fought back. You risked everything to be a better man. And you can be. You are. You may not see it, but I do. I believe in you, Spike.' It is ironic, therefore, that when Buffy finally does tell Spike she loves him, in 'Chosen', Spike refuses

THE GOOD AND THE MONSTROUS: *BUFFY*

to believe her, but thanks her for saying it – while slowly incinerating in a deliberate self-sacrifice to vanquish the Turok-Han.

Spike's acquisition of a soul is a crucial moment. Buffy's encounter with him in 'Beneath You', crazed by the consequences of his actions and tormented by the First, is a tragic scene, taking place in a chapel. He says to her:

> It's what you wanted, right? And – and now everybody's in here, talking. Everything I did . . . everyone I – and him . . . and it . . . the other, the thing beneath – beneath you. . . . Why does a man do what he mustn't? For her. To be hers. To be the kind of man who would nev – to be a kind of man. . . . She shall look on him with forgiveness, and everybody will forgive and love. He will be loved.

Spike has regained his soul, the 'spark', and 'all it does is burn'; he is haunted by the voices of those he has killed and the deeds he has committed. Following his stammered utterances to Buffy above, he drapes himself across the chapel's cross. As the soul burns inside him, so the cross burns his skin. Is this a rejection of vampiric flesh by the cross, or the rejection of the cross by vampiric flesh? There is a correspondence between the soul, the cross, and Spike's embrace of both in his search for love and forgiveness, which implies they are caught up in the same symbolic field. Spike's inner torment caused by his desire for redemption is externalized in this image of crucifixion in fire. This prefigures Spike's ultimate redemption in the final episode of the season, when Spike disintegrates in flames while destroying the hordes of the First.

In one sense, there appears to be an essentialist thrust to the notion that possessing a soul creates a profound differentiation in state of being: it implies that souls confer an innate nature marking the human off from the vampire. However, this is no simple equation of ensoulment with moral goodness: there are plenty of human villains in *Buffy*, and no small number of demons who appear to problematize the notion that the demonic is per se evil – Whistler, for example. The defining feature of having a soul is not, then, polarization along a good/evil axis. Buffy is in other respects able to acknowledge this, informing Riley that it is not as simple as 'demons bad, people good' ('New Moon Rising'). Perhaps more significantly, a principle characteristic of a soul appears to be the capacity for guilt. Both Angel and Spike find ensoulment a path of suffering rather than easy redemption, for their past actions haunt them. This is theologically significant: as also indicated in Chapter Eight, Genesis 2–3 in the Bible creates an association between being in the image of God, knowledge of good and evil, and the capacity to feel shame. Traditional interpretations have emphasized the sexual dimension to both the knowledge and the shame, based on the couple's realization of nakedness and desire to cover themselves following consumption of the fruit (Gen. 3.7). However, this can be read synecdochally to stand for development into moral awareness and responsibility. This correlate between capacity for shame or guilt and moral accountability is replayed in *Buffy* through the metaphysical distinction between the souled and the unsouled.

Angel, of course, is *Buffy*'s first ensouled vampire. Abbott reads him, particularly in his own spin-off series, as a hybrid of Angel/Angelus in whom vampire and human are in constant conflict; he is a 'self-defining existentialist protagonist'.[38] The same could be said of all the main characters in *Buffy*. For existentialist philosophers such as Jean-Paul Sartre, existence precedes essence in human being.[39] Sartre distinguished between being-in-itself (*l'en-soi*), and being-for-itself (*le pour-soi*). Being-in-itself simply is, with no reason or purpose for its own existence. This is the world of external objects. Being-for-itself, to the contrary, represents conscious being and self-presence; it has no absolute nature because it is characterized by freedom of choice. In a world without God, for Sartre, it is a mistake to attribute an 'essence' to human nature; it is in the process of existing that human nature defines (and redefines) itself. This constitutes a radical freedom; concomitantly, it also constitutes a radical responsibility. Persons, having choices, are responsible for their behaviour. This responsibility extends towards consideration of the impact of choices upon others. While no objective authority tells us what to do, we must still evaluate the value and significance of the choices that we make – the more so, indeed, for those choices are our own.

Vampires in *Buffy* are present to themselves – they are conscious – and Drusilla tells us that vampires can in fact love 'quite well. If not wisely' ('Crush'). But do they have moral choice, or are their choices wholly defined by their vampire nature? Spike presents the most complex case in point here. Wilcox argues that even where Spike has no soul, he nevertheless repeatedly *does* good, and is shown to be capable of not only goodness but also change and love.[40] This development is possible pre-soul because

---

38   Stacey Abbott, 'Walking the Fine Line Between Angel and Angelus', *Slayage: The Online International Journal of Buffy Studies* 3, no. 1 (2002). Online: http://www.slayageonline.com/essays/slayage9/Abbott.htm

39   See Jean-Paul Sartre and Carol Macomber, *Existentialism is a Humanism* (New Haven, CT: Yale University Press, 2007); Jean-Paul Sartre, *Being and Nothingness*, trans. Hazel E. Barnes (London: Routledge, 1970).

40   Wilcox, '"Every Night I Save You": Buffy, Spike, Sex, and Redemption', 87.

of the inhibiting influence of the chip, which prevents him from harming humans; but Spike's positive choices for the benefit of others cannot simply be ascribed to the restraining power of the chip. Wilcox therefore likens the chip to psychiatric medication which provides a respite allowing space for development in other areas. Thus Spike, even more than Angel, hybridizes the border between the vampire and the human.

Cox draws out how entrenched the Scooby Gang are in their belief that Spike is irredeemable and therefore *cannot* fully respect or appreciate his 'kind, respectful, affectionate and compassionate'[41] actions in Seasons Five and Six because they are firmly attached to the theory that without a soul can be no goodness.[42] This is despite, for example, his continuing protection of Dawn; his compassion to both Dawn and Buffy following the death of Joyce; and his anonymous floral tribute for Joyce. Cox is disturbed by the philosophical hierarchy implicit in this automatic equation between worth and ensoulment.[43] 'You're beneath me', Buffy informs Spike in 'Fool for Love'. 'You're not a man', Giles tells him, when Spike has protested that a man can change. 'You're a thing. An evil, disgusting thing' ('Smashed').

Not every character accepts this worldview. 'Joyce didn't treat me like I was a freak', Spike tells Xander in 'Forever'. Dawn shrugs off the distinction between the chip and a soul ('. . . same diff' – 'Crush'), raising the question of whether the source of moral action is consequential. It is Spike himself who provides the counter-argument to this, in Season Seven's 'Sleeper'. He expostulates to Buffy, who suspects him of trying to 'off' a woman but being prevented by the chip:

> No, not the chip! Not the chip, dammit. You honestly think I'd go to the end of the underworld and back to get my soul and then – Buffy, I can barely live with what I did. It haunts me. All of it. If you think that I would add to the body count now, you are crazy.

Therefore the difference between the chip and the soul is fundamentally to do with moral guilt and responsibility, and not just a matter of moral action. Giles, while temporarily transformed into a demon in 'A New Man', also aligns conscience with both humanity and the soul: 'I have a soul! I have a

41 J. Renée Cox, 'Got Myself a Soul? The Puzzling Treatment of the Soul in *Buffy*', in Emily Dial-Driver *et al.* (eds), *The Truth of* Buffy*: Essays on Fiction Illuminating Reality* (Jefferson, NC: McFarland, 2008), 24–37 (30).
42 Ibid., 31.
43 Ibid., 31–32.

conscience! I am a human being', he shouts. Humanity, the quintessential state of being ensouled, is also defined by Giles as responsive to love and reason, and 'can be redeemed, or more importantly wants to be redeemed' ('Beauty and the Beasts'). The *wanting* implicates choice in the possibility of redemption. Significantly in existentialist terms, Spike chooses the burden of a soul, and for love: 'This chip – they did to me. I couldn't help it. But the soul, I got on my own – for you' ('Sleeper'). So, at heart, it is love that leads to Spike's transformation into a fully moral agent.

Even vampire nature in *Buffy* is therefore capable of modification, although generally presented as a given beyond choice or moral agency: in that respect, Angel and Spike are exceptions that underline the rule. As the double to humanity, however, vampire nature stands for humanity's own pre-conscious drives and desires, and capacity for 'inhumane' behaviour. In its need to follow the vampiric imperative, it reminds us of our own non-rational impulses. The 'Otherness' of the vampire is not an unreachable Otherness, but an intimate one, mirroring metamorphosis into, or habitation of, a darkness always already potentially present in human being.

This is repeatedly emphasized in *Buffy* through the sheer number of 'doublings' the series presents. Almost every significant character at some point makes an appearance in their 'dark' persona. There are not only Angel/Angelus, and the changing faces of Spike; there are Buffy/Faith, Willow/Dark Willow, Anya/Anyanka, Xander/Vamp Xander. These 'dark' appearances are not confined to the alternative universe from 'The Wish' (where we have Vamp Xander and Vamp Willow), nor only effected through external agency (being turned into a demon or vampire wholly against one's will). They are also played out within the realm of choice, albeit conditioned choice, most visible at the transition points – where, for example, 'scary-veiny Willow' turns back into 'crayon-breaky Willow' ('Grave'), or Anyanka seeks to undo the death of the frat boys ('Selfless').

Nor is it only 'dark' doubles that populate the series. In an interesting subversion of gender roles, Xander's 'doubling' also confronts him with his own fears of *lack* of power ('The Replacement'). Buffy confronts her disempowered self in 'Helpless' and 'Halloween', and a self not living the life of a Slayer in 'Anne' and 'Normal Again'. 'Tabula Rasa' confounds everybody's identities through loss of memory. In his crazed state in Season Seven, Spike's identity, fractured, proliferates. Ultimately, then, the multiple, complex and shifting nature of identity is a recurrent theme. From this unstable locality of fragmented desires and fragmented selves, the human imperative is to choose.

If existential emphasis on choice is valorized in human being, how does this relate to overarching cosmologies of good and evil? No singular, beneficent and originary God features in the Buffyverse. There is, however, a 'First Evil'. This First Evil is, ironically, the nearest in nature to God, but inverted. The First is unique, beyond conception, non-corporeal and primal – even 'pure' ('Bring on the Night'). It takes on the form of people who have died to torment and deceive the living. It has gathered an army – the Harbingers of Death – to destroy the Slayer line once and for all. It also unleashes the über-vampiric in the hope of outnumbering humanity and destroying the dialectical balance between good and evil. It has certain correspondences with Satan in Christian mythology – its primary mode of attack is deception and manipulation. The First transcends ontological categorizations of god or demon. It exists before the demonic Old Ones and the Powers That Be. It tells Buffy:

> You think you can fight me? I'm not a demon, little girl. I am something that you can't even conceive. The First Evil. Beyond sin, beyond death. I am the thing the darkness fears. You'll never see me, but I am everywhere. Every being, every thought, every drop of hate –
>
> ('Amends')

The First claims to be the originator of evil. However, as Buffy's mother tells her in a dream, to destroy the First will not destroy evil, which is always here, and self-perpetuating: 'Buffy, evil isn't coming, it's already here. Evil is always here. Don't you know? It's everywhere' ('Bring on the Night'). This is most probably another apparition of the First, since Joyce appears to be trying to convince Buffy that the First is in consequence not worth fighting: evil is 'natural'. However, Buffy remains determined to fight it, even if the fight is perpetual.

The primal nature of the First Evil appears as a radical reversal of the Christian mythos in which an original graced state gave way to a fallen one because of human disobedience and misuse of free will. According to Christian orthodoxy as established by the fourth-century church father Augustine of Hippo, evil as such did not exist: it was, rather, the absence of good. This was in response to the dualism of the Manichees,.a Gnostic group who asserted the existence of both good and evil, interlocked in a cosmic struggle. For Augustine, a perfectly good God could not be the source of evil; as God was the source of everything that is, evil could not, as such, exist. Is the implication of the Buffyverse, then, the radical opposite of this? That the 'true' nature of the world is evil, and evil has a 'reality' that goodness lacks?

I would argue that such an interpretation does not do justice to the embodied rather than explicitly articulated metaphysics of the Buffyverse. The 'First Evil', it seems to me, is a metaphor for the reality of evil: not as ontological essence, but as manifested material force. The need to come to terms with the dark potentiality of human being is a constant theme throughout the series. 'From beneath you, it devours' is the refrain uttered of the First Evil. This is a mirror of what Buffy tells Spike, reinforcing his position as her dark double: 'You're beneath me' ('Fool for Love'). Spike, at that point the soulless vampire, is also cast as analogue for human capacity for evil, eating away from within. But Spike, let us not forget, is also the one not devoured by his evil but rather consumed by sunlight in a transcendent death which closes the Hellmouth. The capacity for human goodness, heroism, love and community is thus set against the capacity for human moral failure and even monstrosity. Human beings are shown to be conflicted, confused and confusing. Yet they keep on fighting, as Anya observes in both bewilderment and admiration ('End of Days').

The radical confusion and uncertainty of the human condition is demonstrated in the episode 'Normal Again', which functions meta-fictively to undermine the narrative reality of the entirety of the Buffyverse. Following being spiked by a demon, Buffy finds herself shifting erratically in and out of a conventional reality, in which she is not the Slayer, there are no vampires, and her parents are together and still alive. In the 'reality' of Buffyverse, she is suffering from hallucinations because of demon venom. In the conventional 'reality', she is in a psychiatric clinic, hallucinating her life as the Slayer, having been suffering from 'an undifferentiated type of schizophrenia' for six years. Her awakening is attributed by the doctors to breakdown in her secondary world: 'Your sister, your friends, all of those people you created in Sunnydale, they aren't as comforting as they once were. Are they? They're coming apart.' This is Season Six; things are indeed, coming apart. In a particularly sophisticated move, we learn that Buffy had awakened in the world of the psychiatric hospital once before – the previous summer, which correlates with the time of her death in the Buffyverse. Her friend-constructs, the doctor tells her, pulled her back into that reality. Shifting confusingly between the two realities, it is in the end presented as a choice of Buffy's to return to her life as a Slayer to rescue Willow from a demon. The final shot, however, is of Buffy's parents sobbing: Buffy is unresponsive and catatonic. Which is the really 'real'? According to the title, Buffy is normal *again*. To which reality does this refer?

This fundamental lack of ontological certainty is the basis of human

existence and undermines the essential validity of any authoritarian pro-
nouncements. In the Buffyverse, this reinforces rather than undermines
the necessity for human choice and moral accountability. The monstrous
is all around, welling up from within as well as without. In some senses,
Whedon offers us a dark vision of the human. It is a long way from the
Enlightenment's 'man of reason'. The god Glory says in disgust of humans
that they are 'meat-baggy slaves' to hormones, pheromones and feelings
('The Weight of the World'). She goes on to say that humans are no more
than puppets. The whole thrust of the Buffyverse refutes this. Choice,
and moral choice, is of paramount significance. Humanity is shown not
only through its monstrous doubles, but also in its capacity to transcend
the uncertain and drive-driven nature of its own existence, its own inner
demons, and to act altruistically and even heroically in love and compassion. This is *despite* the difficulty and pain which so often feature in human
being. The answer to that problem is voiced by a vampire, Spike, when
Buffy is expressing her existential despair: live, he tells her. This means
more than 'going through the motions': it means to engage in life; to
participate; to care. Furthermore, the reality of human power to *resist* evil
is defiantly voiced by Buffy in Season Seven's 'Bring on the Night':

> I'm beyond tired. I'm beyond scared. I'm standing on the mouth of hell,
> and it is gonna swallow me whole. And it'll choke on me. We're not ready?
> They're not ready. . . . From now on, we won't just face our worst fears, we
> will seek them out. We will find them, and cut out their hearts one by one,
> until The First shows itself for what it really is. And I'll kill it myself. There
> is only one thing on this earth more powerful than evil, and that's us. Any
> questions?

The wording here is significant: what can defeat evil is 'us'. That is to say,
it is not the Slayer, the singular hero, one Chosen One against the forces of
darkness who has the power to defeat evil. It is in community, and sharing,
and solidarity that evil can be defeated. Giles says that only Buffy could
have the strength to defeat the First: he was right, and he was wrong. On
her own Buffy could not have achieved it. It was in having the strength
and insight to relinquish and share her power that Buffy's capacity to
defeat the First ultimately lay. In such a context, again, it is choice that is
presented as the most important determinant, albeit not on a level playing
field, but rather a shifting and sometimes opaque landscape, rhizomati-
cally shot through with drives and desires. Evil is metonymically presented
as the First. There is no such comparable figure in the Buffyverse standing
for goodness. But the spirit of goodness is nevertheless manifest, in every

human choice for good that is made. For choice is what we are left with, even though we may choose in the same way that vampires – and humans for that matter – love: 'quite well. If not wisely.'

CONCLUSION: SHADOWS OF THE DIVINE

> Why this proliferation of marvellous characters at this particular point in time? Is it a phenomenon in tune with the dark side of our *fin de siècle* collective consciousness, still fraught with apocalyptic fears . . .? Are stories of encounters with fearsome phantoms a way of engaging our deep-seated anxieties, putting our spectral enemies to rest by battling them in our imaginations . . .?[1]

THE EXPLORATION OF THESE four fantasy texts – *Buffy the Vampire Slayer*, *Earthsea*, *Harry Potter* and *His Dark Materials* – has shown them to be threaded through with a rich and deep set of spiritual themes and concerns. To round off this analysis, I will conclude by summarizing the kinds of spiritual preoccupations, values and predicaments found in engaging with these texts. I will then draw attention to some of the areas where resonance with contemporary spiritual conditions, outlined in Chapter One, can be discerned.

The first thematic focus was the 'transforming self' (Chapters Two and Three), examined in relation to the *Harry Potter* series and *The Tombs of Atuan* from Le Guin's *Earthsea* series. The model of the 'hero's journey' proposed by Joseph Campbell[2] was taken as the primary analytic frame for considering the transformation of the self in the *Harry Potter* series. Campbell's schema – at its most basic, that of 'Separation, Initiation

1   Millicent Lenz and Peter Hunt, *Alternative Worlds in Fantasy Fiction* (London and New York, NY: Continuum, 2001), 138.
2   Joseph Campbell, *The Hero with a Thousand Faces* (Novato, CA: New World Library, 2008).

and Return' – allowed the hero quest to be related both to spiritual concerns and to psychoanalytical theories. These were seen to be deeply intertwined, for the model of spiritual actualization implicit in this mode of analysis took personal maturation and expansion of the consciousness as constitutive of spiritual growth and development. The hero journey for Campbell was seen to be only superficially over-ground; in fact, it is a journey to inner depths, involving travelling a road of many trials, the overcoming of hidden blockages and the revivification of forgotten powers. This includes encountering and reconciling with feminine and masculine archetypes, in order to achieve apotheosis; this is a mode of spiritual transcendence which enables the hero to focus on the centrality of universal love and to recognize the divine in the other, and the other in the self. Endowed with their own power, the hero is then available for the transfiguration of the world. Opaque materiality gives way to shadows of an immanent eternity. The hero, therefore, represents the disclosure of the divine both within and outside of our selves. Heroes may call for emulation, or offer themselves as object of contemplation; they represent human potentiality – a potentiality residing in all of us, and able to be expressed in the self-discovery and self-development inherent in 'normal' existence. The hero journey acts, then, as a model of and analogue for the spiritual quest. The spiritual journey is related to psychoanalytical development and transformation.

Heroes also participate in the archetypal, understood not necessarily as residing in a Jungian collective unconscious, but as social and/or psychoanalytical in origin and nature. These culturally resonant thought-forms add depth and texture to images and figures who tap into them, fostering a spiritual dimension in terms of accessing deep-rooted concepts of meaning and purpose. The tendency of fantastic literature to make use of mythic tropes further encourages the reading of fantastic heroes in a spiritual key, for myths typically evoke a transcendent dimension. This is partly achieved through the epic and cosmic character of mythic temporality. In the *Harry Potter* series, Harry's self-transcendence and therefore spiritual apotheosis was related to three specific aspects of his personal development: his relations with his father-figures (particularly James, Dumbledore, Voledemort and Snape); his attainment of control over his own destiny, which included a willingness to sacrifice himself for the sake of others as a personal choice; and his reconciliation with death. Coming to terms with death involves coming to terms with the immanence of existence and an embrace of history. This spiritual and personal transformation was mapped against Campbell's hero quest, and also shown to have Christological sub-texts in places.

Le Guin's *Tombs of Atuan* was examined by way of counterpart to the analysis of Harry as hero. Feminist critics such as Pearson and Pope have pointed out the ways in which Campbell's model in particular, but also heroic literature in general, tends to operate on understandings of heroism which assume a masculine protagonist and patriarchal values.[3] This is often the case even where female characters have a lead role. Life-challenges and patterns of psychoanalytic development tend to follow theorizations based on the masculine; 'patriarchal' qualities that are valorized include physical characteristics, achievement as a warrior, the establishment of manhood, and detached rationality over emotionality; archetypes typically emerge from a patriarchal milieu and figure the female as, for example, the sexual temptress, the devouring mother, or the wicked witch. Campbell himself was keen to retain a space for female heroism, and advocates an understanding of motherhood as heroic. Strategies such as these are, of course, important in reclaiming realms of activity traditionally associated with the female as potentially heroic. However, the danger is restricting the heroic capacity of the female to these traditional realms. Campbell's own discourse emphasizes the bodily nature of the female's transition from maiden to mother, over against the psychoanalytic nature of male heroic development. This returns women once more to the realms of passivity and the non-cognitive.

Writers and critics have looked to refigure the female hero and open up different vistas for self-actualization and spiritual transformation. Le Guin, indeed, is one such writer who embraced a feminist consciousness and offered subsequent critical commentary upon her presentation of the female protagonist in *The Tombs of Atuan*, arguing that she had not sufficiently foregrounded her, but left her as complementary to the male hero. It is thus necessary to consider heroic models from a perspective attentive to gendered dynamics, both to identify co-optation into patriarchal symbol-structures, and to discern ways of reading 'against the grain'. Pope and Pearson offer a revised account of the hero which seeks to incorporate those marginalized by factors such as ethnicity and social status as well as gender, and to develop less limited understandings and symbolizations of the spiritual and psychological basis of human life. They maintain that the journey of self-discovery at archetypal level is the same, but that situational differentiation may be required (for example, psychoanalytically, the nature of reconciliation required with male and female principles may well differ). The female, at heart, embarks on a journey of self-discovery

3   Carol Pearson and Katherine Pope, *The Female Hero in American and British Literature* (New York, NY: R.R. Bowker, 1981).

in the same way as the male, but her challenges and achievements may diverge contextually. Ultimately, though, she has entered a transcendent mode of existence, whereby transcendence is understood as a becoming of the self into vitality and power, rather than stagnation or subsistence. It is noted that recognition of situational difference is important but without care may risk reinforcing traditional role boundaries and demarcations, and exclude individuals and groups from the broader vistas of the heroic landscape. However, we may end with a model of the hero which incorporates the multiple; which emphasizes relationality and partnership; and lays more emphasis on *becoming* rather than *being* in heroic identity. The return of Le Guin to *Earthsea* many years later offers us a model of this spiral pattern of heroic becoming, with the movement between the adolescent Tenar of *Tombs* and the middle-aged Tenar of *Tehanu* and *The Other Wind*, and the parallel iterations of Ged as Archmage and farmer.

Metaphysical frameworks were examined in relation to *His Dark Materials*, and again, *Earthsea* (Chapters Four and Five). *His Dark Materials* offers particular interest in that the story arc explicitly deals with a bankrupt organized religion, in the shape of a corrupt Church which is based around a false God, the Authority. The trilogy offers a damning critique of this institutional Church, yet overflows with spiritual and religious themes, in pursuit of the narrative construction of a humanistic 'Republic of Heaven' rather than a 'Kingdom of Heaven'. In his reworking of Milton's *Paradise Lost*, Pullman has presented a fictionalized metaphysics of sin, death, love, free will, the self, and the fundamental nature of the universe, to name but a few dimensions of this. Culturally and philosophically speaking, *His Dark Materials* is firmly located in a post-Christian and humanist universe of the West. However, it is suggested that nevertheless the kind of metaphysics here narrativized has points of resonance with aspects of Eastern traditions, namely Buddhism. No causal connection is postulated; nor is it postulated that the moral and metaphysical framework of *His Dark Materials* can be labelled 'Buddhist'. In a cultural context of hybridization, however, it does show how elements of similarity between Pullman's brand of humanism and Buddhist thought can be identified. It is also suggestive of the reasons why Asian wisdom traditions have often been selectively assimilated into Western spiritual thought, for it shows how predicaments within a world constructed by a Judaeo-Christian metaphysic may appear to be 'solved', or never presented in the first place, in different religio-cultural locations.

Pullman is seeking to establish the human person as a free and democratic citizen, rather than the subject of a transcendent divine. He also wants to revalue sensuality and materiality and rejects otherworldly belief systems. He recognizes that a universe without God may be construed as meaningless and alienating, and concludes from this that what is required is a new story and a new myth: this constitutes a re-mythologization to find new ways of endowing life with purpose, value, joy and meaning. This is the driving impetus behind his construction of the 'Republic of Heaven'. One key element in Pullman's metaphysics within *His Dark Materials* is the concept of Dust; this is a metaphor for compassion, knowledge, wisdom and consciousness which bridges the divide between matter and spirit. All being is interconnected and knowledge is not dependent upon a disjunction between knower and known; rather it is participatory, open and contingent. The self, likewise, is presented as differentiated but not dualistically so; it is dynamic and relational. In *His Dark Materials*, the dissolution of the self at death is presented positively as a return to source; by contrast, the world of the dead is an artificial extension of existence akin to a prison camp. It is significant that the dead are freed from this place by the telling of true stories. This becomes, indeed, an ethical imperative: Pullman's non-theistic universe has a strong moral driver and an ethic of care, duty and communal responsibility. The deposing of the Authority has far from led to a world stripped of meaning, purpose and ethical ground. To this extent, *His Dark Materials* presents us with a magisterial vision of a humanistic worldview which is nevertheless spiritually and ethically rich.

Earthsea presents us with a metaphysics at once radically different and strangely similar. The metaphysical and cosmological basis of *Earthsea* was developed further in the last three books of the sextuplet as a direct response to Le Guin's own more developed feminist consciousness, highlighting the extent to which metaphysical frameworks are intimately entwined with socio-political concerns and issues. Le Guin imagines her new world order as a field to reconstruct a cosmological order more hospitable to the non-traditionally heroic. Underpinning the entire sequence is a philosophy drawn from Le Guin's own Taoist leanings. This is reflective of her emphasis on connection rather than separation in sacrality, and model of the world as network of complementary forces which are not dualistically opposed, but dynamically interdependent. It is a positive construction of a universe without 'God' in the traditional monotheistic sense. Unity with nature, with community and with cosmos are key themes. Self-development and the leading of virtuous lives are important, with action arising from a place of balance and harmony rather than striving and ego. Taoist themes of complementarity and balance thoroughly permeate *Earthsea*. There are also resonances with Jungian philosophies of psychic integration through balancing and reconciliation of apparently opposing polarities.

Le Guin's universe in *Earthsea* has an articulated ontological base in the connection between word and being: in a move directly contradictory of postmodern understandings of signification, language secures reality and there is not merely correspondence but identity between true naming and true being. Old Speech, the language of truth and reality, is the basis of magic. Loss of truth in words and names leads to the loss of creativity, magic and 'light'. The wound in the world which causes this loss is precipitated by a breaching of the boundary between death and life; being depends upon non-being, and to collapse the distinction leads to a collapse in meaning and the possibility of truth. Creation is fundamentally dependent upon differentiation, and an eternal becoming. From death, comes rebirth. Language, and command of language, is one of the points where Le Guin in her later trilogy felt impelled to make a feminist intervention: for she had established a socio-political world in which only men had real access to the use of Old Speech and the accompanying High Magic. Women were denied access to this language of creativity, being and power. This is indicative of the extent to which socio-political inequities can be projected into the metaphysical sphere, and vice versa: the positing of different metaphysical locations for men and women is then used to legitimate differentiation in the socio-political order. Le Guin overcomes this in her later trilogy through a complex cosmology based upon the relationship between humans and dragons, understood as initially one species which later chooses to go in different directions. It is female figures, Therru and Irian, who reclaim this heritage and become dragon. Dragons are representative of potentiality, transformation, freedom, vitality and transcendence. They do not learn the Old Speech: the Old Speech is constitutive of their nature and being, inserting the dragon into the metaphysics of creation itself. This symbolic revalorization of the female is paralleled by a remodelling of the hero figure in the shape of a domesticated, middle-aged Tenar, a Ged who has lost all his magely powers, and Therru: an abused girl-child. It is Therru, the disempowered, who ascends to fly on gulfs of sunlit air in her dragon-nature.

Metaphysics, then, cannot be divorced from socio-politics. In the 'Transforming Worlds' section (Chapters Six and Seven), socio-politics are specifically examined, using *Buffy the Vampire Slayer* and *Harry Potter* as textual examples. *Buffy* is posited upon power dynamics, again inclusive of but not reducible to matters of gender. The concept of a little blonde girl monster-slayer is a deliberate reversal of traditional horror film tropes. The initial school setting allows for a contextualizing metaphor of 'high school as hell', which again prioritizes distributions of power. This is significant for understanding models of self and of self-in-relation, which are key aspects of any spiritual vision. *Buffy* utilizes a playful and postmodern style to undermine and recode traditional constructs; it is an ironic pastiche which deliberately blurs the boundaries between reality and fiction. To an extent *Buffy* models the carnivalesque – a mocking questioning of norms, hierarchies and structures. Institutional authority is presented, generally, as negative, lacking in insight or oppressive; in the interstices thrive the sub-cultures of youth and monsters, in liminal spaces which offer the possibility of systemic disruption. The focus on sub-cultures both undermines any concept of singular, unified power structures and reveals relations between the transgressive and the normalized. The transgressive is an important element in *Buffy*, coded in its representations of gender, sexuality and the monstrous. Its space is detraditioned: its vampiric mythology is dislocated from religious settings, although Whedon freely admits to the deployment of Christian symbolism. However, the frame for this is cultural rather than confessional. There is no divine presence, no divine authority. The vampires are not stains on the proper, divinely ordained cosmic order, but dangerous pollutants threatening human well-being: not unholy, but simply undead.

An important way in which institutional authority is undermined is in the presentation of relations between Buffy and her Watchers' Council. Buffy, as an individual, is iconoclastic – unable to adhere to traditional models of the Slayer. Importantly, one aspect of her failure to stick to the norm here is her refusal to act as a solitary monad, but rather to be situated in a network of family and friends. Her friends, the Scooby Gang, come to represent an alternative organizational dynamic. While the Watchers' Council are bound by tradition and hierarchy (with clear parallels to religious organizations), the Scooby Gang models a more anarchic and democratic mode of operating. This is tied in with Buffy's refusal to expel emotions from her decision-making processes – it is all part of a rejection of traditional, rational and hierarchical models of power. The militaristic Initiative also acts as a symbol of the dangers of this kind of instrumentalized authoritative structure; their invention-gone-wrong, Adam, is defeated by the Scooby Gang's participatory, collaborative mode of working. When Buffy strays into leading on a militaristic model, she herself is rejected. The importance both of recognizing limits to the proper exercise of power, and of acting from a place of love, wisdom and responsibility, are constantly affirmed. This model of adaptive action is set against the law of patriarchy. This is underscored by the account of Slayer lineage, in which the Shadow-Men staked a woman in the desert to be violated, infused with demonic power and to be ever after their tool. Buffy rejects the possibility of a gift of power from the Shadow-Men and takes instead a gift from the hidden female Guardians, who bestow upon her the scythe which is so important in the final victory. So, also, is Buffy's transformation of the Slayer lineage through the radical redistribution of power, endowing Slayer capacity upon every Potential. This power-sharing is pivotal both in the defeat of the First Evil and in the construction of a new, polyphonic economy of power. In terms of establishing this new order, it is also significant when Willow corrects Xander: they did not 'save' the world – a messianic religious trope – they 'changed' it. However, *Buffy* is by no means incognizant of the difficult negotiations faced in changing power structures from within it. Buffy's own location as an icon of typical Barbie-doll femininity cuts chiastically across her location as the Slayer. This can be read mimetically to show how the very incongruity in Buffy's persona begins to unravel the patriarchal stereotypes and open up space for new possibilities for gender-becoming. Thus, as a show, *Buffy* subverts normative patterns of power and authority at both individual and social levels, offering glimpses of alternative modes of being which are more empowering for individuals and co-operative for groups.

The *Harry Potter* series is rich with socio-political concerns and issues, and has received considerable critical attention in this respect. This is partly because of the close analogue between the 'fantasy' world of Harry Potter and the 'real' world. The Muggle, non-magical fictional world is obviously a direct analogue. However, within the world of *Potter* the magical world is an *indirect* analogue. By juxtaposing the two, Rowling is able to make highly pertinent socio-political commentary. This is relevant to spiritual concerns given the premise that spirituality is always rooted within and has implications for socio-political contexts. Questions such as who and what are considered valuable in life, what counts as markers of success or achievement, and what models of self and relation are espoused can be accessed through such a socio-political analysis. The world of *Potter* can be seen to be deeply socially stratified along a number of lines: this includes the continuum between Muggle and Magical, and within the magical world, between human and non-human. This type of stratification appears at face-value to lend support to the critics who would see in *Potter* a retrogressive traditionalism and nostalgia at work, which is socio-politically conservative and privileges hereditary privilege and wealth over the ostensible liberal rhetoric claiming to value each for their own merits. In so doing, the texts work to support authoritative and hierarchical structures.

However, it can also be claimed that in fact Rowling is presenting a deeply satirical and politicized work, and that her representations of social stratification actually amount to a sustained critique of it. The politics of both Thatcherism and New Labour appear to haunt the text in the presentation of the Ministry. The blood purity motif is of key importance and receives sustained attention throughout the series; indeed, it is a major plot hinge in the cause of the hostilities between Death Eater factions and the Order. Against this structural hierarchy of aristocratic privilege, primary protagonists such as Hagrid and Dumbledore affirm that this is not significant, and that it is what one chooses to be that defines who one is. Rowling's presentation of the blood purity issue here can be related to a number of racialized discourses of oppression, including that of Nazi Germany. The position of Snape, Voldemort and Harry as half-bloods helps to deconstruct the boundary as an ideological construct. As Voldemort is Harry's double, the importance of choice in 'destiny' is thereby reaffirmed. In a similar vein, Dumbledore tells Harry that the prophecy cannot constrain him to act against his will, and that it was by choosing to act upon it that Voldemort had initiated its truth. However, freedom to choose is less evident in the fracture line between the human and non-human magical worlds; the situation of the house-elves can act to represent confinement and oppression based on class, ethnicity or gender. Dobby is of central significance here, as holding out the possibility that emancipation is possible – not only in terms of being socially emancipated, but in consciousness also. The world of *Potter* does indeed represent a number of seemingly intractable stratifications – along blood, class, species and wealth. There is critical controversy regarding Rowling's presentation of gender. However, it can be said that the presentation of such situations does not amount to an endorsement of them; rather, it shows the 'dance' between fantasy and reality, and enables the former to make critical and subversive comment upon the former.

The final thematic area selected for exploration was the idea of the good and the monstrous, considered in relation to *His Dark Materials* and *Buffy* (Chapters Eight and Nine). A revaluation of fundamental notions of good and sin is a pivotal structuring principle in *His Dark Materials*, which overall can be seen as an inversion of the Fall narrative of Genesis 3. Pullman follows the line that this is a 'fortunate fall', actually indicating an accession to maturity in terms of both sexuality and consciousness. It is a coming of age, and a coming into power. While there are strands of thought within the Christian tradition which would endorse such a reading, Pullman's account is deliberately set against the Christian narrative as a humanistic alternative. Good and evil are not independent forces, but simply names for what people do. There is no God: the Authority is a fraud. While the Church in *His Dark Materials* is a fictional construct, there are sufficient echoes of Christianity to cause religious controversy around his wholly negative ecclesiastical portrayal. A central abomination practised by the Church is intercision, the rivening of daemon from human. This is related to Pullman's inversion of the Fall narrative. The settling of Dust upon children at puberty is related by the Church to original sin; as the severance of the dæmon appears to stop the settling of Dust, the Church is experimenting with the brutal practice of forcible separation. Pullman's re-reading of the Fall narrative, by contrast, sees in this moment the development of humanity into the fullest image of what it really means to be human.

Lyra is symbolically positioned as Mother Eve, but revalued as saviour rather than cause of humanity's downfall. Mary Malone's role is to act the serpent – again cast in a positive and salvific rather than destructive light. Mary's name is obviously important here, since in traditional Christianity it is Mary who 'redeems' Eve by bearing the ultimate Redeemer, Christ; this Mary facilitates the means by which Eve/Lyra can save the universe. It is also of note that, as in freeing the dead, the telling of true stories is the means to redemption. The redemptive nature of the feminine principle is also an important aspect of Pullman's narrative (mirrored in the significance of the Angel Xaphania, who arguably represents *Sophia*, the feminine divine wisdom principle in Christianity). The salvation of the multiverse is, though, effected through a conjunction of masculine and feminine. Will, working in partnership with Lyra, is also appropriately named. The nature and understanding of human will are central aspects of the Fall narrative. Traditionally, it is the exercise of human will which caused the Fall, and thus the advent of human sin. It is this freedom of human will that preserves God from the charge of creating evil. In Pullman's revisioned version, God does not enter the equation. This does not diminish human responsibility for action; the appropriate exercise of the will is then a fundamental feature of the constitution of the subject. It is related to what is implied in Pullman's account of 'knowing good and evil': namely, self-awareness and moral agency. Therefore, 'Will' is an appropriate model for what it means to be a citizen of Pullman's humanist Republic of Heaven, as a morally responsible agent. However, Pullman's account is also cognizant of the importance of limits upon the will: power should not be exercised in an unrestrained manner, but tempered by compassion, wisdom and duty. This is true also of knowledge: while acquisition and pursuit of knowledge is presented as a good in itself, a cautionary note is sounded concerning its appropriate use. Pullman's environmental concerns come to the fore here, since it is misuse of technical knowledge through the creation and inappropriate use of the 'subtle knife' which has been causing ecological disruption. Pullman's emphasis on limitation and duty is most potently figured in the conclusion, where Will and Lyra necessarily choose to live apart in their separate worlds. This has caused some critics to see in his ending both a disappointing failure to promulgate a new, libidinal and creative economy of human existence and a return to traditional models of social and economic order.

A central theme of *Buffy the Vampire Slayer* is the construction of the monstrous. It is the monstrous that secures the identity of the good; the monstrous represents that which cultures reject and fear. In this way, what is figured as monstrous acts to both mirror and critique human being. Monsters both confirm cultural classifications, and disturb their boundaries. The fragility of the border between the good and the monstrous is thereby exposed. The vampire acts as an externalization of humanity's own shadow-side: in this respect, it is humanity's double, and stands for its relations with its own instinctual desires and drives, including the death-drive. The vampire also figures both transgressive desire and alienation. The vampire interrogates conceptions of what it means to be human. This is especially significant for a universe which is not religiously constituted, and where there is no 'blueprint' of theological anthropology to secure human identity, nature and purpose. In *Buffy*, the borderline been the human and the monstrous is even further challenged by the presence of 'hybrids': vampires with souls. This also underlines identity as multiple, fractured and shifting. It further shows how intimately interconnected the vampire and human are. Human capacity for evil and atrocity is hard to ignore: the vampire figures that dark, destructive side to human nature. As death-in-life, it also elicits abjection: that which we seek to eject but from which we cannot part. However, an interesting feature of recent vampiric representation, including in *Buffy*, is its coding as supra-human, glamorous, heroic and sexually desirable. One aspect of this relates love and sex to death: a not uncommon psychoanalytical move. Beyond this, however, the vampire in some respects is presented as the 'authentically' human in its existential struggle with a divided self and with alienation. In *Buffy*, Angel and Spike are paradigmatic representatives of this.

Buffy challenges simplistic categorizations of 'good' and 'evil'; there are human villains and helpful demons. This raises the question of what, exactly, the significance of the soul is. We know it *is* significant from the story arcs regarding Angel and Spike. Ultimately, it seems that the soul is a signifier not for moral goodness but for the capacity for moral responsibility, agency and remorse. This plays, once more, into interpretations of Genesis 3, which relate knowledge of good and evil to the ability to feel shame. This is consistent with existentialist philosophies, which foreground freedom of choice and a concomitant moral responsibility, rather than fixity of nature. Human being is also related in *Buffy* to love, and a desire for redemption: in this respect Spike's love for Buffy and desire for his soul again positions him, as vampire, as authentic agent and Buffy's dark-double. The First Evil might appear to suggest an originary and essential evil in the Buffyverse; however, I have suggested that it is better understood as a metonym for the reality of evil, as a manifested material force rather than as a primal being. *Buffy* therefore presents a model of the human which has the capacity for self-transcendence through acts of love, heroism and community-oriented action, but which is also conflicted, multiple and threaded through with transgressive drives and desires. The human condition is fundamentally uncertain, undermining the validity of authoritarian monological claims. But within this indistinct and ambiguous landscape, the spirit of goodness is also manifest in human choices.

These fantasy texts, then, resonate deeply with spiritual questions and concerns. Each has its own unique emphases and narrative constructions, and taken as a set they cannot be reduced to a list of common elements or elaborated into an overarching system. Nevertheless, certain common themes and issues do emerge. All four, for example, lay considerable emphasis on the significance of both human choice and human responsibility, in universes with no discernible transcendent external authority providing 'answers' or promising salvation. All are rooted in a robust sense of ethical commitment; the significance of personal engagement and discernment in ethical matters is forefronted, and while there is a clear sense of the importance of 'good' and 'evil' action, these are not ontologically secured or embodied in some transcendent entity. The closest to such a being is the First Evil in *Buffy*, which, as intimated above, I read in a metonymic rather than originary key. None of the four works feature a monotheistic God, although there are 'smaller' gods in Buffy. However, *His Dark Materials* is the only work which explicitly disavows the existence of an ultimate divine. The others pass over this in silence.

There is a concern in all four texts with the place of women and/or a 'feminine' symbolic. This is most controversially expressed in *Harry Potter*, where critics hold that Rowling fails to provide adequate representation of women. It is thoroughly central in the other three. Death is a preoccupation in each text, and the necessity of reconciling with mortality. *Earthsea* and *His Dark Materials* share a very similar account of an 'artificial' afterlife, from which true death – dissolution – is a welcome relief. *Buffy* and *Harry Potter* both feature afterlives but they are left enigmatic in nature. *Earthsea* and *His Dark Materials* also share an anxiety for ecological balance. In all four texts, love and community are emphasized as primary contexts for living.

The subject is shown as capable of self-transcendence in acts of love, including protagonists offering themselves up for sacrificial death in *Buffy* and *Harry Potter* – in both cases with Christological sub-texts. In *His Dark Materials*, it is Asriel and Mrs Coulter who fall sacrificially into the abyss. The sacrifice of Will and Lyra is their own love for each other on the altar of duty. In *Earthsea*, the philosophy reflects Le Guin's own Taoist principles, and sacrifice is not valorized. Nevertheless, Ged risks and loses his powers as Archmage in service to the community. Self-transcendence is also attained through the subjects developing their full potentiality, a process shared by the reader in the course of the narrative journey. In *Earthsea*, it is potently symbolized by Therru becoming dragon. In *Buffy*, it is ironically the relinquishment of her isolated power which enables Buffy to self-transcend her 'destiny' as Slayer. The importance of not only self-transcendence but self-limitation is also recurrently shown. In *Harry Potter* and *Earthsea*, for example, it is the quest for immortality which represents a foundational breach of proper human limits. All four include narrative arcs which draw attention to the necessity of self-limitation in the use of power and knowledge.

It is argued, therefore, that we see here potent models of the authentic journey of the self emerge, which are evocative of spiritual journeying both within and outside of traditional religious frameworks. A wide range of other themes and issues integral to spiritual life and reflection are also present in the texts, including the nature of human being (both socio-politically and metaphysically), the importance of choice, self-limitation, good, evil, death, and the significance of love and community. The world-views are humanistic, with the divine in the guise of a transcendent God either silent or absent. Nevertheless, none of the works presents a reductive materialism. The emphasis is this-worldly, and on self-spirituality in the sense of realizing one's own authentic potential. Such a model of self-spirituality need not be interpreted as selfishly individualistic: the expansion of selves presented are part of a journey to selves more open and relational with others. A distinct tendency to valorize dehierarchalization and anti-authoritarianism is also notable.

In Chapter One it was noted that Carrette and King worried that consumerism was overtaking religious forms and that a dominance of individualistic and capitalistic spiritualities would arise, in detriment to social living and social justice, and called for a counter-discourse to set against it.[4] The kinds of spiritualities emergent in these texts fit, I suggest,

---

4   Jeremy R. Carrette and Richard King, *Selling Spirituality: The Silent Takeover of Religion* (London: Taylor & Francis, 2005).

with the kind of socially oriented, justice-seeking spirituality which Carrette and King favour. The spiritual values implicit and explicit in the texts resonate with established religious models of ethical and compassionate behaviour. There is, however, no ultimate metaphysical referent in these texts – even the ontological basis of language in *Earthsea* was shown to be unstable, and Dust in Pullman to be contingently present. The reader will, inevitably, frame the texts with her or his own spiritual and metaphysical reference points; the reception of *Harry Potter* and *His Dark Materials* demonstrates this well, with some audiences perceiving them as 'anti-religious', and others as congruent with religious perspectives and frameworks when understood as works of fiction and metaphor.

The contingent, immanent, anti-dualistic, anti-dogmatic worldviews do resonate with postmodern spiritualities. So too does the lack of ontological certainty and fractured identities evident in, for example, the Buffyverse. The strong continuing commitment to ethical frameworks raises the perennial postmodern dilemma, namely, the source of ethics in a groundless universe. The narratives present ethical action emerging from personal responsibility, duty or love, the capacity for which is located in what it means to be human. However, where to be human is not to exist as a fixed essence, it highlights once more the significance of choice. Lacking the Authority, we are the authors. The concept of self-authoring works well with the kind of analysis I have undertaken, considering spiritualities as narrated. In reading the texts, the reader becomes co-narrator. The possibility is always open to read in the mode of resistance, negotiation or even perhaps sometimes self-transformation.

For those constructing their spiritualities outside of formal traditions, the model of the bricoleur can be applied, whereby one assembles from the brightest pieces available the narrative of one's life. This is a mode of mythopoesis. These texts, which as fantasy literature might also be deemed forms of mythopoesis, are some of the fragments which may enter into the bricolage. Literature, including fantasy literature, allows one to explore possibilities imaginatively, disclosing how things might be, or how we might be. In Chapter One, Todorov's theory of the fantastic was mentioned; the fantastic in his particular analysis represents the hesitation, or interruption, between the uncanny and the marvellous. I suggest that the concept of the fantastic as hesitation might be applied by analogy to reading fantasy texts in this mode: poised between a spiritual and a secular which do not part, but do not collapse into one another. In this negotiation between immanence and transcendence, we may find shadows of the divine.

BIBLIOGRAPHY

Abbott, Stacey. 'A Little Less Ritual and a Little More Fun: The Modern Vampire in *Buffy the Vampire Slayer*'. *Slayage: The Online International Journal of Buffy Studies* 1, no. 3 (2001). Online: http://www.slayageonline.com/essays/slayage3/sabbott.htm
——'Walking the Fine Line Between Angel and Angelus', *Slayage: The Online International Journal of Buffy Studies* 3, no. 1 (2003). Online: http://www.slayageonline.com/essays/slayage9/Abbott.htm
Acocella, Joan. 'Under the Spell', *The New Yorker* (31 July 2000): 74–78.
Alderman, Naomi and Annette Seidel-Arpaci. 'Imaginary Para-Sites of the Soul: Vampires and Representations of "Blackness" and "Jewishness" in the Buffy/Angelverse'. *Slayage: The Online International Journal of Buffy Studies* 3, no. 2 (2003). Online: http://www.slayageonline.com/essays/slayage10/Alderman_&_Seidel-Arpaci.htm
Alexander, Jenny. 'A Vampire Is Being Beaten: DeSade through the Looking Glass in *Buffy* and *Angel*', *Slayage: The Online International Journal of Buffy Studies* 4, no. 3 (2004). Online: http://www.slayageonline.com/essays/slayage15/Alexander.htmJoan
Almond, Philip C. *The British Discovery of Buddhism*. Cambridge: Cambridge University Press, 1988.
Altizer, Thomas J. J. *The New Apocalypse: The Radical Christian Vision of William Blake*. Aurora, CO: The Davies Group, 2000.
Attebury, Brian. *The Fantasy Tradition in American Literature: From Irving to Le Guin*. Bloomington, IN: Indiana University Press, 1980.
Augustine. de natura and gratia iii, 3–iv, 4. In *The Christian Theology Reader*, edited by Alister E. McGrath. Oxford: Wiley-Blackwell, 2006.
Badiner, Allan Hunt (ed.). *Dharma Gaia*. Berkeley, CA: Parallax Press, 1990.
Bakhtin, Mikhail. *Problems of Dostoevsky's Poetics*, translated by Caryl Emerson. Minneapolis, MN: University of Minnesota Press, 1984.
——*Rabelais and His World*, translated by Hélène Iswolsky. Bloomington, IN: Indiana University Press, 1984.
Barbaccia, Holly G. 'Buffy in the "Terrible House"'. *Slayage: The Online International Journal of Buffy Studies* 1, no. 4 (2001). Online: http://www.slayageonline.com/essays/slayage4/barbaccia.htm
Barfield, Steven. 'Fantasy and the Interpretation of Fantasy in Harry Potter'. *The Washington and Jefferson College Review* 54 (Fall 2004): 24–32.
Baureithel, Ulrike. 'The origin of the world'. *signandsight.com* (16 June 2009). Online: http://www.signandsight.com/features/1885.html
Berger, Peter. *A Far Glory: The Quest for Faith in an Age of Credulity*. New York, NY: Free Press, 1992.

Bieszk, Patricia. 'Vampire Hip: Style as Subcultural Expression in *Buffy the Vampire Slayer*'. *Refractory: A Journal of Entertainment Media* (4 February 2005). Online: http://blogs.arts.unimelb.edu.au/refractory/2005/02/04/vampire-hip-style-as-subcultural-expression-in-buffy-the-vampire-slayer-patricia-bieszk/

Bird, Sharon R. 'Welcome to the Men's Club: Homosociality and the Maintenance of Hegemonic Masculinity'. *Gender and Society* 10, no. 2 (April 1996): 120–32.

Black, Sharon. 'The Magic of Harry Potter: Symbols and Heroes of Fantasy'. *Children's Literature in Education* 34, no. 3 (2003): 237–47.

Blake, William. 'Eternity'. In *The Complete Poetry and Prose of William Blake*, edited by David V. Erdman. New York, NY: Doubleday, 1982.

Bowman, Laurel. '*Buffy the Vampire Slayer*: The Greek Hero Revisited' (2002). Online: http://web.uvic.ca/~lbowman/buffy/buffythehero.html

Bradney, Anthony. '"I Made a Promise to a Lady": Law and Love in *BtVS*'. *Slayage: The Online International Journal of Buffy Studies* 3, no. 2 (2003). Online: http://www.slayageonline.com/essays/slayage10/Bradney.htm

Braidotti, Rosi. 'On the feminist female subject or from she-self to she-other'. In *Beyond Equality and Difference: Citizenship, Feminist Politics and Female Subjectivity*, edited by G. Bock and S. James. London: Routledge, 1992: 176–92.

Brannon, Julie Sloan. '"It's about Power": Buffy, Foucault, and the Quest for Self'. *Slayage: The Online International Journal of Buffy Studies* 6, no. 4 (2006). Online: http://slayageonline.com/essays/slayage24/Brannon.htm

Breton, Rob and Lindsey McMaster. 'Dissing the Age of MOO: Initiatives, Alternatives, and Rationality'. *Slayage: The Online International Journal of Buffy Studies* 1, no. 1 (2001). Online: http://slayageonline.com/essays/slayage1/bretonmcmaster.htm

Bruce, Steve. *Religion in the Modern World: from Cathedrals to Cults*. Oxford: Oxford University Press, 1996.

——*God is Dead: Secularization in the West*. Oxford: Oxford University Press, 2002.

Byatt, A. S. 'Harry Potter and the Childish Adult', *The New York Times* (7 July 2003). New York edition, A13.

Callander, Michelle. 'Bram Stoker's *Buffy*: Traditional Gothic and Contemporary Culture'. *Slayage: The Online International Journal of Buffy Studies* 1, no. 3 (2001). Online: http://slayageonline.com/essays/slayage3/callander.html

Campbell, Joseph. *The Hero with a Thousand Faces*. Novato, CA: New World Library, 2008.

Campbell, Joseph and Bill Moyers. *The Power of Myth*, edited by Betty Sue Flowers. New York, NY: Doubleday, 1988.

Carlyle, Thomas. *Sartor Resartus (1831). Lectures on Heroes (1840)*. London: Chapman and Hall, 1858.

Carrette, Jeremy R. and Richard King, *Selling Spirituality: The Silent Takeover of Religion*. London: Taylor & Francis, 2005.

Chevalier, Noel. 'The Liberty Tree and the Whomping Willow: Political Justice, Magical Science, and Harry Potter'. *The Lion and the Unicorn* 29, no. 3 (2005): 397–415.

Clute, John and John Grant (eds). *The Encyclopedia of Fantasy*. New York, NY: St Martin's Griffin, 1999.

Colás, Santiago. 'Telling True Stories, or The Immanent Ethics of Material Spirit (and Spiritual Matter) in Philip Pullman's *His Dark Materials*'. *Discourse* 27, no. 1 (2005): 34–66.

Comoletti, Laura B. and Michael D. C. Drout. 'How They Do Things with Words: Language, Power, Gender, and the Priestly Wizards of Ursula K. Le Guin's Earthsea Books'. *Children's Literature* 29 (2001): 113–41.

Cox, Renée. 'Got Myself a Soul? The Puzzling Treatment of the Soul in *Buffy*'. In *The Truth of* Buffy: *Essays on Fiction Illuminating Reality*, edited by Emily Dial-Driver, Sally Emmons-Featherston, Jim Ford and Carolyn Anne Taylor. Jefferson, NC: McFarland, 2008: 24–37.

Crosby, Janice C. *Cauldron of Changes: Feminist Spirituality in Fantastic Fiction*. Jefferson, NC: McFarland, 2000.

Crow, John H. and Richard D. Erlich. 'Shadows in Earthsea: Le Guin's Uses of a Jungian Archetype'. In *Ursula K. Le Guin*, edited by Joseph D. Olander and Martin Harry Greenburg. Edinburgh: Paul Harris, 1979: 220–24.

Damour, Lisa. 'Harry Potter and the Acquisition of Knowledge'. In *Reading Harry Potter*, edited by Giselle Liza Anatol. Columbia, MO and London: University of Missouri Press, 2004: 15–24.

David, Robert G. *The Arctic in the British Imagination, 1818–1914*. Manchester: Manchester University Press, 2000.

Davidson, MaryJanice. *Undead and Unwed*. New York, NY: Berkley Books, 2004.

Davie, Grace. 'Prospects for Religion in the Modern World.' *The Ecumenical Review* 52, no. 4 (2000): 455–64.

Day, William Patrick. *Vampire Legends in Contemporary American Culture*. Lexington, KY: University Press of Kentucky, 2002.

de Beauvoir, Simone. *The Second Sex*. New York, NY: Knopf, 1971.

Deleuze, Gilles and Félix Guattari. *Anti-Oedipus: Capitalism and Schizophrenia*. London and New York, NY: Continuum International Publishing Group, 2004.

Dewey, John. *The Quest for Certainty*. New York, NY: Minton, Balch & Co., 1929.

Dobbelaere, K. 'Some Trends in European Sociology of Religion'. *Sociological Analysis* 48 (1987): 107–37.

Dundes, Alan. 'Folkloristics in the Twenty-First Century (AFS Invited Presidential Plenary Address, 2004)'. *Journal of American Folklore* 118, no. 470 (2005): 385–408.

Erickson, Greg. '"Religion Freaky" or a "Bunch of Men Who Died?" The (A)theology of *Buffy*'. *Slayage: The Online International Journal of Buffy Studies* 4, nos 1–2 (2004). Online: http://www.slayageonline.com/Numbers/slayage13_14.htm

——'"Sometimes You Need a Story": American Christianity, Vampires and Buffy'. In *Fighting the Forces: What's at Stake in* Buffy the Vampire Slayer, edited by Rhonda V. Wilcox and David Lavery. Lanham, MD: Rowman & Littlefield, 2002: 108–19.

Erlich, Richard D. 'Le Guin and God: Quarreling with the One, Critiquing Pure Reason'. *Extrapolation* 47, no. 3 (Winter 2006): 351–80.

'Faith and Fantasy'. *Encounter*. ABC Radio National (24 March 2002). Online: http://www.abc.net.au/rn/relig/enc/stories/s510312.htm

Falconer, Rachel. *The Crossover Novel: Contemporary Children's Fiction and its Adult Readership*. London: Taylor & Francis, 2008.

Ferrara, Mark S. 'Ch'an Buddhism and the Prophetic Poems of William Blake'. *Journal of Chinese Philosophy* 24, no. 1 (1997): 59–73.

Feuerbach, Ludwig. *The Essence of Christianity*, translated by Marian Evans. New York, NY: Calvin Blanchard, 1855.

Fiorenza, Elisabeth Schüssler. *Jesus: Miriam's Child, Sophia's Prophet*. London and New York, NY: Continuum, 1995.

Foucault, Michel. 'Truth and Method'. In *The Foucault Reader*, edited by Paul Rabinow. New York, NY: Pantheon Books, 1984: 31–120.

Freitas, Donna and Jason King. *Killing the Imposter God*. San Francisco, CA: Jossey Bass, 2007.

Frye, Herman Northrop. *Fearful Symmetry: A Study of William Blake*. Princeton, NJ: Princeton University Press, 1947.

Geertz, Clifford. *Interpretation of Cultures*. New York, NY: Basic Books, 1977.

Gill, Eric and Anthony Lundsgaarde. 'State Welfare Spending and Religiosity: a Cross-National Analysis'. *Rationality and Society* 16, no. 4 (2004): 399–436.

Gilligan, Carol. *In a Different Voice: Psychological Theory and Women's Development*. Cambridge, MA: Harvard University Press, 1982.

Gooderham, David. 'Fantasizing It as It Is: Religious Language in Philip Pullman's Trilogy, *His Dark Materials*'. *Children's Literature* 31, no. 1 (2003): 155–75.

Graeber, David. *Fragments of an Anarchist Anthropology*. Chicago, IL: Prickly Paradigm Press, 2004.

Graham, Elaine L. *Representations of the Post/human: Monsters, Aliens and Others in Popular Culture*. Manchester: Manchester University Press, 2002.

Grant, John. 'Gulliver Unravels: Generic Fantasy and the Loss of Subversion'. *Extrapolation* 41, no. 1 (Spring 2000): 21–27.

Greeley, Andrew M. *Religious Change in America*. Cambridge, MA: Harvard University Press, 1989.

Gresh, Lois H. *Exploring Philip Pullman's* His Dark Materials*: An Unauthorized Adventure through* The Golden Compass, The Subtle Knife, *and* The Amber Spyglass. London: Macmillan, 2007.

Granger, John. *Looking for God in Harry Potter*. Carol Stream, IL: Tyndale House Publishers, 2006.

Grimes, M. Katherine. 'Harry Potter: Fairy Tale Prince, Real Boy and Archetypal Hero'. In *The Ivory Tower and Harry Potter: Perspectives on a Literary Phenomenon*, edited by Lana A. Whited. Columbia, MO and London: University of Missouri Press, 2004: 89–122.

Grosz, Elizabeth A. *Sexual Subversions*. London and Sydney: Allen & Unwin, 1989.

Hallaway, Tate. *Tall, Dark and Dead*. New York, NY: Berkley Books, 2006.

Hampson, Daphne. *After Christianity*. London: SCM Press, 1996.

Harrison, Jane Ellen *Prolegomena to the Study of Greek Religion*. Princeton, NJ: Princeton University Press, 1991.

Hartney, Christopher. 'Imperial and Epic'. In *The Buddha of Suburbia*, edited by Carole M. Cusack, Christopher Hartney and Frances Di Lauro. Sydney: RLA Press, 2005.

Hebdige, Dick. *Subculture: The Meaning of Style*. London and New York, NY: Routledge, 1979.

Heelas, Paul. *The New Age Movement*. Oxford: Wiley-Blackwell, 1996.

Heelas, Paul and Linda Woodhead. *The Spiritual Revolution: Why Religion is Giving Way to Spirituality*. Oxford: Wiley-Blackwell, 2005.

Heilman, Elizabeth E. (ed.). *Critical Perspectives on Harry Potter*, 2nd edn. Oxford and New York, NY: Routledge, 2008.

Henderson, Joseph. 'Ancient Myths and Modern Man'. In *Man and His Symbols*, edited by Carl Gustav Jung and Marie-Luise von Franz. London: Doubleday, 1964: 104–57.

Hinton, Sofrina. 'Confluence: The Quest for Self in *Buffy the Vampire Slayer*', *Phase Five* 1, no. 2 (25 November 2002). Online: http://www.bibliora.com/P5_0302/html/confluence.html

Hopkins, S. *Girl Heroes: The New Force in Popular Culture*. Sydney: Pluto Press, 2002.

Hume, David. *Dialogues concerning Natural Religion and Other Writings*, edited by Dorothy Coleman. Cambridge: Cambridge University Press, 2007.

Irigaray, Luce. *An Ethics of Sexual Difference*, translated by Carolyn Burke and Gillian C. Gill. London: Athlone Press, 1993.

——*This Sex Which is Not One*, translated by Catherine Porter. Ithaca, NY: Cornell University Press, 1985.

Jackson, Rosemary. *Fantasy: Literature of Subversion*. London: Routledge, 1981.

Johnson, Elizabeth A. *Friends of God and Prophets: A Feminist Theological Reading of the Communion*. London: Continuum, 1998.
——*She Who Is: The Mystery of God in Feminist Theological Discourse*. New York, NY: Crossroad, 1992.
Jung, Carl Gustav. *Psychology and the East*. Princeton, NJ: Princeton University Press, 1978.
Kay, David N. *Tibetan and Zen Buddhism in Britain*. London: Routledge, 2004.
Keller, Tatiana. 'Feminist Issues in Earthsea: *Tehanu: the Last Book of Earthsea*'. The New York Review of Science Fiction 28 (December 1990): 14–16.
Kerényi, Karl. *Dionysos*. Princeton, NJ: Princeton University Press, 1996.
Kierkegaard, Søren. *Fear and Trembling*, edited by C. Stephen Evans and Sylvia Walsh, translated by Sylvia Walsh. Cambridge: Cambridge University Press, 2006.
Kristeva, Julia. 'Place Names'. In *Desire in Language*, edited by Leon S. Roudiez, translated by Thomas Gore, Leon Roudiez and Alice Jardine. New York, NY: Columbia University Press, 1980: 271–94.
——*Powers of Horror*, translated by Leon S. Roudiez. New York, NY: Columbia University Press, 1982.
——'Women's Time', translated by Alice Jardine and Harry Blake. *Signs* 7, no. 1 (1981): 13–35.
Lacoss, Jann. 'Of Magicals and Muggles: Reversals and Revulsions at Hogwarts'. In *The Ivory Tower and Harry Potter: Perspectives on a Literary Phenomenon*, edited by Lana A. Whited. Columbia, MO and London: University of Missouri Press, 2004: 67–88.
Laetz, Brian and Joshua J. Johnston. 'What is Fantasy'. *Philosophy and Literature* 32, no. 1 (2008): 161–72.
Le Guin, Ursula K. 'Dragonfly'. In Ursula K. Le Guin, *Tales from Earthsea*. London: Orion, 2001: 197–265.
——*Earthsea Revisioned*. Cambridge, MA: Children's Literature New England, 1993.
——*Language of the Night: Essays on Fantasy and Science Fiction*, edited and with introductions by Susan Wood, 2nd edn. London: The Women's Press, 1989.
——*The Beginning Place*. London: Harper & Row, 1980.
——'The Carrier-Bag Theory of Fiction'. In *Women of Vision*, edited by Denise Du Point. New York, NY: St Martins Press, 1988: 1–9.
——'The Feminine and the Tao: an interview with Ursula K. LeGuin'. Interview by Brenda Peterson. *Embrace the Moon: School of Tijiquan and Qigong*, 2003. Online: http://www.embracethemoon.com/perspectives/leguin.htm
——*The Earthsea Quartet: A Wizard Of Earthsea; The Tombs of Atuan; The Farthest Shore; Tehanu*. London: Puffin, 1992.
——*The Lathe of Heaven*. New York, NY: Scribner's, 1971.
——'The Ones Who Walk Away from Omelas'. In Ursula K. Le Guin, *The Wind's Twelve Quarters*. London: Victor Gollancz, 1975: 275–84.
——*The Other Wind*. San Diego, CA: Harcourt & Brace, 2001.
Leane, Elizabeth, 'Locating the Thing: The Antarctic as Alien Space in John W. Campbell's "Who Goes There?"', *Science Fiction Studies* 32, no. 2 (July 2005): 225–39.
Lenz, Millicent and Peter Hunt. *Alternative Worlds in Fantasy Fiction*. London and New York, NY: Continuum, 2001.
Lewis, C. S. *The Last Battle*. London: The Bodley Head, 1967.
Limon, John. *Stand-up Comedy in Theory, or, Abjection in America*. Durham, NC: Duke University Press, 2000.
Lindow, Sandra J. *Becoming Dragon: The Transcendence of the Damaged Child in the Fiction of Ursula K. Le Guin*. Brownsville, TX: The University of Texas, 2003.

Littlefield, Holly. 'Unlearning Patriarchy: Ursula Le Guin's Feminist Consciousness in *The Tombs of Atuan* and *Tehanu*'. *Extrapolation* 36, no. 3 (Fall 1995): 244–58.

Lloyd, Genevieve. *The Man of Reason: 'Male' and 'Female' in Western Philosophy*. London: Routledge, 1993.

Locke, John. *An Essay Concerning Human Understanding* (Stilwell, KS: Digireads.com Publishing, 2008), 204.

Loy, David and Linda Goodhew. *The Dharma of Dragons and Dæmons: Buddhist Themes in Modern Fantasy Fiction*. Somerville, MA: Wisdom Publications, 2004.

McDaniel, Kathryn N. 'The Elfin Mystique: Fantasy and Feminism in J. K. Rowling's Harry Potter Series'. In *Past Watchful Dragons: Fantasy and Faith in the World of C. S. Lewis*, edited by Amy H. Sturgis. Altadena, CA: Mythopoeic Press, 2007: 183–207.

McLean, Susan. 'The Power of Women in Ursula K. Le Guin's *Tehanu*'. *Extrapolation* 38, no. 2 (1997): 110–18.

Colin N. Manlove. *Modern Fantasy: Five Studies*. Cambridge: Cambridge University Press, 1978.

——'The Elusiveness of Fantasy'. In *The Shape of the Fantastic: Selected Essays from the Seventh International Conference on the Fantastic in the Arts*, edited by O. H. Saciuk. Westport, CT: Greenwood Press, 1990: 53–65.

Martin, David. *A General Theory of Secularization*. New York, NY: Harper & Row, 1978.

Meacham, Steve. 'The Shed Where God Died'. *The Sydney Morning Herald* (13 December 2003). Online: http://www.smh.com.au/ articles/2003/12/12/1071125644900.html

Mendlesohn, Farah. 'Crowning the King: Harry Potter and the Construction of Authority'. In *The Ivory Tower and Harry Potter: Perspectives on a Literary Phenomenon*, edited by Lana A. Whited. Columbia, MO and London: University of Missouri Press, 2004: 159–82.

Mills, Alice. 'Archetypes and the Unconscious in *Harry Potter* and Diana Wynne Jones' *Fire and Hemlock* and *Dogsbody*'. In *Reading Harry Potter*, edited by Giselle Liza Anatol. Columbia, MO and London: University of Missouri Press, 2004: 3–14.

——'Burning Women in Ursula K. Le Guin's *Tehanu: The Last Book of Earthsea*'. *New York Review of Science Fiction* 7, no. 1 (1995): 3–7.

Money, Mary Alice. 'The Undemonization of Supporting Characters in *Buffy*'. In *Fighting the Forces: What's at Stake in* Buffy the Vampire Slayer, edited by Rhonda V. Wilcox and David Lavery. Lanham, MD: Rowman & Littlefield, 2002: 98–120.

Moorcock, Michael. *Wizardry and Wild Romance: A Study of Epic Fantasy*. London: Gollancz, 2004.

Müller, F. M. *Lectures on the Origin and Growth of Religion*. London: Longmans, Green, 1878.

Nagapriya. *Exploring Karma and Rebirth*. Birmingham: Windhorse Publications, 2004.

Nelson, Victoria. 'Symmes Hole, or The South Polar Romance'. *Raritan: A Quarterly Review* 17, no. 2 (Fall 1997): 136–66.

Nietzsche, Friedrich Wilhelm. *Beyond Good and Evil*, translated by Walter Kaufmann. New York, NY: Vintage Books, 1966.

——*The Antichrist*, translated by H. L. Mencken. Whitefish, MT: Kessinger Publishing, 2004.

——*Thus Spake Zarathustra*, translated by R. J. Hollingdale. Harmondsworth: Penguin, 1961.

Nodelman, Perry. 'Reinventing the Past: Gender in Ursula K. Le Guin's *Tehanu* and the Earthsea "Trilogy"', *Children's Literature* 23 (1995): 179–201.

Norris, Pippa and Ronald Inglehart. *Sacred and Secular: Religion and Politics Worldwide.* Cambridge: Cambridge University Press, 2004.

Olsen, Lance. 'The Country Nobody Visits: Varieties of Fantasy in Strand's Poetry'. In *The Shape of the Fantastic: Selected Essays from the Seventh International Conference on the Fantastic in the Arts.* Westport, CT: Greenwood Press, 1990.

Owen, Susan A. 'Vampires, Postmodernity and Postfeminism: *Buffy the Vampire Slayer'. Journal of Popular Film and Television* 27, no. 2 (Summer 1999): 24–31.

Pagels, Elaine H. *Adam, Eve, and the Serpent.* New York, NY: Vintage Books, 1989.

——*The Gnostic Gospels.* New York, NY: Vintage Books, 1989.

——*The Origin of Satan.* New York, NY: Vintage Books, 1996.

Parsons, Wendy and Catriona Nicholson. 'Talking to Philip Pullman: An Interview'. *The Lion and the Unicorn* 23, no. 1 (January 1999): 116–34.

Partridge, Christopher Hugh. *The Re-Enchantment of the West: Alternative Spiritualities, Sacralization, Popular Culture and Occulture*, vol. 1. London: Continuum, 2005.

Pearson, Carol and Katherine Pope. *The Female Hero in American and British Literature.* New York, NY: R.R. Bowker, 1981.

Pender, Patricia. '"I'm Buffy and You're . . . History": The Postmodern Politics of *Buffy'.* In *Fighting the Forces: What's at Stake in* Buffy the Vampire Slayer, edited by Rhonda V. Wilcox and David Lavery. Lanham, MD: Rowman & Littlefield, 2002: 35–44.

Pennington, John. 'From Elfland to Hogwarts, or the Aesthetic Trouble with Harry Potter', *The Lion and the Unicorn* 26, no. 1 (2002): 78–97.

Philippopoulos-Mihalopoulos, Andreas. 'Between Light and Darkness: Earthsea and the Name of Utopia'. *Contemporary Justice Review* 8, no. 1 (2005): 45–57.

Pinsent, Pat. 'Unexpected Allies? Pullman and the Feminist Theologies'. In *His Dark Materials Illuminated: Critical Essays on Philip Pullman's Trilogy*, edited by Millicent Lenz and Carole Scott. Detroit, MI: Wayne State University Press, 1995: 199–211.

Plantinga, Alvin. *God, Freedom, and Evil.* Grand Rapids, MI: Eerdmans, 1977.

Playdon, Zoe-Jane. 'What you are, what's to come: Feminisms, citizenship and the divine in *Buffy'.* In *Reading the Vampire Slayer: The New, Updated, Unofficial Guide to* Buffy *and* Angel, edited by Roz Kaveney. London: Tauris Parke, 2004: 156–94.

Powers, Douglas. 'Buddhism and Modernity: An Ancient Tradition Faces the Twenty-First Century'. *Religion East and West* 1, no. 1 (2001): 67–76.

Pratt, Annis. *Archetypal Patterns in Women's Fiction.* Bloomington, IN: Indiana University Press, 1981.

Pratt, James Bissett. *The Pilgrimage of Buddhism and a Buddhist Pilgrimage.* New Delhi: Asian Educational Services, 1996.

Protevi, John. *Political Physics: Deleuze, Derrida and the Body Politic.* London: Continuum, 2001.

Pullman, Philip. 'A Dark Agenda?'. Interview by Susan Roberts. *Surefish: the community website from Christian Aid* (November 2002). Online: http://www.surefish.co.uk/culture/features/pullman_interview.htm

——'Are You There. God? It's me'. *Book* (December 2002). Online: http://web.archive.org/web/20050211151440/http://www.bookmagazine.com/issue25/inthemargins.shtml

——'Carnegie Medal Acceptance Speech'. *Philip Pullman: His Dark Materials.* Online: http://www.randomhouse.com/features/pullman/author/carnegie.html

——'I am of the Devil's party'. Interview by Helena de Bertodano. *Telegraph.co.uk* (29 January 2002). Online: http://www.telegraph.co.uk/culture/donotmigrate/3572490/I-am-of-the-Devils-party.html

——'Identity crisis'. *Guardian* (19 November 2005). Online: http://docs.newsbank. com/s/InfoWeb/aggdocs/UKNB/10E015E661AFB3F8/10499C0CF00BD483

——'Interview with Philip Pullman'. Interview by Joan Bakewell. *Belief* series, BBC Radio 3 (23 September 2006).

——'Philip Pullman – the extended e-mail interview'. Interview by Peter T. Chattaway, *Filmchat* (28 November 2007). Online: http://filmchatblog.blogspot. com/2007/11/philip-pullman-extended-e-mail.html

——'Philip Pullman: New Brand of Environmentalism'. Interview by Andrew Simms. *Telegraph.co.uk* (19 January 2008). Online: http://www.telegraph.co.uk/ earth/3322329/Philip-Pullman-new-brand-of-environmentalism.html

——*The Amber Spyglass*. London: Scholastic, 2001.

——'The Republic of Heaven'. *The Horn Book Magazine* (December 2001). Online: http://www.hbook.com/magazine/articles/2001/nov01_pullman.asp

——*The Subtle Knife*. London: Scholastic, 2007.

——'The Worlds: Religion'. In *Philip Pullman: Other Writing*. Online: http://www. philip-pullman.com/pages/content/index.asp?PageID=110

Pye, Martin. *Skilful Means: a Concept in Mahayana Buddhism*. London: Routledge, 2008.

Raine, Kathleen. *Blake and Tradition*, 2 vols. London: Taylor & Francis, 2002.

Reed, Toni. *Demon-lovers and their Victims in British Fiction*. Lexington, KY: University Press of Kentucky, 1988.

Rescher, Nicholas. *G. W. Leibniz's Monadology: an Edition for Students*. London: Routledge, 1992.

Rice, Anne. 'Essay on Earlier Works'. *Anne's Bookshelf* (15 August 2007). Online: http://www.annerice.com/Bookshelf-EarlierWorks.html

Ricoeur, Paul. *Time and Narrative*, translated by Kathleen Blarney and David Pellauer. 3 vols. Chicago, IL: University of Chicago Press, 1985.

Riess, Jana. *What Would Buffy Do?* San Francisco, CA: Jossey-Bass, 2004.

Robertson, Roland. 'Global Millennialism: A Postmortem on Secularization'. In *Religion, Globalization and Culture*, edited by Peter Beyer and Lori G. Beaman. Leiden: Brill, 2007: 9–34.

Robinson, Christopher L. 'The Violence of the Name: Patronymy in Earthsea'. *Extrapolation* 49, no. 3 (Winter 2008): 385–409.

Robinson, Hilary. *Reading Art, Reading Irigaray: The Politics of Art by Women*. London: I.B.Tauris, 2006.

Roof, Wade Clark. *Spiritual Marketplace: Baby Boomers and the Remaking of American Religion*. Princeton, NJ: Princeton University Press, 2001.

Rottensteiner, Franz. 'Review: Le Guin's Fantasy'. *Science Fiction Studies* 8, no. 1 (1981): 87–90.

Rowling, J. K. *Harry Potter and the Chamber of Secrets*. London: Bloomsbury, 1998.

——'*Harry Potter and the Chamber of Secrets*, Audio Interview: J. K. Rowling', interview by Steve Head (13 November 2002). Online: http://ffmovies.ign.com/ filmforce/audio/press_conf_jk.mp3

——*Harry Potter and the Deathly Hallows*. London: Bloomsbury, 2007.

——*Harry Potter and the Goblet of Fire*. London: Bloomsbury, 2000.

——*Harry Potter and the Half-Blood Prince*. London: Bloomsbury, 2005.

——*Harry Potter and the Order of the Phoenix*. London: Bloomsbury, 2003.

——*Harry Potter and the Philosopher's Stone*. London: Bloomsbury, 1997.

——*Harry Potter and the Prisoner of Azkaban*. London: Bloomsbury, 1999.

——Interview by Evan Solomon, CBCNewsWorld: *Hot Type* (13 July 2000).

——'J. K. Rowling Official Site. Section: F. A. Q'. Online: http://www.jkrowling.com/ textonly/en/faq_view.cfm?id=58

——'J. K. Rowling Official Site. Section: Characters'. Online: http://www.jkrowling. com/en/index.cfm

Ruether, Rosemary Radford. *Sexism and God-talk: Toward a Feminist Theology*. Boston, MA: Beacon Press, 1983.

Russell, Mary Harris. 'Eve, Again! Mother Eve!'. In *His Dark Materials Illuminated: Critical Essays on Philip Pullman's Trilogy*, edited by Millicent Lenz and Carole Scott. Detroit, MI: Wayne State University Press, 1995: 212–22.

Sandner, David. *Fantastic Literature: A Critical Reader*. London: Praeger, 2004.

Sanyal, Mithu M. *Vulva: Die Enthüllung des unsichtbaren Geschlechts*. Berlin: Wagenbach, 2009.

Sartre, Jean-Paul. *Being and Nothingness*, translated by Hazel E. Barnes. London: Routledge, 1970.

Sartre, Jean-Paul and Carol Macomber, *Existentialism is a Humanism*. New Haven, CT: Yale University Press, 2007.

Schneiders, Sandra M. *Beyond Patching: Faith and Feminism in the Catholic Church*. New York, NY: Paulist Press, 1991.

Schneiders, Sandra Marie. 'Religion vs. Spirituality: A Contemporary Conundrum'. *Spiritus: A Journal of Christian Spirituality* 3, no. 2 (2003): 163–85.

Schoefer, Christine. 'Harry Potter's Girl Trouble'. *Salon.com* (13 January 2000). Online: http://www.salon.com/books/feature/2000/01/13/potter/index1.html

Scott, Niall (ed.). *Monsters and the Monstrous: Myths and Metaphors of Enduring Evil*. Amsterdam: Rodopi, 2007.

Sebastian, C. D. 'Theory of Psyche in Buddhism: An Appraisal of Buddhist and Scientific Psychology'. *OMEGA: Indian Journal of Science and Religion* 6, no. 1: 39–51.

Segal, Robert Alan. *Hero Myths*. Oxford: Wiley-Blackwell, 2000.

Shantz, Jeff. *Living Anarchy: Theory and Practice in Anarchist Movements*. Palo Alto, CA: Academica Press, 2008.

Sherman, Cordelia. 'The Princess and the Wizard: The Fantasy Worlds of Ursula K. LeGuin and George MacDonald'. *Children's Literature Association Quarterly* 12, no. 1 (1987): 24–28.

Shohet, Lauren. 'Reading Dark Materials'. In *His Dark Materials Illuminated: Critical Essays on Philip Pullman's Trilogy*, edited by Millicent Lenz and Carole Scott. Detroit, MI: Wayne State University Press, 1995: 22–36.

South, James B. 'Buffy the Concept Slayer', interview by Alan Saunders on *The Philosopher's Zone*, ABC Radio National (29 March 2008). Online: http://www.abc. net.au/rn/philosopherszone/stories/2008/2198169.htm

Spaise, Terry L. 'Necrophilia and SM: The Deviant Side of *Buffy the Vampire Slayer*'. *Journal of Popular Culture* 38, no. 4 (May 2005): 744–62.

Stark, Rodney. 'Secularization, R.I.P.'. *Sociology of Religion* 60, no. 3 (1999): 2 49–73.

Stephens, Rebecca. 'Harry and Hierarchy: Book Banning as a Reaction to the Subversion of Authority'. In *Reading Harry Potter*, edited by Giselle Liza Anatol. Columbia, MO and London: University of Missouri Press, 2004: 51–65.

Stevenson, Gregory. *Televised Morality*. Lanham, MD: Hamilton Books, 2003.

Swearer, Donald. 'An Assessment of Buddhist Eco-Philosophy'. Center for the Study of World Religions, Harvard Divinity School (2005). Online: http://www.hds. harvard.edu/cswr/resources/print/dongguk/swearer.pdf

Todorov, Tzvetan. *The Fantastic: A Structural Approach to a Literary Genre*. Ithaca, NY: Cornell University Press, 1975.

Trites, Roberta Seelinger. 'The Harry Potter Novels as a Test Case for Adolescent Literature'. *Style* 35, no. 3 (Fall 2001): 427–85.

BIBLIOGRAPHY

Tucker, Nicholas. 'The Rise and Rise of Harry Potter'. *Children's Literature in Education* 30, no. 4 (1999): 221–34.

Vaughn, S. 'The Female Hero in Science Fiction and Fantasy: "Carrier-Bag" to "No-Road".' *The Journal of the Fantastic in the Arts* 4, no. 4 (1991): 83–96.

Verjoeven, Martin. 'Buddhism and Science: Probing the Boundaries of Faith and Reason'. *Religion East and West* 1, no. 1 (2001): 77–97.

Waggoner, Diana. *The Hills of Faraway: A Guide to Fantasy*. New York, NY: Atheneum, 1978.

Wall, Derek (ed). *Green History: A Reader in Environmental Literature, Philosophy and Politics*. London: Routledge, 1994.

Wannamaker, Annette. 'Men in Cloaks and High-heeled Boots, Men Wielding Pink Umbrellas: Witchy Masculinities in the Harry Potter Novels'. *The Looking Glass: New Perspectives on Children's Literature* 10, no. 1 (2006). Online: http://www.lib.latrobe.edu.au/ojs/index.php/tlg/article/view/96/81

Weisman, Steven R. 'Editorial Observer; A Novel That Is a Midsummer Night's Dream'. *The New York Times: Opinion* (11 July 2000). Online: http://www.nytimes.com/2000/07/11/opinion/editorial-observer-a-novel-that-is-a-midsummer-nights-dream.html

Westman, Karin E. 'Specters of Thatcherism: Contemporary British Culture in J. K. Rowling's Harry Potter Novels'. In *The Ivory Tower and Harry Potter: Perspectives on a Literary Phenomenon*, edited by Lana A. Whited. Columbia, MO and London: University of Missouri Press, 2004: 305–28.

Whedon, Joss. *Audio Commentary: Buffy the Vampire Slayer, Season One*. DVD. 'Welcome to the Hellmouth' and 'The Harvest', 2001.

Whedon, Joss. 'Joss Whedon – The Man behind the Slayer'. Interview by Laura Miller. *Salon.com* (23 May 2003). Online: http://www.salon.com/entertainment/tv/int/2003/05/20/whedon/index.html

Whorf, B. L. *Language, Thought and Reality: Selected Writings*, edited by J. B. Carroll. Cambridge, MA: MIT Press, 1956.

Wilcox, Rhonda. '"Every Night I Save You": Buffy, Spike, Sex, and Redemption'. In Rhonda Wilcox, *Why Buffy Matters: The Art of* Buffy the Vampire Slayer. London: I.B.Tauris, 2005: 79–89.

Wilson, Eric G. 'Polar Apocalypse in Coleridge and Poe'. *Wordsworth Circle* 35, no. 1 (Winter 2004): 37–44.

Winnubst, Shannon. 'Vampires, Anxieties and Dreams: Race and Sex in the Contemporary United States'. *Hypatia* 18, no. 3 (2003): 1–20.

Woolf, Virginia. *A Room of One's Own*. San Diego, CA: Harcourt & Brace, 1981.

Wulf, Elizabeth. 'Becoming Heroic: Alternative Female Heroes in Suzy McKee Charnas' *The Conqueror's Child*'. *Extrapolation* 46, no. 1 (Spring 2005): 120–32.

Wytenbroek, J. R. 'Taoism in the Fantasies of Ursula K. Le Guin'. In *The Shape of the Fantastic: Selected Essays from the Seventh International Conference on the Fantastic in the Arts*, edited by Olena H. Saciuk. New York, NY: Greenwood Press, 1990: 173–80.

Yeo, Michelle. '*Harry Potter and the Chamber of Secrets*: Feminist interpretations/Jungian dreams'. *Studies in Media and Information Literacy Education* 4, no. 1 (2004). Online: http://www.utpjournals.com/simile

Zimmerman, Virginia. 'Harry Potter and the Gift of Time'. *Children's Literature* 37 (2009): 194–215.

INDEX

Note: Entries preceded by an asterisk (*) denote fictional characters.

Abbott, Stacey 108,
  111–12, 182
abjection 54, 172–3, 175,
  176–7
Acocella, Joan 130
*Adam 109, 115–16
afterlife 200
  see also death
*Akaren 88
*Alder 101
Alderman, Naomi 107
Alexander, Jenny 178
alternative spirituality 12
Altizer, Thomas J. J. 67
Andersen, Hans Christian
  134
*Angel 105, 114, 174
Angel series 170
angels 78
*Anya 116–17
apotheosis 39–41
archetypes 26, 38, 46, 54,
  96, 98
*Arha *see* Tenar
aristocracy, in *Harry Potter*
  130–1, 197
*Arren 88, 100
*Asriel 80, 152, 165
atonement 39–41
Attebery, Brian 6
Augustine of Hippo 156,
  185
aurora borealis 151–2
*Authority, The 152–3
authority structures 4,
  130–1

Bainbridge, Walter 17
Bakhtin, Mikhail 104, 126
balance 86

*Balthamos 66
Barbaccia, Holly G. 113
Barfield, Steven 145–6
Bastian, Adolph 23
Beauvoir, Simone de 49
Berger, Peter 16
Bieszk, Patricia 105–6
*Bird 76
birthright 134–5
Blake, William 64, 66–7,
  77–80, 81, 154
blood 111, 140–1
blood purity 131–6, 197
*Borisovitch, Semyon
  150–1
Bradney, Anthony 115
Brannon, Julie Sloan 119,
  120, 121–2
Breton, Rob 105, 116
bricolage 10, 20, 202
Bruce, Steve 2, 14, 18
Buddhism 65–8, 71–4,
  77–9, 81–3
*Buffy 3, 194
  death 109, 179
  fear of being monstrous
    178
  and friends 116–17
  iconoclasm 112–14,
    195–6
  relationship with Spike
    176–81
Buffy the Vampire Slayer
  103–27, 168–88, 194–5,
  199–200
  (film) 2, 103
  (TV series) 2, 103–4,
    106, 178
Byatt, A. S. 130, 145
*Byrnison, Iorek 150, 166

Campbell, Joseph 23–31,
  36, 38–40, 42, 47–8,
  189–90
Carlyle, Thomas 25
Carrette, Jeremy R. 8–9,
  201–2
Chevalier, Noel 145
choice 17, 134–6, 156, 158,
  185, 187
  see also free will
Christian mythology
  107–9
Chronicles of Narnia 69–70
  The Last Battle 69–70
Church, in *His Dark
  Materials* 148, 192–3,
  197–8
class (social) 130, 131,
  136, 138
*Cob 87, 89
Colás, Santiago 75
coming of age 50–1, 100,
  112–13, 120, 191, 197
Comoletti, Laura B. 93
Comte, Auguste 13
consumerism 8, 18, 201–2
*Coulter, Mrs 149–50, 152
Cox, J. Renée 183
creation 72
Crosby, Janice C. 45

dæmons (in *His Dark
  Materials*) 76, 148–9,
  157
  see also intercision
Damour, Lisa 32
Dark Lord 3
David, Robert G. 151
Davie, Grace 15–16
*Dawn 116–17, 121

INDEX

Day, William Patrick 171, 174
death
  in *Earthsea* 85, 87, 89, 102
  in *Harry Potter* 41–3
  in *His Dark Materials* 76, 193
death of God 68–9
deep ecology 171
Deleuze, Gilles 105
demons (in *Buffy*) 110, 111, 169–70
Derrida, Jacques 90
desires 82
Dewey, John 74
discourses 9, 11
*Dobby 137, 197
Dracula 107
dragons 96–8, 100, 101, 194
Drout, Michael D. C. 93
*Dumbledore 33, 34–5, 40, 41
Dundes, Alan 23
*Duny 3–4
*Dursley, Dudley 29, 37
*Dursley, Petunia 37
*Dursley, Vernon 29, 33
*Dursley family 130–1
Dust 71–3, 149, 150, 161–3, 193
duty 82

Earthsea cycle 3–4, 45–62, 84–102, 194
  The Farthest Shore 85, 88, 100
  The Other Wind 46, 85, 101
  Tales from Earthsea 46, 92–3
  Tehanu 45–6, 61, 93–100
  The Tombs of Atuan 45–62, 191
  A Wizard of Earthsea 3–4, 86–7
ecology 165, 171
enlightenment 77, 80
environmentalism 80–1
Erickson, Gregory 108, 170
Erlich, Richard D. 85
escapism 7–8
ethics 202
  in *His Dark Materials* 166
  see also morality
ethnicity 46, 138

Eve 156, 160–1, 164, 198
evil 187
  see also *First Evil; good, the, *and* evil

fairy tales 134
*Faith 122, 177
Falconer, Rachel 41, 145
Fall, the 63, 65, 79–80, 147, 165, 197–8
fantastic, the 5–6, 202
fantasy
  definition 5
  Harry Potter as satiric 145–6
  as literary genre 5–7
  as subversive 1
father figures 39–41, 190
*Feldt, Lena 150
femininity *see* gender
feminist consciousness 4
  and Campbell's work 36, 47–9
Ferrara, Mark S. 67
Feuerbach, Ludwig 13, 158
*First Evil 169, 185–7, 196, 200
Foucault, Charles 9, 120, 121
fragmentation 1–2
free will 156–8, 185, 197, 198
freedom 60, 84, 97, 137–9
Freud, Sigmund 13, 32
Frye, Northrop 25, 67

*Ged 4, 50, 55–61, 87, 88, 92, 94, 100
Geertz, Clifford 11–12
gender 84–5, 93, 102
  in *Harry Potter* 139–42, 167
  politics 46
  roles 4
George, Stefan 152
*Giles 113, 115, 183–4
Gilligan, Carol 101
*Ginny 140
globalization 16–17
Gnostics 163, 164, 185
God
  death of 68–9
  existence of 110
  goddess-figure 36
good, the 4
  and evil 150, 157–8, 197, 199–200
  and the monstrous 168–88

Gooderham, David 166–7
Goodhew, Linda 66, 78
Graeber, David 115
Graham, Elaine L. 169
Green philosophy 81
Gresh, Lois H. 73
Grimes, M. Katherine 23
*Grindelwald 42
*Grumman, Stanislaus 148
Guattari, Felix 105

*Hagrid 29
Hahn, Johann Georg von 23
Hampson, Daphne 10
Harrison, Jane Ellen 154
Harry Potter 22–44, 128–46, 196–7
  and the Chamber of Secrets 33, 132–3, 140
  and the Order of the Phoenix 34, 35
  and the Philosopher's Stone 33, 35
  and the Prisoner of Azkaban 32
  for references to the character, see *Potter, Harry
Harry Potter series 196–7
Hartney, Christopher 65
heaven 110
  see also Republic of Heaven
Heelas, Paul 2, 12, 18–19
heredity 131–6, 142
*Hermione 3, 138, 139
hero myths 23–4
  and gender 46–8, 93, 94, 191
hero quest 4, 26, 39–41, 44–8, 190
hero's journey 23–31, 36, 38, 42, 134, 189–90
  and female heroism 47–8, 58
heroines 49
His Dark Materials 63–83, 147–67, 197–9
  The Amber Spyglass 65
  Northern Lights 151–2
Hogwarts 30
house-elves 137–9
Hume, David 157

identity 81
individualism 14–15, 82

Inglehart, Ronald 16–17
intercision 148–9, 198
*Iorek, *see* *Byrnison, Iorek
*Irian 92–3, 101–2
Irigaray, Luce 123–5
*Ivy 95

Jackson, Rosemary 146
*James 35
Jung, Carl 23, 26, 87, 193
  see also archetypes;
    shadows

*Kalessin 93, 97, 101
karma 82
Keller, Tatiana 98–9
Kendal Project 18–19
*Kendra 113
Kierkegaard, Søren 68
King, Richard 8–9, 201–2
Kleist, Heinrich von 64
knowledge 74–5, 79–80,
  166–7, 198
Kristeva, Julia 27, 55, 91–2,
  171–2, 175, 176

labyrinth 51–2
Lacoss, Jann 23
language 88, 89–90, 194
Lao Tzu 85–6
Le Guin, Ursula K. 1
  Earthsea Revisited 46
  and gender 84
  The Lathe of Heaven 85
  on myth 27
  religious beliefs 85–8, 193
  see also Earthsea cycle
Leane, Elizabeth 151
Leibniz, Gottfried
  Wilhelm 71–2
Lenz, Millicent 163
lesbian sex 106
*LeStrange, Bellatrix 37–8
Lewis, C. S. 69–70
*Lily 36–7
Lindow, Sandra J. 99–100
love 117–18
  and vampires 182
Loy, David 66, 78
*Lupin 33
*Lyra 74–7, 150, 153, 155,
  161, 164–5, 198

magic 93, 129
*Malfoy, Draco 132
*Malone, Mary 71–2,
  159–62, 198
Manlove, Colin N. 5

marginalization 105
Martin, David 15
Marx, Karl 13
Mary 159–60, 198
masculinity *see* gender
materialism 73, 83
McDaniel, Kathryn N. 138
McLean, Susan 100–1
McMaster, Lindsey 105,
  116
Mendlesohn, Farah 129–31,
  134–5, 137, 142–3
metaphysics 192–4
*Metatron 152
Mills, Alice 31–2, 33, 34,
  35, 37, 96–8
Milton, John 63, 64, 72
mimesis 124–6
modernity 14
monads 72
Money, Mary Alice 118
monsters 109
  and the good 4, 168–88,
    199
morality 82, 131
*Moss 94–5, 99
motherhood 48
Müller, Friedrich 13
myth, definitions 27
mythology
  Christian 107–9
  polar 151–2
mythopoesis 27, 140

Nagapriya 79, 82
names 90–2
Narnia 69–70
necrophilia 173–4
Nelson, Victoria 151
Ness, Peter Van 9–10
New Age spiritualities 12,
  18, 174
Nietzsche, Friedrich
  Wilhelm 68–9, 147, 179
Nodelman, Perry 55–7
Norris, Pippa 16–17
North, the 150–2
nostalgia 130, 145

occult, the 19–20
Oedipal motifs 23, 31–2,
  34
*Ogion 91–2, 93
Orpheus myth 153–4

Pagel, Elaine 164
Pan myth 155
*Pantalaimon 154–5

parody 124
*Parry, Will 76, 155, 158–9,
  198
Partridge, Christopher
  19–20
patriarchy 113, 118–19,
  140
Pearson, Carol 48–9, 191
*Pekkala, Serafina 80, 164
Pender, Patricia 122–3
Pennington, John 144
Philippopoulis-
  Mihalopoulos, Andreas
  89
Pinsent, Pat 163
Plantinga, Alvin 157
Playdon, Zoe-Jane 108,
  116
Pope, Katherine 48–9, 191
*Post, Gwendolyn 104
postmodernity 171
*Potter, Ginny 140
*Potter, Harry 22–44
  'chosen' status 136
  heredity and success
    142–4
  self-sacrifice 190
  self-transcendence 190
*Potter, James 32
power 4, 9
  in *Buffy* 97–8, 101, 103,
    115–20, 126, 170,
    194–6
Powers, Douglas 66, 82
Principe, Walter 8
progress 13
Prometheus myth 165
Propp, Vladimir 23
psychic integration 193
psychoanalytic theory 23,
  31–2, 190
Pullman, Philip
  on human identity 81
  on knowledge 81, 157
  materialism 73, 77
  religious beliefs 63–70
  *see also His Dark
    Materials*

quest *see* hero quest
*Quirrell 35

Raglan, Fitzroy Richard
  Somerset 23
Raine, Kathleen 154
Rank, Otto 23
rational choice theory 17
rationalism 116

INDEX

rationality 14–15
rebirth 78–9
redemption 184, 198
religion
  absence in *Harry Potter*
    129
  in *Buffy* 110, 193
  definition 11–12
  and spirituality 11–12
  in the thought of Joss
    Whedon 107–8
  in the thought of Philip
    Pullman 63–70
Republic of Heaven 63, 68,
  70–1, 82, 148, 193
Rice, Anne 174–5
Ricoeur, Paul 27, 42
*Riddle, Tom 33–5, 41,
  140
Robertson, Roland 16
Robinson, Christopher L.
  90–2
*Ron 3
Roof, Wade Clark 12
Rottensteiner, Franz 7
Rowling, Joanne K. 3
  portrayed as Hermione
    138
  see also Harry Potter
Russell, Mary Harris 153,
  162

sacralization 13
sacred, the 85
sacrifice 85–6, 95, 109,
  118, 150, 179
sadomasochism 177–8
salvation 57
Sandner, David 1
Sanyal, Mithu M. 54
Sartre, Jean-Paul 182
Schneiders, Sandra Marie
  9–10
Schoefer, Christine 139, 141
secularization 13–16, 18,
  109
Segal, Robert Alan 25–6
*Segoy 93
Seidal-Arpeci, Annette
  107
self 75–6
self-discovery 48–9
self-integration 10
self-knowledge 158
self-sacrifice 181, 190
self-spirituality 12
self-transcendence 10–11,
  41, 190, 200–1

self-transformation 22–44,
  46, 99
serpents 159–60
shadows (Jungian) 177
Shantz, Jeff 115
Shohet, Lauren 155–6
sin 156, 198
*Sirius 33
*Skadi, Ruta 148, 149
slavery 137–9
snakes 159–60
*Snape, Severus 35, 41, 135
*Snyder 104
social power relations 4, 9
social stratification 4, 144,
  196
socio-political issues 194,
  196–7
soul 75–6, 180–1, 183–4,
  199
South, James B. 121
Spaise, Terry L. 174
*Sparrowhawk 4
*Spike 105, 112, 117–18,
  186
  relationship with Buffy
    176–81
  spiritual journey 1, 4, 12
    see also hero's journey
spirituality 83
  definitions 8–12
  and religion 11–12, 64
  and socio-political
    domain 12, 19
Stark, Rodney 14, 17, 18
Stoker, Bram 107
stories 76–7, 161, 193
sub-cultures 105–6, 195
subjective experience 19
submyth 27
substitutionary death
  109
subtle knife 166
Swearer, Donald 81

Taoism 85–8, 193
taproot texts 6
*Tara 106, 116–17
*Tehanu 93, 99, 101–2
*Tenar 4, 45–62, 92, 93–5,
  194
*Therru 93–5, 97, 194
time 55
Todorov, Tzvetan 6, 202
Tolkien, J. R. R. 143
traces 42–3
trust 57
truth 68, 74–80, 90, 194

Tucker, Nicholas 130
Tylor, Edward 23

'vagina dentata' 54
vampires 107, 111–12,
  169–76, 184, 199
  and love 182
Vaughn, Sue 61
virtue 66
Vogler, Christopher 26
*Voldemort 33–5, 40–1, 43,
  135–6
  see also *Riddle, Tom
vulva 54

Wall, Derek 81
*Walsh, Maggie 104, 109
Wannamaker, Annette
  141–2
*Weasley, Ginny 38, 39
*Weasley, Mrs 37–8
Weber, Max 2, 13
Weisman, Steven R. 128
*Wesley 114
Westman, Karin E. 131–2,
  137–8
Whedon, Joss 3, 103
  atheism 107–8
Whorf, Benjamin Lee 89
Wilcox, Rhonda 173, 177,
  182
*Wilkins, Mayor 104
*Will *see* *Parry, Will
*Willow 105, 106, 110–11,
  115, 170
Wilson, Eric G. 151
*Winky 137, 138
Winnubst, Shannon 171
Wisdom 163
witches 94, 150
woman, as temptress 38–9
women
  in the *Buffy* series 123–5
  as heroes 46–8, 93, 94,
    191
  sexuality 106, 141
  see also gender
wonder 5
Woodhead, Linda 12, 19
Wulf, Elizabeth 61
Wytenbroek, J. R. 86–7, 88

*Xander 105, 115, 122
*Xaphania 82, 163–4, 198

Yeo, Michelle 139

Zimmerman, Virginia 42

216